Social Work

A PROFESSION OF MANY FACES

SPECIAL EDITION FOR MICHIGAN STATE UNIVERSITY

Armando T. Morales

Bradford W. Sheafor

Malcolm E. Scott

Taken From:
Social Work: A Profession of Many Faces, Twelfth Edition
by Armando T. Morales, Bradford W. Sheafor, Malcolm E. Scott

Custom Publishing

New York Boston San Francisco
London Toronto Sydney Tokyo Singapore Madrid
Mexico City Munich Paris Cape Town Hong Kong Montreal

Cover Art: *One from Many*, by Robin McDonald-Foley

Taken from:

Social Work: A Profession of Many Faces, Twelfth Edition
by Armando T. Morales, Bradford W. Sheafor, Malcolm E. Scott
Copyright © 2010 by Pearson Education, Inc.
Published by Allyn & Bacon
Boston, Massachusetts 02116

This special edition published in cooperation with Pearson Custom Publishing.

Printed in the United States of America

10 9 8 7 6 5 4 3 2 1

2009720007

WH

**Pearson
Custom Publishing**
is a division of

www.pearsonhighered.com

ISBN 10: 0-558-39619-4
ISBN 13: 978-0-558-39619-0

Contents

part five
Social Work Practice with Vulnerable Populations 250

chapter 21

Social Work Practice with Muslims in the United States 385

chapter 23

Social Work Practice with Indigenous Peoples and Tribal Communities 437

Social Welfare: A Response to Human Need

Prefatory Comment

The Preamble to the Constitution of the United States asserts that this nation was formed to "insure domestic tranquility, provide for the common defense, promote the general welfare, and secure the blessings of liberty to ourselves and our posterity...." In the months and years since the terrorist attacks on September 11, 2001, our tranquility has surely been broken, the commitment to providing common defense has been translated into preemptive strikes against Iraq, and many of the blessings of liberty have been compromised in the name of homeland security. In this context, the main focus of social work, promoting the general welfare (or well-being of the people) has been difficult to achieve. Indeed, people's perceptions of what constitutes well-being have changed, and the country's willingness to share its resources is increasingly characterized by self-interest and a response to special interests, rather than a promotion of the welfare of all of its members. The altruism that once flourished in the United States has diminished.

Human needs periodically change. Sometimes there is gradual change that occurs incrementally over time, and at other times dramatic change occurs quickly, such as in response to a local disaster or the terrorist attacks on September 11, 2001. It is within the context of these changing needs through the decades that new programs and services were developed and several new professions, including social work, emerged to assume responsibility for helping to "promote the general welfare" of the nation's people.

Although each person has his or her unique constellation of needs, some needs are common to all people. Logically, efforts should be made to address the most basic needs and then, if there is sufficient commitment and resources, to deal with those of lesser priority. Abraham Maslow suggests the following priorities, or *hierarchy of human needs,* beginning with the most basic:[1]

▶ *Physiological survival needs:* nourishment, rest, and warmth
▶ *Safety needs:* preservation of life and sense of security
▶ *Belongingness needs:* to be a part of a group and to love and be loved
▶ *Esteem needs:* approval, respect, acceptance, and appreciation from others
▶ *Self-actualization needs:* opportunity to fulfill one's potential

A society must decide which of these needs it will attempt to serve and which needs individuals and families should be expected to meet themselves. The more basic the need, the more likely it is that society will make some provision for meeting that need.

Although individual philosophies vary regarding how much responsibility the society should take for responding to human needs, two basic philosophies dominate thinking in the United States and shape political debate. A *conservative* philosophy argues for placing primary responsibility for maintaining the well-being of people with the individual and family, depends on the market system to drive the economy, and tends toward a protectionist national view of issues. In contrast, a *liberal* position favors a more substantial role for government and other social structures in meeting basic needs and in the use of social programs to redistribute income and at least partially influence the economy, and it expects the government to actively address global issues. Thus, the political climate at any time will affect the degree to which the society will take responsibility for the welfare of its members and embrace social programs to maximize the well-being of its citizens. When a more conservative orientation is dominant, the society is most likely to assume responsibility for only the most basic needs (e.g., physiological survival and safety). Social programs would typically be limited to activities such as food programs, provision for the homeless, and intervention in cases of child abuse. If a more liberal orientation dominates, the society would be viewed as needing to also address belongingness, esteem, and/or self-actualization needs. Thus there would likely be support for additional social programs such as family counseling, mental health, services to persons with disabilities, and even for programs aimed at changing social structures to try to prevent social problems from emerging.

Social Welfare Programs

Society's organized efforts to meet some human needs are labeled *social welfare*. The term *social*, when applied to humans, addresses the interactions of individuals or groups with other people, groups, organizations, or communities. The term *welfare* implies concern for the well-being of people. Social welfare programs, then, are developed to help people function more satisfactorily in their interactions with others and thus to lead more fulfilling lives. A useful definition of *social welfare* is the translation of society's dominant social philosophies into social policies, to be carried out by a system of human services agencies and delivered by human services professionals, in order to meet the socially related needs of individuals, families and other households, groups, and/or communities through programs offering social provisions, personal services, and/or social action.

In its early years, the United States was largely rural, and the economy was based on family farms and local trade. Except in the cases of widows and orphans or persons experiencing major physical disabilities or mental illnesses, the social programs were typically of limited scope. With the transition to an industrial society in the 1800s, the family, and particularly the extended family, could not meet many of the needs of its members. Family members often had to move to distant locations to find jobs, making the mutual support one might expect from family members less available. Also, the work depended more on the specialized skills in the use of machines than on an individual's manual labor, and those without suitable skills or intelligence became expendable. Life was further complicated by competition for jobs, with large numbers of skilled immigrants also seeking to enter the labor market. In this environment, social welfare programs began to expand because many individuals and families could no longer be self-sufficient.

More recently, the economy has become more global and increasingly tied to electronic technology, which again is altering the structure of the society. Families are no longer required to work as a unit to survive, although the general well-being of their members often depends on multiple breadwinners. In addition, individuals can work somewhat in isolation (often in a home office) and thus their opportunity for regular social interaction with colleagues is lessened. Further, a few people who are highly skilled in the use of technology can complete work that once required many laborers (for example, through mechanized farming or robotics), leading to job displacement—especially for those experiencing educational, emotional, or mental disabilities or one of the several forms of discrimination. These and other trends that have disenfranchised segments of the population have moved social welfare programs from a relatively minor role in U.S. society to an increasingly central place.

The Evolution of Social Welfare

An index of a nation's continued commitment to its people is its investment in social programs. These programs are the mechanisms by which public concerns are translated into assistance for people. They are expressed in laws and other policies that represent the society's plans to provide for an identified need. In the United States, social welfare programs have been subject to ever-changing philosophies, and consequently support for these programs has increased and decreased at various periods. Knowledge of the evolution of social welfare provides an important context for understanding the work of social workers today.

Colonial Times to the Great Depression

Picture life in the rural United States in the 1700s, when land was plowed and families worked to tame the wilderness. Although there were many trials and tribulations in that agricultural society, the person with average intelligence and a willingness to work hard could usually succeed. Given an open frontier and liberal government policies for staking a claim to fertile land, an individual could readily acquire property and produce at least the necessities of life. Each member had sharply defined roles that contributed to the family's welfare, people survived, and, in time, usually prospered. All members (i.e., grandparents, children, and other relatives) performed the required work and, perhaps as important, were needed. Even the person who was mentally or physically disabled could find meaningful ways to contribute. The "American Dream" became a reality for most (unless one was of African, Asian, Mexican, or Native American background) in this simple agrarian society.

The family was not usually completely independent and self-supporting. For mutual protection, social interaction, and opportunity to trade the goods they produced, families would band together into loosely knit communities. Trade centers eventually emerged as small towns; a market economy evolved; and merchants opened stores, bought and sold products, and extended credit to people until their products were ready for market. Efforts to meet human needs in this environment can best be characterized as *mutual aid*. When special problems arose, neighbors and the community responded. The barn that burned was quickly rebuilt, widows and orphans were cared for, and the sick were tended to. People shared what they had with needy friends and neighbors, knowing that the favor would be returned some day. In this preindustrial society, the quality of life depended on the "grace of God and hard work." Society rarely needed to respond to unmet human needs, but, when it did, churches and synagogues usually provided that service.

Conditions began to change in the mid-1800s and early 1900s when industrialization and urbanization created rapid and dramatic changes in both the family and the market system. People congregated in cities where there were jobs, the individual breadwinner rather than the family unit became the key to survival, and interactions with others were increasingly characterized by impersonality. Those from the vulnerable population groups (e.g., immigrants, the aged, minorities, women, persons with disabilities), in particular, experienced reduced opportunity for employment or, if employed, access to meaningful and personally rewarding jobs. Not only were social problems increased, but, with the changed roles of the family and market system, society had to create new ways to respond to human needs.

Early social welfare programs were heavily influenced by the *Puritan ethic,* which argued that only those people with a moral defect required assistance. According to Puritan reasoning, those who failed did so because they suffered from a moral weakness and were viewed as sinful. It is not uncommon even today for clients to feel that their troubles represent God's means of punishing them for some sin or act of immoral behavior. Following the same philosophy, grudging taxpayers often resent contributing to human services when they believe the client is morally at fault for needing assistance. This view, however, does not take into consideration the structural factors in the society that contribute to or even may cause an individual's problems.

The United States was not settled by wealthy people. When social needs were addressed by this developing society, small voluntary organizations were formed to provide services. If voluntary organizations did not meet needs, town meetings were held and actions taken to provide assistance, thus creating the first public social services. Any assistance was considered charity, not a right. Requests for help were either supported or rejected, depending on the judgments made by the townsfolk.

The philosophy derived from the *French Enlightenment* of the eighteenth century contradicted the Puritan view. It argued that people are inherently good and that need for assistance is not related to morality. People needing help were judged as deserving of assistance depending on the causes of their problems.

The *worthy poor* were viewed as good people who required help because they were afflicted with an ailment or were women and children left destitute by the death or desertion of the breadwinning husband and father. The *unworthy poor* were thought to have flaws of character. That one's plight may have been caused by others, by chance, or even by structural conditions in the society was only beginning to be recognized.

There were, of course, those who held a sympathetic view of persons in need and attempted to reform the punitive and uncaring approaches to providing services. One of the first great social reformers, Dorothea Dix, chronicled the deplorable conditions in prisons and almshouses (also referred to as "poor farms") and sought to establish government responsibility for meeting human needs. Her effective lobbying contributed to the passage of a bill in the U.S. Congress to grant federal land to states to help them finance care for the mentally ill. The veto of that bill in 1854 by President Franklin Pierce established a precedent that was to dominate thinking about society's responsibility for social welfare for the next three-quarters of a century—that the federal government should play no part in providing human services. As late as 1930, President Herbert Hoover relied on the precedent established by the Pierce Veto. When he approved an appropriation of $45 million to feed livestock in Arkansas during a drought while opposing an additional $25 million to feed the farmers who raised that livestock.[2]

Other social reformers, too, began to advocate for programs to meet needs—mostly through voluntary associations such as the Charity Organization Societies, Settlement Houses, the Mental Hygiene Movement, and programs to assist former slaves to integrate into the dominant society. When the federal government refused to engage in providing human services, the states sporadically offered services, with several states creating state charity boards or public welfare departments. However, not until the Great Depression of the 1930s led to severe economic crisis and the ensuing New Deal programs of President Franklin D. Roosevelt was it recognized that private philanthropy, even in combination with limited state and local government support, could not adequately address the major human needs.

This picture of life in the United States is based largely on the experience of the white European immigrant. But what if one were African American, Mexican American, or Native American? Certainly life was different for these segments of the population. Consider, for example, the experience of African Americans in the 1800s. Families brought to this nation as slaves often had little control over their lives or their ability to function as a family unit. In slave families, males were often demeaned and females sexually abused, and family members were frequently sold as property to other slave owners. Even after emancipation, few social programs were available to meet even basic needs as the former slaves either remained as sharecroppers in the South or struggled to meet their basic needs in the discriminatory society in the North.

Similarly, the movement of people from Mexico into the Southwest United States in the mid-eighteenth and nineteenth centuries was characterized by discrimination and hardship. The United States had purchased and acquired by military force nearly one million square miles of Mexican territory. The Mexicans, who subsequently became Mexican Americans because of U.S. birth, were subjected to extensive acts of brutality at the hands of the Texas Rangers and lynchings by Anglo Americans who resented their competition for farming, grazing, and water rights.[3]

Native Americans, too, lived a different experience. As the westward movement progressed, the original Americans increasingly had their cultural identity eroded through treaties (often to be broken later) and government policies that dramatically changed the Native Americans' way of life. Policies during this period were intended to accomplish *extermination* of the Native Americans through war, lack of disease control, provision of alcohol, and slavery; lead to *expulsion* from their land; *excluded* them from their tribal life by sending young people to "Indian schools"; and *assimilated* them into the larger society by destroying tribal collective action.

These three racial/ethnic groups clearly did not participate in the "American Dream," although their labor played a significant role in the growing economic prosperity of the nation.

The Great Depression to the 21st Century

The Great Depression was also the great equalizer. People who had previously been successful suddenly required help. These were able-bodied people of European descent who needed assistance. Could they be blamed for their condition, or did other factors contribute to their troubles? In this case, it was the deterioration of the worldwide economy that forced many people into poverty. U.S. society began to recognize that indeed there were structural factors in modern society responsible for many social problems. With the Pierce Veto now defunct, the government began an unprecedented period of expansion in social welfare that became inclusive of many more people.

World War II rallied the United States to a common cause and helped people recognize their interdependence. Each person was counted on to contribute to the common good during wartime conditions, and the nation could ill afford to create "throwaway" people by failing to provide for their basic needs. By the 1960s, economic recovery was complete, and a brief period of prosperity and responsiveness to human needs followed. The Kennedy and Johnson administrations fostered the War on Poverty and Great Society programs, and the Human Rights Revolution was in its heyday. These activities focused public concern on the poor, minorities, women, the aged, people who were mentally and physically disabled, and other population groups that had previously been largely ignored. Legislation protecting civil rights and creating massive social programs was passed; court decisions validated the new legislation, and a vast array of new social programs emerged.

The bloom on social programs began to fade in the middle of the 1970s, and public apathy replaced public concern. Under the Carter administration, a deteriorating economy was accompanied by a growing political conservatism, and the continued commitment to human services was placed in direct competition with military buildup and the maintenance of U.S. superpower status. By the 1980s, the time was ripe for conservatives to attempt to dismantle the social programs that had developed over the past two decades. President Ronald Reagan's effort to limit the federal government's social programs echoed the political rhetoric based on the distrust of government that characterized the conservative philosophy, mixed with punitive, moralistic views regarding the recipients of human services that revealed vestiges of the Puritan philosophy. The Reagan administration had only moderate influence over expenditures for "mandated" social programs such as Social Security but was able to decrease by almost 15 percent the expenditures on "discretionary" social programs.

The Reagan administration attempted not only to cut federal expenditures but also to shift responsibility to state and local governments or, where possible, to the private sector of the human services. However, the combination of a more liberal Congress and a series of Supreme Court decisions that protected most of the gains made in human services and civil rights during the prior two decades partially blunted the radical changes that President Reagan promised. In the 1990s, implementation of President Clinton's moderate social agenda of health and welfare reform was diminished somewhat by a very conservative Congress, leaving little opportunity to roll back the decreased support for human services. Health care reform failed completely, and welfare reform was characterized by stringent employment-training requirements and a maximum of financial aid for five years, elimination of any benefits for noncitizens, the shift of more responsibility to state governments, and the reduction of benefits for out-of-wedlock children. According to the Urban Institute, the outcome of this reform after eight years was mixed with the number of financial assistance recipients declining and, as one indicator, the overall well-being of poor children remaining unchanged.[4]

Social Welfare in the Early 2000s

Our historical review of social programs indicates that, in the early stages of U.S. society's development, the expectation was that the individual would take care of himself or herself or, if not, that the families would ensure that their members' needs were met. Laws placed primary responsibility on the family unit for caring for its members, and, to a larger extent than in many societies, these laws have protected the sanctity of the family's decisions about how to achieve this goal. If this expectation could have been fulfilled, there may not have been the need for a social welfare institution, or perhaps society would reluctantly intervene only in cases where family members were being damaged (e.g., child abuse or neglect, domestic violence, elder maltreatment).

U.S. society evolved, however, in a way that the family became unable to meet many social needs, and voluntary social services provided by religious or voluntary human services agencies began to expand. Today, these contributions amount to only a small portion (3.2 percent) of the total expenditures on human resources, yet they are particularly important because they are relatively flexible funds that can be used to respond to changing needs. Although some of these important human services continue to be offered under the auspices of religious organizations, most are now related to secular nonprofit human service organizations, such as those typically associated with the United Way or those that raise their own funds to supplement client fees. As revealed in Table 2.1, these private nonprofit organizations are more likely to contribute their resources to educational programs rather than to health or human services programs, and they simply do not have the funds to support income maintenance programs, except for emergency food, clothing, and shelter.

Table 2.1

Government and Private Sector Allocations to Health, Education, and Social Welfare (in billions of dollars)

	Federal Government 2007	State/Local Government 2005	Private/ Nonprofit 2006	Total
Health, hospitals, Medicare	$ 642.1B	$ 170.2B	$ 20.2B	$ 832.5B
Elementary, secondary, and higher education and job training	70.2	689.4	33.8	793.4
Human services (e.g., social services, criminal justice, housing, and food and nutrition assistance)	115.3	76.4	24.4	216.1
Income security (cash assistance, other public welfare except Social Security)	271.8	362.0	0	633.8
Total	$ 1,099.4B	$ 1,298.0B	$ 78.4B	$ 2,675.8B
% Total Expenditures	44.4%	52.4%	3.2%	100.0%

Sources: Federal Government. Office of Budget Management. Fiscal Year 2009 Budget. Table 3.2. Outlays by Function and Subfunction: 1962–2009. http://www.whitehouse.gov/omb/budget/fy2009/pdf/hist.pdf; State & Local Government. U.S. Census Bureau. Summary of State & Local Government Finances by Level of Government: 2005. http://www.census.gov/govs/estimate/0500ussl_1.html; Private/Nonprofit. *GivingUSA 2007: The Annual Report on Philanthropy for the Year 2006, 52nd Annual Issue.* GivingUSA Foundation. http:givingusa.org/downloads, p. 27.

Local and state governments were the next line of defense. Today, city, county, and state governments supply 52.4 percent of the funds that underwrite the health, education, and social welfare programs in the United States. These government units focus largely on education at all levels (see Table 2.1), but they also provide significant support in other human resource areas.

Finally, the federal government provides a large portion of all human resource funding. The massive social programs that evolved have made it evident that voluntary and local government resources are insufficient to provide for people's most basic needs. Although controversy continues over the extent of participation and the role of the federal government in providing human resources, today more than $1,099 billion is invested annually in health, income security, and other programs. The rationale for this extensive involvement of the federal government is that many human problems are created by national and international factors such as enormous national debt, chronic unemployment, pervasive discrimination, inflation, the international trade deficit, and even the volatile price of goods and services on the worldwide market. Local areas have little, if any, influence over these factors, and it is necessary to create national programs to equalize the burden of responding to the needs of the victims of these largely uncontrollable events.

The federal government outlays for *discretionary programs* (i.e., those where the president and Congress have some choice regarding the allocation of federal funds) are an indicator of public priorities. Discretionary expenditures have changed substantially since the initiation of the Afghanistan and Iraq wars, shifting the emphasis from enhancing the quality of life in the United States to supporting the war effort. At the end of the Clinton Administration in 1999, and prior to the initiation of those wars, the National Defense allocation was $275 billion, or 48.2 percent of the discretionary program outlays. The budget for 2009 estimates the Defense budget will be $670 billion, or 55.4 percent of the total.[5] Many other areas of government support are, therefore, not growing in proportion to defense, including education, health, housing, and income security programs.

An outcome of the varied patterns of funding for human services has resulted in a patchwork of programs, and it is often difficult for potential clients to navigate through the collection of services. Social workers perform an important role in helping people find their way through the maze of human services. The de-emphasis on federal programs in the areas of health and income security should not detract from appreciation of the programs provided at the state and local levels of government or from voluntary contributions from individuals, foundations, and businesses. As Table 2.1 indicates, almost $2.5 trillion are spent each year on health, education, income security, and other human services. That amounts to more than $8,144 for each of the 303 million people in the United States in 2008. The United States in many respects is a generous nation.

Purpose and Goals for Social Programs

Social programs are created to accomplish three general purposes. First, most are designed for the *remediation* of a social problem. When a sufficient number of people experience difficulty in a particular aspect of social functioning, social programs are created to provide services intended to correct that problem—or at least to help the clients deal with it more effectively. Remediation programs include services such as income support for the poor, counseling for the mentally ill, and job training for the displaced worker. Remediation has historically been the central form of human service.

A second general purpose of human services has evolved more recently—the *enhancement* of social functioning. In this form of social program, the emphasis is on the growth and development of clients in a particular area of functioning without a "problem" having necessarily been identified. Well-baby clinics, parent-effectiveness training, and various youth recreation programs are all examples of social programs designed for personal enhancement.

Finally, the purpose of some social programs is the *prevention* of social problems. As opposed to treating symptoms, prevention programs attempt to identify the basic causes of difficulties in social functioning and seek to stimulate changes that will keep problems from ever developing. Prevention programs, for example, might include helping parents learn appropriate ways to discipline children or conducting community education to make the public aware of the negative impact racism, sexism, or poverty has on the growth and development of children.

Social programs have been created to serve at least four specific goals. The goal of some social programs is to facilitate the *socialization* of people to the accepted norms and behaviors of society. Such programs are designed to help people develop the knowledge and skills to become full participating and contributing members of society and include, for example, such programs as scouting, Boys Clubs and Girls Clubs, and YMCA or YWCA activities. Another goal of social programs is to assist in *social integration*, where people are helped to become more successful in interacting with the world around them. Counseling, therapy, and rehabilitation programs, for example, attempt to achieve this goal. A third goal of social programs is, at times, to provide *social control* by removing people from situations when they might place themselves or others at risk, or when they require some period of isolation from their usual surroundings in order to address problems. Examples of these programs are found in mental hospitals and correctional facilities. Finally, some programs are intended to achieve *social change,* that is, to express the conscience of society by stimulating changes that will enhance the overall quality of life. For example, public education to encourage the practice of safe sex to reduce the risk of AIDS and the solicitation of employers to hire persons who are developmentally disabled are activities that help to bring about social changes that benefit the society.

Social Program Conceptions

The design of social programs also reflects differing perceptions about who should be served and when services should be given. The most basic programs are based on a *safety net approach* and are planned as a way for society to assist people when other social institutions have failed to resolve specific problems. An alternative conception of social programs, the *social utilities approach,* views human services as society's frontline in addressing common human needs.

The Safety Net Approach.   This conception views human services as a safety net that saves people who have not had their needs met by their primary resources such as the family or employment/economic systems. This approach begins with the presumption that a predefined problem exists—for example, a family's income is too low, a person's behavior is deviant, a child is at risk. Services are then provided to address the problems, and, when a satisfactory level of problem reduction is achieved, the services are terminated. One negative aspect of such programs is that, to be eligible for a safety net program, a client must also take on the stigma of having failed in some aspect of social functioning. Further, at times clients must be terminated from service because they have reached a predefined level of functioning, even though the service providers may recognize that the clients would benefit from additional assistance.

Safety net programs are thought of as *residual* because they are designed to deal with the residue of human problems—that is, those problems that are left after all other processes of helping are exhausted. Programs based on this approach are also *selective* in the sense that they are designed to serve a specific population experiencing a specific need. Finally, safety net programs are *time-limited* in the sense that services are terminated when a problem is solved (or at least reduced), a predetermined level of functioning is achieved, or a time limit for service reached.

The Social Utilities Approach.   The social utilities conception of human services views social programs as one of society's primary social institutions for meeting needs. Like public utilities for water and electricity, these social utilities are available to all people who wish to make use of them. They do not assume that the person who receives services is at fault or has necessarily failed if he or she requires services. Rather, this concept recognizes that society creates conditions where all people can benefit from social programs, whether the program is designed to help people solve problems or enhance already adequate functioning.

Social utility programs are *universal* in the sense that they do not have strict eligibility requirements. Such programs are also based on an *institutional* conception of human services that considers social programs a regular or institutionalized way of meeting human needs. They do not assume that the individual, family, or any other social institution has failed if, for example, parents place a child in day care, if a young person joins a scouting program, or if a senior citizen takes advantage of a senior center's lunch program.

Human Services Program Categories

It is also useful to recognize that social programs can be divided into three distinct categories: social provisions, personal services, and social action. In a developed nation, all of these program categories are required.

Social Provisions.   This category of social programs is designed to meet the most fundamental needs of the population, and such programs are typically viewed as part of the safety net. *Social provisions* are the tangible resources given to persons in need, either as cash or as direct benefits, such as food, clothing, or housing.

Social provisions are the most costly programs in outlay of actual dollars. As social programs have evolved, governmental agencies have assumed the primary responsibility for providing these services, and the private sector has taken the role of providing backup for those people who slip through the mesh of the public safety net. Such major social provision programs as Temporary Assistance to Needy Families (TANF), Supplemental Security Income (SSI), food stamps, low-rent public housing, and many others are provided under governmental auspices. Meals and lodging for transients and the homeless, emergency food programs, financial aid in response to crisis situations, shelters for battered wives, and many other social provision programs, however, are offered by voluntary social agencies.

Personal Services.   The personal services category of programs includes both problem-solving and enhancement programs. Unlike social provisions, *personal services* are intangible services that help people resolve issues in their social functioning. Examples of personal service programs are marriage and family counseling, child protection services, client advocacy, family therapy, care for the disabled, job training, family planning and abortion counseling, foster care programs, human service brokering and referral activities, and many other programs aimed at helping clients strengthen their social functioning.

Social Action.   When one works with people, it quickly becomes evident that it is often insufficient just to help a person or group cope with an unjust world. Efforts must be made to create a more just and supportive environment. For example, it is not enough to help a woman understand and cope with discrimination in the workplace. Although these activities may be important for her ability to keep her job, they do not resolve the basic problem, and they place the burden of change and adjustment on the victim. *Social action* programs help change conditions that create difficulties in social functioning. They require specialized knowledge and skill to effect change in organizations and communities. These efforts involve fact finding, analysis of community needs, research and interpretation of data, and other efforts to inform and mobilize the public to action in order to achieve change.

 ## The Successes and Failures of Human Service Programs

It is not possible to fully assess the array of human service programs in the United States in this overview chapter. The poverty rate is perhaps the most revealing single indicator of quality of life because severely limited income is clearly associated with many social problems that affect people's well-being, including health, disabilities, mental health, nutrition, housing conditions, and so on.

To what extent, then, have there been improvements in the rates of poverty[*] in the United States in recent years? Beginning with the end of the War on Poverty (approximately in the year 1970) and ending near the conclusion of G. W. Bush's final term, with the exception of older people, the black population, and to some degree households headed by single mothers, we find little change in poverty rates (see Table 2.2). Several consistent patterns stand out in these data, however, that will be developed further in this book. First, children under age 18 are highly vulnerable to poverty. Poverty has been substantially reduced for older people but has increased for children and youth. Second, the white non-Hispanic population has experienced less poverty than any other racial or ethnic group. Third, the poverty rate for married couples is considerably less than for households headed by single parents, and if the single parent is a female the rate more than doubles than if the single parent is a male. Finally, poverty is highest in the central cities of urban areas and in rural areas. The escape of the wealthy to the suburbs is evident in these data. The picture is more complex on closer examination. A cross tabulation of these data for children under age 18, for example, reveals that young males experience less poverty than young females, white children are less likely to live in poverty than are children of color, children living with married parents are much better off than those living with a single parent, and children residing in the suburbs are much less likely to

---

[*]The experience of poverty is much more than living on a limited income, yet income is used as the single indicator of the degree of deprivation an individual or family experiences. The poverty threshold is adjusted annually by the federal government to reflect the minimum amount of money required by families of different sizes to be able to afford nutritious food, obtain adequate housing, sufficiently clothe family members for work and school, and provide needed health care. The poverty threshold in 2007, for example, was approximately $10,787 for a single-person household, $14,291 for a single parent with one child, and $19,157 for the typical two-parent family with two children. As a reference point, the median income for all families in 2007 was $44,389. Poverty thresholds for households of various sizes can be found at http://www.census.gov/hhes/www/poverty/threshld/thresh07.html.

Table 2.2

Percent of Individuals Below the Poverty Level by Age, Race and Ethnicity, Family Relationship, and Location of Residence: 1970 to 2006

	2006	2000	1990	1980	1970
Total Population	**12.3 %**	**11.3 %**	**13.5 %**	**13.0 %**	**12.6 %**
Children under age 18	17.6	16.2	20.6	18.3	15.1
Adults ages 18–64	10.8	9.6	10.7	10.1	9.0
Older adults ages 65 and over	9.4	9.9	12.2	15.7	24.6
White, non-Hispanic	8.2	7.4	8.8	9.1	7.3 (1973)*
Asian & Pacific Islander	10.3	9.9	12.2	**	**
Black	24.3	22.5	31.9	32.5	33.6
Hispanic	20.6	21.5	28.1	25.7	21.9 (1973)*
Married Couple	4.9	4.7	5.7	6.2	ND
Male householder (no wife present)	13.3	11.3	12.0	11.0	ND
Female householder (no husband)	28.3	25.4	33.4	32.7	32.5
Central city	16.1	16.3	19.0	17.2	14.2
Not central city (suburbs)	9.1	7.8	8.7	8.2	7.1
Nonmetropolitan area (rural)	15.2	13.4	16.3	15.4	16.9

* Classification revised in 1973.

** Data first reported in 1987.

Source: DeNavas-Walt, Carmen, Bernadette D. Proctor, and Jessica Smith. U.S. Census Bureau, Population Reports, P60-233, *Income, Poverty, and Health Insurance Coverage in the United States: 2006*, Washington, D.C.: U.S. Government Printing Office, 2007. Tables B1, B2, and B3.

experience poverty than other children. In short, these data suggest that the person at greatest risk for experiencing poverty would be a young female of color, living with a single mother in the central city of an urban area or in rural America.

These consistent patterns do not happen by chance. The data in Table 2.2 represent the culmination of laws, policies, norms, and cultural patterns that characterize life in the United States. Factors such as racism (and the opposite side of that coin, "white privilege"), sexism, and the other "isms" that separate people in this society play out in the rates of poverty and other social indicators (see Part Five of this book). Social workers are committed to helping individuals and families whose lives reflect these conditions. Although some individuals and families may have contributed to making their own situations more difficult, social workers are also committed to examining these patterns and their causes in order to bring about changes in the cultural patterns and structures that will help to prevent such unfair and disproportionate opportunities that limit people from achieving a high quality, fulfilling, and satisfying life.

Concluding
Comment
The United States was formed with a goal of joining people to promote, among other things, the general welfare of all citizens. At times that goal has taken a back seat to individual and corporate interests, but at other times, when national leadership has had support for strengthening its social programs, the nation has come closer to realizing that objective. All people, however, do not equally experience that goal. If the United States is to remain strong and minimize the likelihood of attacks from internal or external terrorists—or by foreign powers—it must find ways to share the benefits of civilization with its own and other citizens.

More effective provision of social programs will require skilled professionals to help clients achieve more desirable levels of social functioning. Social workers are one of the groups of professional helpers who are central to the efforts to improve the general well-being of people. By examining Box 2.1, we can observe how the social programs that have evolved in the United States underpin the practice of a child welfare worker, Demetria, as she carried out the work in the case situation described in Chapter 1.

Box 2.1

Social Welfare Programs Accessed by Demetria

In dealing with the case of Joseph Miles in Chapter 1, the social worker, Demetria, was able to make a difference in the lives of the Miles family because a number of social welfare programs were available in the community. As described in this chapter, the case involved at least three of the basic needs described by Maslow: *physiological survival needs* (the family's financial problems led to concern about adequate food and heat), *safety needs* (Joseph's bruising, whether from family violence or gang activity), and *belongingness needs* (Joseph's isolation from family and peers). Given the report that these fundamental needs may not have been met—or perhaps that the problems were caused—by Joseph's family, the society stepped in to protect a vulnerable child who may have been in danger by giving the authority and responsibility to the child welfare division to investigate.

There was no indication in the way Demetria investigated that she was influenced by the *Puritan ethic,* which would lead her to make moral judgments about why the family needed help, or even the *French Enlightenment* philosophy, which would judge the Miles family worthy or unworthy for the reasons they were poor. Rather, because a child was at risk—and indeed the whole family was at risk—several *safety net programs* were called into play. The child protection service represented by Demetria falls into the *personal services* category of social programs, while Medicaid and food stamps help the family secure *social provisions.* All of these programs were provided by a *government* or *public agency,* the county Social Welfare Department, of which the Child Welfare Division was one unit. The referral of Joseph to the teen group at the Boys and Girls Club (a *private, nonprofit agency*) was another *personal service* activity, aimed at *socialization* to more acceptable norms of behavior for a 12-year-old boy. This counseling program was open to any child in the community, with or without a defined "problem," and thus would be viewed as a *social utility program.* Finally, the recommendation by Demetria's supervisor to place the lack of resources to address employment problems on the agenda of the next local National Association of Social Workers meeting for discussion could, if the problem is determined to be widespread, lead to *social action* to correct that problem. Without these programs, Demetria would have been of limited help to this family.

KEY WORDS AND CONCEPTS

Hierarchy of needs
Social welfare
Mutual aid philosophy
Puritan ethic
Social program goals (i.e., socialization, social integration, social control, and social action)

Social program conceptions (i.e., safety net, social utilities)
French Enlightenment philosophy
Human service program categories (i.e., social provisions, personal services, social action)

SUGGESTED INFORMATION SOURCES

Day, Phyllis J. *A New History of Social Welfare,* 5th Edition. Boston: Allyn and Bacon, 2006.

Ehrenreich, Barbara. *Nickel and Dimed: On (Not) Getting By in America.* New York: Henry Holt, 2001.

Herrick, John M., and Paul H. Stuart, eds. *Encyclopedia of Social Welfare History in North America.* Thousand Oaks, CA: Sage Publications, 2004.

Katz, Michael B. *The Price of Citizenship: Redefining the American Welfare State.* New York: Metropolitan Books, 2001.

Trattner, Walter I. *From Poor Law to Welfare State,* 6th Edition. New York: Free Press, 1999.

ENDNOTES

1. Abraham H. Maslow, *Motivation and Personality* (New York: Harper & Row, 1970), pp. 25–28.
2. Harold L. Wilensky and Charles N. Lebeaux, *Industrial Society and Social Welfare* (New York: Free Press, 1965), p. 42.
3. Armando Morales, *Ando Sangrando (I Am Bleeding): A Study of Mexican American-Police Conflict* (La Puente, CA: Perspectiva Publications, 1972), p. 11.
4. Olivia A. Golden, *Assessing the New Federalism: Eight Years Later* (Washington, D.C.: The Urban Institute, 2005), p. 18.
5. U.S. Office of Budget, *Budget of the United States Government: Fiscal Year 2009.* Historical Table 8.7.

Social Work: A Comprehensive Helping Profession

Prefatory Comment

The human services have become a central part of the fabric of U.S. society. Founded on the commitment to promote the general welfare of its people, society has gradually assumed increasing responsibility for ensuring that people have access to assistance in meeting their basic needs. This assistance takes the form of various social programs that are delivered by people who possess a variety of helping skills. The ability to help others is highly valued in all societies, whether provided to family and friends or others in one's community. In highly developed societies, including the United States, much of this helping has become so complex that human services programs require highly trained professionals. It is within this context that social work was born.

What is perhaps the most basic form of helping has been termed *natural helping*. Before reaching a social worker or other professional helpers, clients often have been counseled or assisted in some way by family, friends, neighbors, or volunteers. Natural helping is based on a mutual relationship among equals, and the helper draws heavily on intuition and life experience to guide the helping process. The complexity of many social issues and the extensive knowledge and skill required to effectively provide some human services today exceed what natural helpers can typically accomplish. This has resulted in the emergence of several occupations, known as human services professions, that deliver more complicated services to people in need.

Professional helping is different from natural helping in that it is a disciplined approach focused on the needs of the client, and it requires specific knowledge, values, and skills to guide the helping activity. Both natural and professional helping are valid means of assisting people in resolving issues related to their social functioning. In fact, many helping professionals first became interested in these careers because they were successful natural helpers and found the experience rewarding. Social workers often work closely with natural helping networks (i.e., both family members and friends) during the change process and as a source of support after professional service is terminated. However, natural helpers are not a substitute for competent professional help in addressing serious problems or gaining access to needed services.

Social work is the most comprehensive of human service occupations and, through time, has become recognized as the profession that centers its attention on helping people improve their social functioning. In simplest terms, social workers help people strengthen their interaction with various aspects of their world—their children, parents, spouse or other loved one, family, friends, coworkers, or even organizations and whole communities. Social work is also committed to changing factors in the society that diminish the quality of life for all people, but especially for those persons who are most vulnerable to social problems.

Social work's mission of serving both people and the social environment is ambitious. To fulfill that mission, social workers must possess a broad range of knowledge about the functioning of people and social institutions, as well as have a variety of skills for facilitating change in how individuals, organizations, and other social structures operate. This comprehensive mission has made social work an often misunderstood profession. Like the fable of the blind men examining the elephant with each believing that the whole elephant is like the leg, trunk, or ear that he examined, too often people observe one example of social work and conclude that it represents the whole of professional activity. To appreciate the full scope of this profession, it is useful to examine its most fundamental characteristics—the themes that characterize social work.

The Central Themes Underpinning Social Work

Five themes capture the character of social work. No one theme is unique to this profession, but in combination they provide a foundation on which to build understanding of social workers and their practice.

A Commitment to Social Betterment

Belief in the fundamental importance of improving the quality of social interaction for all people, that is, *social betterment,* is a central value of the social worker. The social work profession has taken the position that all people should have the opportunity for assistance in meeting their social needs.

Social work has maintained an idealism about the ability and responsibility of this society to provide opportunities and resources that allow each person to lead a full and rewarding life. It has been particularly concerned with the underdog—the most vulnerable people in the society. This idealism must not be confused with naivete. Social workers are often the most knowledgeable people in the community about the plight of the poor, the abused, the lonely, and others who for a variety of reasons are out of the mainstream of society or experiencing social problems. When social workers express their desire for changes that contribute to the social betterment of people, it is often viewed as a threat by those who want to protect the status quo.

A Goal to Enhance Social Functioning

Social workers take the position that social betterment involves more than addressing problems—it also involves assisting those who want to improve some aspect of their lives, even though it may not be considered "a problem." Social work, then, is concerned with helping people enhance their *social functioning*, that is, the manner in which they interact with people and social institutions.

Social workers help people and social institutions change in relation to a rapidly changing world. The technology explosion, information explosion, population explosion, and even the threat of nuclear explosion dramatically affect people's lives. Those who can readily adapt to these changes—and are not limited by discrimination because of race; cultural background; gender; age; or physical, emotional, or intellectual abilities—seldom use the services of social workers. Others who have become victims of this too rapidly changing world and its unstable social institutions, however, are likely to require professional help in dealing with this change.

An Action Orientation

Social work is a profession of doers. Social workers are not satisfied just to examine social issues. Rather, they take action to prevent problems from developing, attack problematic situations that can be changed, and help people deal with troublesome situations that cannot be changed. To do this, social workers provide services that include such activities as individual counseling, family and group therapy, linking people to the network of services in a community, fund raising, and even social action. Indeed, social work is an applied science.

An Appreciation for Human Diversity

To deal effectively with the wide range of change to which social work is committed, it has become a profession characterized by *diversity*—diversity of clientele, diversity of knowledge and skills, and diversity of services provided. In addition, social workers themselves come in all shapes, colors, ages, and descriptions.

Social workers view diversity as positive. They consider human difference desirable and appreciate the richness that can be offered to a society through the culture, language, and traditions of various ethnic, racial, and cultural groups. They value the unique perspectives of persons of different gender, sexual orientation, or age groups, and they recognize and develop the strengths of persons who have been disadvantaged. What's more, social workers view their own diversity as an enriching quality that has created a dynamic profession that can respond to human needs in an ever-changing world.

A Versatile Practice Perspective

The wide range of human conditions with which social workers deal, the variety of settings in which they are employed, the extensive scope of services they provide, and the diverse populations they serve make it unrealistic to expect that a single practice approach could adequately support social work. Rather, the social worker must have a comprehensive repertoire of knowledge and techniques that can be used to meet the unique needs of individual clients and client groups.

The versatile social worker, then, must have a solid foundation of knowledge about the behavior of people and social institutions in order to understand clients' situations. He or she also needs to understand that differing beliefs may affect the way people will interpret and react to those situations. And, finally, the social worker must have mastered a number of helping techniques from which he or she can imaginatively select to help individuals, families, groups, organizations, and communities improve their social functioning.

How do these themes affect social work practice? The following case example* is just one of many situations where a social worker might help a client:

> Karoline Truesdale, a school social worker, interviewed Kathy and Jim Swan in anticipation of the Swans' oldest son, Danny, beginning school in the fall. The Swans responded to Ms. Truesdale's invitation to the parents of all prospective kindergartners to talk over any concerns they might have about their children's schooling. When making the appointment, Kathy Swan indicated that her son Danny was near the cut-off age for entering school and may not be ready yet for kindergarten. When questioned further, Kathy expressed considerable ambivalence indicating that having him in school would help to relieve other burdens at home but may be too much for Danny.

Karoline's notes from the interview contained the following information:

> Kathy Swan is 20 years old and about to deliver her third child. She indicates that they did not need another mouth to feed at this time, but "accidents happen" and she will attempt to cope with this additional child when the baby is born (although she already appears physically and emotionally depleted). Jim is 21 years old and holds a temporary job earning minimum wage. He moved the family to the city because "money in agriculture has gone to hell" and a maintenance job was available at a manufacturing plant here. However, he was laid off after three months when the plant's workforce was reduced. Jim is angry that he moved the family for this job, yet the company felt no obligation to keep him on. He stated that "people in the country don't treat others like that." He is also worried that his temporary job will last only a few more weeks and commented that Kathy "spends money on those kids like it was going out of style." Jim said in no uncertain terms that he did not want and they could not afford another baby, but Kathy had refused to even consider an abortion.
>
> The children are quite active, and Danny pays little attention to Kathy's constant requests that he calm down. When Jim attempts to control Danny, Kathy accuses him of being too physical in his discipline. When questioned about this, Jim reported that his dad "beat me plenty and that sure got results." Kathy complains that Jim does not appreciate the difficulty of being home with the children all of the time, and she objects to the increasing amount of time he is away in the evenings. Jim replied rather pointedly that "it is not much fun being at home anymore." Tension between Kathy and Jim was evident.
>
> When questioned about their social contacts since moving to the city, both Kathy and Jim reported that it had been hard to make friends. They knew "everyone in town"

---

*Sonia Nornes and Bradford W. Sheafor originally developed this case material for the Fort Collins (Colorado) Family Support Alliance.

before they moved, but it is different now. With his changing employment, Jim has not made any real friends at work, and Kathy feels isolated at home since Jim takes the car to work each day, and the bus is her only means of transportation. She did indicate that one neighbor has been friendly, and they have met two couples they liked at church.

When asked specifically about Danny, Kathy reported that he has been ill frequently with colds and chronic ear infections. She hesitantly described his behavior as troublesome and hoped the school's structure would help him. Kathy described a Sunday school teacher who called him hyperactive and suggested that she not take him to Sunday school anymore. Kathy wondered if there was some kind of treatment that would help Danny and allowed that she was "about at the end of her rope with that child."

It was clear to Karoline that both Kathy and Jim wanted Danny to begin school. But was Danny ready for school—and would the school be ready for Danny? Would Danny's entering school be best for him? Would it resolve the family's problems? Are there other things that could be done to help this family and, perhaps, prevent other problems from emerging?

Within the strict definition of her job, Karoline could assist the Swans in reaching a decision about school attendance and complete her service to this family. With her "social betterment" concern, however, resolution of only the question about Danny's entering school would not be sufficient. As a social worker, Karoline would hope to help the Swan family address some of the more basic issues they face in order to improve the overall quality of their lives.

Social workers are not experts on all problems clients may experience. Karoline's experience, for example, would not prepare her to make judgments about Danny's health and the possible relationship between his chronic colds and ear infections and his behavior problems. She might refer the Swans to a low-cost medical clinic where a diagnosis of Danny's health problems can be made. She is, however, an expert in "social functioning" and can help Jim and Kathy Swan work on their parenting skills, strengthen the quality of their communication, assist them in developing social relationships in the community, and, perhaps, help Jim obtain job training and stable employment. Karoline's "action orientation" would not allow her to procrastinate. She would be anxious to engage this family in assessing the issues it faces and would support Kathy and Jim as they take action to resolve them.

The Swan family represents at least one form of "human diversity." They are a rural family attempting to adapt to an urban environment. Karoline knows that it will take time and probably some help to make this adjustment. She will explore strengths that may have been derived from their rural background. Perhaps Jim's skills in gardening and machinery repair would prove to be an asset in some lines of employment. Also, their rural friendliness may prove beneficial in establishing new social relationships, and they might be helped to build friendships through their church or neighborhood, or to use other resources where they can find informal sources of support (i.e., natural helping).

Service to the Swan family will require considerable practice "versatility." Karoline will need to assist the family in problem solving around whether or not to send Danny to school. She will hopefully engage them in more in-depth family counseling. She might invite them to join a parents' group she leads to discuss child-rearing practices, link them with medical and psychological testing services for Danny, and help Mr. Swan obtain job training. If Danny does attend school next year, Karoline might work closely with his teacher and Mrs. Swan to monitor Danny's progress and address any problems in his social functioning that may arise. If he does not attend school, an alternative program might be found where he can develop the socialization skills required in the classroom. Clearly, a wide range of practice activities would be needed, and Karoline must be versatile in her practice to apply them.

The Mission of Social Work

While social work practice requires considerable variation in activity, at a more abstract level the profession has consistently maintained that its fundamental *mission* is directly serving people in need and, at the same time, making social institutions more responsive to people. Although this unique mission has been steadfastly held for more than a century, it has been difficult to develop public understanding of its uniqueness among the helping professions. One way to understand this profession is to examine its three primary purposes: caring, counseling, and changing.

Caring

At times the best knowledge social workers can muster is inadequate to prevent or resolve the many problems encountered by the disabled, elderly, terminally ill, and other persons with limited capacity for social functioning. Social workers recognize that certain conditions in life cannot be corrected. Yet the victims of these conditions deserve not only humane but high-quality care.

Caring that makes people comfortable and helps them cope with their limitations is frequently the most valuable service a social worker can provide. Sometimes caring takes the form of arranging for meals to be delivered or for income to be supplemented, and ensuring that adequate housing is provided. At other times, the person and/or family may require help to better adjust to an unchangeable situation like a disability or terminal illness. There is also an important leadership role for social work in helping communities create the necessary services to provide such care. The fundamental intention of caring for those in need is a central purpose of social work practice.

Counseling

Another thrust of social work practice has been to provide treatment for individuals and families experiencing problems in social functioning. Depending on client needs, direct services ranging from psychosocial therapy to behavioral modification, reality therapy, crisis intervention, and various group and family therapy approaches are used by social workers.[1] These approaches do not automatically cure social problems in the same way a physician might prescribe a medication to cure an infection. In fact, most social workers would argue that at best they can only help clients find a way to resolve their issues. The contribution the social worker makes is the ability to engage the client in actively working toward change, to accurately assess the individual and societal factors that have created the need for change, to select appropriate techniques for a given client and situation, and to use these techniques effectively in conjunction with the clients to accomplish the desired results.

Changing the Society

Social change is the third primary purpose of social work. Social workers are committed to reforming existing laws, procedures, and attitudes until they are more responsive to human needs. Many pioneer social workers were reformers who worked to improve conditions in slums, hospitals, and poorhouses. Today, social workers actively influence social legislation in an effort to create new social programs or to change factors that contribute to damaging social conditions such as racism, sexism, and poverty.

Social workers also seek to change negative public attitudes about the more vulnerable members of society by providing public education and facilitating the empowerment of the affected members of the population to advocate for their own interests. Social workers, then, bring about change in the society by representing the interests of their clientele and/or helping clients persuade decision makers at the local, state, or national levels to respond to human needs.

The mission of social work is captured in the following three-part statement. Social work's mission includes:

▶ Caring for those who must live with an unchangeable social problem
▶ Counseling people addressing their social problems by helping them change and/or attempt to change the condition that causes the problem
▶ Changing conditions in the society that make some people more vulnerable to social problems

This mission, however, does not in itself clearly distinguish social work from other helping-oriented occupations. To gain further clarity, one must examine definitions of social work.

Defining Social Work

Unfortunately, social work has been hard to define. Different dictionary definitions treat social work as a set of skills, a job title, or even an activity that might be performed by volunteers. None treat this as a profession with extensive academic and practice experience required for the work. These definitions typically fail to distinguish social workers from others who engage in similar activities. Therefore, it is informative to examine how social workers define themselves.

Three concerted efforts have been made by the social work profession to arrive at a clear definition of social work. The first occurred in the 1920s when the American Association of Social Workers convened a series of meetings of key agency executives in Milford, Pennsylvania. These representatives from a range of practice settings identified several factors that appeared to be common to all social work practice, but they could not agree on a concise definition of social work. However, the Milford Conference encouraged further efforts at articulating a definition of social work when it concluded that social work's common features were more substantial than the differences.[2]

The 1950s brought a second surge of interest in developing a clear conception of social work. The merger of several specialized social work practice organizations and the more generic American Association of Social Workers into the National Association of Social Workers (NASW) was completed in 1955. For a time, a spirit of unity dominated the social work profession, and the effort to find a definition of social work that would reflect the commonality in diverse practice activities began in earnest. A critical step was the publication of the "Working Definition of Social Work Practice" in 1958. Although not yet providing a comprehensive definition of social work, the document established an important basis for subsequent definitions by identifying three common goals of social work practice:[3]

1. To assist individuals and groups to identify and resolve or minimize problems arising out of disequilibrium between themselves and their environment.
2. To identify potential areas of disequilibrium between individuals or groups and the environment in order to prevent the occurrence of disequilibrium.
3. To seek out, identify, and strengthen the maximum potential of individuals, groups, and communities.

Thus, the "Working Definition" established that social workers are concerned with curative or treatment goals, as well as emphasizing the importance of social change or prevention. In addition, the definition recognized the focus of social work on the interactions between people and their environments and the responsibility of social workers to provide services to people as individuals, as parts of various groups, and as members of communities.

Third, in the 1970s and 1980s, NASW published three special issues of its major journal, *Social Work,* that generated substantial debate and discussion about the nature of social work.[4] This activity enhanced understanding of the central features that characterize social work but did not lead to a definitive description of this profession.

Although NASW has never formally adopted a definition of social work, a one-sentence definition developed by one of its committees has gained widespread acceptance.

Social work is the professional activity of helping individuals, groups, or communities enhance or restore their capacity for social functioning and creating societal conditions favorable to that goal.[5]

This statement provides a clear and concise "dictionary definition" of the profession. It draws important boundaries around social work. First, social work is considered professional activity. Professional activity requires a particular body of knowledge, values, and skills, as well as a discrete purpose that guides one's practice activities. When practice is judged professional, community sanction to perform these tasks is assumed to be present, and the profession, in turn, is expected to be accountable to the public for the quality of services provided.

Second, this definition captures a uniqueness of social work. It makes clear that social workers serve a range of client systems that include individuals, families or other household units, groups, organizations, neighborhoods, communities, and even larger units of society. For social work, the identification of one's client is tricky because a client or target of practice activity may range from an individual to a state or nation. The unique activities of the social worker are directed toward helping all of those systems interact more effectively and therefore require professional education as preparation.

Finally, the last part of the definition concerns social work's *dual focus on person and environment.* Social workers help people enhance or restore their capacity for social functioning. At the same time, they work to change societal conditions that may help or hinder people from improving their social functioning. Herein lies another uniqueness of social work. Whereas some professions focus on change in the person and others on changing the environment, social work's attention is directed to the connections between person and environment.

When working with clients, social workers must take into consideration both the characteristics of the person and the impinging forces from the environment. In contrast, the physician is primarily prepared to treat physical aspects of the individual, and the attorney is largely concerned with the operation of the legal system in the larger environment (although both the physician and attorney should give secondary attention to other, related systems). Social work recognizes that each person brings to the helping situation a set of behaviors, needs, and beliefs that are the result of his or her unique experiences from birth. Yet it also recognizes that whatever is brought to the situation must be related to the world as that person confronts it. By focusing on transactions between the person and his or her environment, social interaction can be improved.

Figure 3.1 depicts this unique focus of social work. Social workers operate at the boundary between people and their environment. They are not prepared to deal with all boundary matters. Rather, they address those matters that are judged problematic or have been selected as a way to contribute to the enhancement of social functioning. In sum, social workers temporarily enter the lives of their clients to help them improve their transactions with important elements of their environment. To further understand social work, it is instructive to examine the approaches social workers use when assisting their clients or advocating for social change.

Figure 3.1

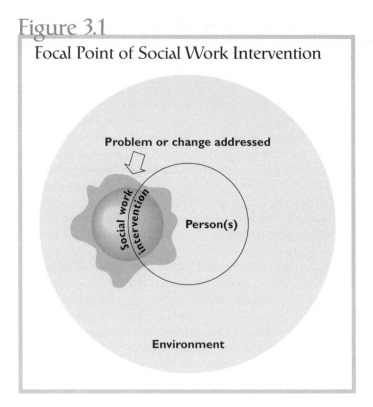

Focal Point of Social Work Intervention

Problem or change addressed

Social work intervention

Person(s)

Environment

Social Work Practice Approaches

Arriving at a practice approach that is sufficiently flexible and encompassing to relate to this complex profession has proven difficult. In fact, social work might be characterized as a profession in search of a practice approach. That search began with the development of several distinct practice methods.

Traditional Practice Methods

The first practice method to develop, *social casework,* was described in the 1917 classic social work book, *Social Diagnosis.*[6] In this book, Mary Richmond focused on the requirements for effective practice with individuals and families, regardless of the type of problem presented. The book filled an important void in social work by introducing a literature describing social work practice. The principles of social casework identified by Richmond were enthusiastically adopted by social workers, and the profession moved its primary focus to work with individuals and families. The popularity of Freudian psychology in the 1920s and 1930s also directed social work toward considering the individual primarily responsible for his or her condition, rather than viewing problems in the structure of society as also contributing to people's issues. Abbott noted that Richmond later expressed concern over this trend to overemphasize the person side of the person-environment mission of social work:

> The good social worker, says Miss Richmond, doesn't go on helping people out of a ditch. Pretty soon she begins to find out what ought to be done to get rid of the ditch.[7]

Social workers concerned with providing services to groups took longer to develop a set of guiding principles, partially because those social workers disagreed among themselves as to whether they should identify professionally with the emerging field of social work. This disagreement was resolved in the 1930s in favor of identifying with social work, and thus a second distinct method, *social group work,* evolved.

The third practice method to develop was *community organization.* With many social agencies and social programs being created in each community, their coordination and the evaluation of their effectiveness became important and, to meet that need, another distinct practice area emerged. Community organization became the practice method primarily concerned with coordinating the distribution of resources and building linkages among existing services.

In addition to using one of these three primary practice methods in their work, many social workers found themselves responsible for administering social agencies and conducting research on the effectiveness of social programs. By the late 1940s, *administration* and *research* had evolved as practice methods in social work. Viewed as secondary methods, they were seen as a supplement to a person's ability as a caseworker, group worker, or community organizer.

Multimethod Practice Approach

Concurrent with the development of these five distinct practice approaches was the growing commitment to unifying social work as a single profession with a well-established practice method. A major study of social work and social work education, the Hollis–Taylor Report, was concluded in 1951. It recommended that, because the breadth of social work practice required social workers to intervene at more than one level of the client system, social work education should prepare students with a beginning level of competence in each of the five practice methods.[8]

The multimethod practice approach proved a good fit with the varied demands for social work practice but failed to yield the unifying practice theme the profession needed. Practitioners typically identified with a dominant method and used the others sparingly.

Generalist Practice Approach

Supported by concepts drawn from social systems theory, the generalist approach to practice began to emerge in the late 1960s. As Balinsky stated, "The complexity of human problems necessitates a broadly oriented practitioner with a versatile repertoire of methods and skills capable of interacting in any one of a number of systems."[9]

The generalist model provided versatility and met the requirement for a flexible approach to social work practice demanded by the complexity and interrelatedness of human problems.

Generalist practice contains two fundamental components. First, it provides a perspective from which the social worker views the practice situation. Social systems theory helps the social worker to maintain a focus on the interaction between systems—that is, the person–environment transactions—and to continually look for ways to intervene in more than one relevant system. Second, rather than attempting to make the client's situation fit the methodological orientation of the social worker, the situation is viewed as determining the practice approach to be used. Thus, the social worker is required to have a broad knowledge and skills and to have the ability to appropriately select from those basic competencies to meet the needs of clients.

Although many social workers contend that the generalist approach has been part of social work practice since its inception, only recently have there been analysis and explication of this practice approach. With the accreditation requirement that both baccalaureate- and master's-level social workers be prepared as generalist practitioners, there has been a resurgence of activity aimed at clarifying the nature of generalist practice in recent years. In their article titled "Milford Redefined: A Model of Initial and Advanced Generalist Social Work," Schatz, Jenkins, and Sheafor delineate the key elements of generalist social work at both the initial and advanced generalist levels.[10]

This model recognizes that there is a *generic foundation* for all social work, whether generalist or specialist, that includes such factors as knowledge about the social work profession, social work values, the purpose of social work, ethnic/diversity sensitivity, basic communication skills, understanding of human relationships, and others.

The *generalist perspective,* according to this model, (1) is informed by sociobehavioral and ecosystems knowledge; (2) incorporates ideologies that include democracy, humanism, and empowerment; (3) requires a worker to be theoretically and methodologically open when approaching a practice situation; (4) is client centered and problem focused; (5) includes both direct and indirect interventions; and (6) is research-based.

At the *initial generalist* level of practice, the social worker builds on the generic foundation and, using the generalist perspective, must at least be capable of (1) engaging effectively in interpersonal helping, (2) managing change processes, (3) selecting and utilizing multilevel intervention modes, (4) intervening in multiple-sized systems as determined by the practice situation, (5) performing varied practice roles, (6) assessing and examining one's own practice, and (7) functioning successfully within an agency.

The *advanced generalist* social worker engages in more difficult practice tasks and, therefore, operates from an expanded knowledge base about individuals, groups, organizations, and communities that is developed in master's degree programs. The advanced generalist must also develop increased skills to intervene in direct service provision with individuals, families, and groups at one end of the multiple-level practice spectrum and, at the other end, address more complex indirect practice situations such as supervision, administration, program evaluation, and policy development. Finally, the advanced generalist is expected to approach social work practice from an eclectic, but disciplined and systematic, stance and to simultaneously engage in both research and practice evaluation.

Specialist Practice Approaches

In contrast to the generalist, a number of specialized practice approaches have emerged. *Specialist* social work practice is characterized by the application of selected knowledge and skills to a narrowed area of practice based on practice setting, population served, social problems addressed, and/or practice intervention mode used. In other words, this practice approach begins with a preference about the knowledge and skill required for practice in that specialized area and serves clients whose needs fit into those more narrow, but in-depth, worker competencies.

While education for initial generalist practice is offered in baccalaureate programs or the early part of master's-level programs, specialist education has increasingly become the emphasis of the latter part of a master's degree. Master's social work education programs sometimes offer the advanced generalist as their area of concentration but more typically build their curricula on one or more specialty areas. Although individual schools of social work usually focus on only a limited number of specialties, the following illustrates the range of specializations a school might offer.

> *Fields of Practice:* for example, services to families, children, and youth; services to the elderly; health; mental health; developmental disabilities; education; business and industry; neighborhood and community development; income maintenance; employment.
>
> *Problem Areas:* for example, crime and delinquency; substance abuse; developmental disabilities; family violence; mental illness; neighborhood deterioration; poverty; racism; sexism.
>
> *Populations-at-Risk:* for example, children and youth; the aged; women; single parents; ethnic populations; persons in poverty; migrants; gay and lesbian persons; the chronically mentally ill.
>
> *Intervention Methods or Roles:* for example, specific practice approaches with individuals, families, and groups; consultation; community organization; social planning; administration; case management; social policy formulation; research.
>
> *Practice Contexts and Perspectives:* for example, industry; hospitals; schools; rural or urban areas.

Today social work embraces both generalist and specialist approaches to practice. The generalist viewpoint supports the commonality that unites social work into one profession; the specialist approach helps to delineate unique areas for in-depth social work practice.

Social Workers: Their Many Faces

How has the emergence of a profession concerned with helping people change conditions that affect their social functioning played out? First, a fairly specific career pattern has emerged, and, second, a substantial number of people have selected social work as a career.

Career Patterns of Social Workers

Varying career patterns have evolved as the practice of social work has changed over time. The early social workers were volunteers or paid staff who required no specific training or educational program to qualify for the work. When formal education programs were instituted at the turn of the twentieth century, they were training programs located in the larger social agencies. In fact, it was not until 1939 that accreditation standards required that all recognized social work education must be offered in institutions of higher education. There was also controversy over whether appropriate social work education could be offered at the baccalaureate level as well as at the more professionally respectable master's level. The reorganization of social work into one professional association (the National Association of Social Workers, or NASW) and one professional education association (the Council on Social Work Education, or CSWE) in the 1950s yielded a single education-level profession. At that time, only the master's degree from an accredited school of social work was considered "legitimate" social work preparation. Today, the Master of Social Work (MSW) degree still is considered the "terminal practice degree" in social work, but other professional practice levels are now recognized. In 2006, 173 of the 181 accredited programs reported their graduation statistics indicating that 17,209 persons received the MSW degree, making it the dominant qualification for social work practice.[11]

It was not until 1970 that the NASW recognized baccalaureate-level (BSW) social workers as fully professional social workers. The Council on Social Work Education subsequently created accreditation standards, and, by 2006, 433 of the 458 accredited schools throughout the United States reported graduating 12,845 persons with the BSW (at times this may be a BA or a BS degree).[12] Another career level had indeed been established.

Increasingly, social workers are also completing doctoral degrees in social work, either the Doctor of Social Work (DSW) or the Doctor of Philosophy (Ph.D.). In 2006, for example, 293 persons completed a doctorate in social work from the sixty-one reporting schools in the United States.[13] In addition, a number of other social workers also complete doctorates in related disciplines. Most doctoral-level social workers are employed in teaching or research positions, but doctoral programs aimed at preparing people for direct social work are beginning to emerge. Doctoral programs, however, are not subject to accreditation by CSWE and are not recognized as professional practice preparation in social work. Thus, the MSW continues to be viewed as the terminal practice degree.

By 1981, NASW found it necessary to develop a classification system that would help to clarify the various entry points to social work and define the educational and practice requirements at each level. This system sorts out the career levels into four categories: *basic professional* (BSW), *specialized professional* (new MSW), *independent professional* (MSW plus at least two years experience), and *advanced professional* (doctorate or special practice proficiency).[14] NASW's classification scheme has several benefits. First, it identifies and clarifies the practice levels existing in social work and, in general terms, spells out the competencies that both clients and employers can expect from workers at each level. Second, it describes a continuum of social work practice with several entry points based on education and experience. Finally, it suggests a basis for job classification that can increasingly distinguish among the various levels of social work competence and assist agencies in selecting appropriately prepared social workers to fill their positions.

A Snapshot of Today's Social Workers and Their Work

Who are the people who have elected a career in social work? It is difficult to determine accurately the characteristics of today's social workers because a single source based on an agreed upon definition of social work does not exist. NASW reports a membership of approximately 150,000, but given that more than 500,000 social workers graduated from CSWE accredited programs in the past 30 years, it is clear that only a fraction of the qualified social workers have elected to join NASW.[15] All social workers are not required to be licensed, but approximately 310,000[16] hold a state license to practice social work. Based on positions classified by employers as social work jobs, the Bureau of Labor Statistics (BLS) estimates there are approximately 595,000 social workers in the United States. Finally, the most current population survey in which people self-classify their occupation estimates that there are 670,000 to 730,000 social workers.[17] Each estimate is flawed, but it is likely that the BLS estimate is the most accurate representation of the number of practicing social workers in the United States today.

The most current and complete data set regarding social workers and their practice activities was conducted by the NASW Center for Workforce Studies. The 2004 study included a random sample of 10,650 licensed social workers from 48 states and the District of Columbia with a 49.4 percent response rate. Thus it can be considered a good representation of licensed social workers. The social workers reporting in this study were 81 percent female and 86 percent non-Hispanic white persons.[18] One limitation is that a number of states have not embraced the basic social worker (BSW) in their licensing, and many baccalaureate social workers are not licensed—thus only 12 percent of the sample practices at that level.

The data in Table 3.1 indicate that mental health, as a social worker's primary practice area, is almost twice as likely as any other focus of practice. Also, although more than 80 percent of the social workers are employed in some form of organization or agency, the largest single practice setting was private practice. This represents a substantial change over the past few decades in the ability of social workers to attract clients to their independent entrepreneurial practice. Increasingly, social workers must be able to manage their own small business, as well as administer large social agencies. The primary work, or function, social workers perform in these jobs is working directly with clients as individuals or in families and groups.

Table 3.1

Characteristics of Licensed Social Workers: Practice Areas, Employment Settings, and Job Functions

Social Worker Characteristic	Percentage
Primary Practice Area	
Mental Health	37
Children/families/adolescents	19
Medical health	13
Aging	9
Schools	8
Developmental disabilities	3
Addictions	3
Primary Employment Setting	
Private practice (solo or group)	18
Social service agency	15
Behavioral health clinic	9
Hospital/medical center	9
School (preschool through grade 12)	9
Nursing home/residential group care facility	5
Case management agency	2
Courts/justice system	2
Primary Job Function (20 hours or more per week)	
Direct/clinical practice	61
Administration/management	20
Supervision	7
Planning/community organization/social policy	7
Consultation	6
Teaching/training	6

Source: Tracy Whitaker, Toby Weismiller, and Elizabeth Clark, *Assuring the Sufficiency of a Frontline Workforce: A National Study of Licensed Social Workers, Executive Summary* (Washington, D.C.: NASW Center for Workforce Studies, 2006), pp. 15–19.

Who are the clients of social workers? Table 3.2 indicates that social workers must be prepared to work with clients from all age groups—from young children to older adults. Even if a social worker works primarily with one age group, he or she inevitably works with family members and others across the age spectrum. The need for social workers to become culturally competent in working with all racial/ethnic groups is

Table 3.2

Characteristics of Social Workers' Clients

Client Characteristic	Percentage	
Client Age	51% or more of workload	Any part of workload
Children	15	62
Adolescents	15	78
Adults	39	90
Older adults	25	78
Client Race/Ethnicity		
Non-Hispanic white	59	99
Black/African American	10	85
Hispanic/Latino	5	77
Asian/Pacific Islander	1	49
Native American/Alaska Native	1	30
Client Condition	Client issue	
Psychosocial stressors	76	
Medical conditions (acute and chronic)	48	
Co-occurring conditions	42	
Mental illness	39	
Affective conditions	33	
Substance abuse	27	
Physical disabilities	19	
Developmental disabilities	10	

Source: Tracy Whitaker, Toby Weismiller, and Elizabeth Clark, *Assuring the Sufficiency of a Frontline Workforce: A National Study of Licensed Social Workers, Executive Summary* (Washington, D.C.: NASW Center for Workforce Studies, 2006), pp. 15–19.

evident from the data indicating that, although social workers may work primarily with persons of one background, they end up doing some work with persons from all groups. Finally, social workers deal with a wide variety of client conditions. More than two-thirds deal with clients experiencing psychosocial stressors as these are interrelated with other problems, but many social workers also deal with social issues related to medical conditions, mental illness, and many other conditions.

A 2004 member salary survey conducted by NASW helps to provide a picture of the earning power of social workers. The median annual income for social workers in that membership sample was $51,900 for full-time social workers during the calendar year 2003.[19] Previous membership studies indicated that social workers begin at a lower salary level upon completing the professional degree and then reach the median salary at around 15 years of experience. Prior data also indicate that the typical person with a BSW degree earns about $1,000 per month less than the person with an MSW degree, and a person with a doctorate earns about $1,000 per month more than the MSW graduate.[20]

These salary levels are not sufficient in themselves to draw top-quality professionals to this demanding work. While social work wages are considered "high" by the Bureau of Labor Statistics (i.e., in the second highest quartile of earnings for all occupations),[21] social work salaries are relatively low for positions requiring professional preparation. Other rewards from the work must therefore be considered more important than earning power to maintain a competent labor force of social workers. In a substantial analysis of the labor market for social workers, Michael Barth concludes that social workers' "taste" for providing their services is exceptionally strong. Barth indicates that, from an economist's perspective, a strong taste for a profession implies that the worker would seek that work even if it conveys greater risk of low pay and despite the potential of the worker to earn greater pay elsewhere.[22] In short, social workers appear to be more attracted to the opportunity to make a difference in the lives of people than to select a profession that will result in high earning power.

Concluding Comment

Since its inception more than a century ago, social work has emerged as a comprehensive helping profession. From the beginning, social workers sought that elusive common denominator that would depict this profession as clearly as possible and help social work form into a cohesive entity. The characteristic of working simultaneously with both people and their environments to improve social functioning has consistently served as social work's primary mission and thus differentiates social work from the other helping professions. In addition to helping people deal with their environments, social workers also consider it their mission to bring about social change in order to prevent problems or to make social institutions more responsive to the needs of people—especially the most vulnerable members of the society. With this person and environment focus, social workers provide a combination of caring, counseling, and changing activities that help people improve the quality of their lives and, therefore, help the society accomplish its goal of promoting the general welfare. In Box 3.1, the practice activities of Demetria (see Chapter 1), illustrate how her social work orientation plays out in her work with the Miles family.

Data in Table 3.1 indicate that social workers today are employed in a wide range of practice areas, from mental health to addictions; work mostly within the context of some form of agency or organization; and mostly work directly with clients to address social issues. Table 3.2 also reinforces social work's claim to be especially concerned with the persons in society who are most vulnerable to social problems. They work with people of all ages and races or ethnic groups, and they address a wide range of client conditions.

Social work has evolved a career ladder that recognizes professionals at four levels: basic, specialized, independent, and advanced. This classification scheme recognizes that at each of the four levels somewhat different job activities occur. The two entry levels (i.e., basic and specialized professional levels) require that the worker complete the requisite educational preparation represented in the accreditation standards of the Council on Social Work Education. At the latter two levels, additional practice experience and expertise and/or advanced education warrant the recognition.

Box 3.1

Demetria's Social Work Orientation

The case in Chapter 1 revealed a social worker's approach to investigating and beginning service when addressing a possible child abuse or neglect complaint. Demetria, the social worker, had just completed her social work degree, and the report from the school related to Joseph Miles was her first "solo" case. Of course, she had the backup of her supervisor, but nevertheless she was understandably apprehensive about being able to do a good job. Clearly the demands for knowledge and skill were beyond that expected of a *natural helper* or *volunteer.* Complex human issues such as this require a well-equipped *professional helper,* in this case, a professional social worker.

Demetria's work clearly demonstrated a commitment to *social betterment* as she carried her assessment beyond the minimum required to establish or reject the suspected child abuse. She sought to understand and address the multiple issues that were combining to affect Joseph; was *versatile* in her practice approach by addressing individual, family, and community issues; and did something about what she found (an *action orientation*). Because none of the issues in this case were unchangeable, the work did not fall into the *caring* aspect of social work's mission. Most of the effort involved the *counseling* and *changing* functions that social workers address. Fitting Demetria's work into the NASW *definition of social work,* the paraphrasing might read "Demetria's practice was the professional activity of helping Joseph and the Miles family restore their capacity for social functioning and creating a more supportive societal resource for those needing employment assistance."

In the NASW classification of levels of professional social work practice, Demetria was a *basic social worker,* having just completed her BSW preparation, and her supervisor was probably an *independent* or *advanced social worker* according to that classification system. Demetria's practice approach was that of an *initial generalist.* She did not try to fit Joseph and his mom into a specialized method or practice approach. Instead, she started by identifying their issues and drawing on multiple approaches to resolve those issues, such as individual counseling (for Joseph and his mother); involvement in a peer group (for Joseph); referral to other needed resources in the community; and a consideration of social action to improve the community resources.

KEY WORDS AND CONCEPTS

Natural and professional helping
Social betterment
Social functioning
Human diversity
Caring/Counseling/Changing
"Working Definition" of social work
"NASW Definition" of social work

Dual focus on person and environment
Generalist social work practice
Specialist social work practice
Traditional practice methods
NASW classification of practice levels
(basic, specialized, independent,
advanced)

SUGGESTED INFORMATION SOURCES

Canadian Association of Social Workers, http://www.casw-acts.ca.
Corey, Mariane Schneider, and Gerald Corey. *Becoming a Helper,* 4th ed. Pacific Grove, CA: Brooks/Cole, 2003.
LeCroy, Craig W. *The Call to Social Work: Life Stories.* Washington, D.C.: NASW Press, 2002.
National Association of Social Workers, http://www.naswdc.org.
Payne, Malcolm. *What Is Professional Social Work,* 2nd ed. Chicago, IL: Lyceum Books, 2006.

ENDNOTES

1. For a brief description of a number of practice approaches, see Bradford W. Sheafor and Charles R. Horejsi, *Techniques and Guidelines for Social Work Practice,* 7th ed. (Boston: Allyn & Bacon, 2006), Chapter 6.
2. American Association of Social Workers, *Social Casework: Generic and Specific: A Report of the Milford Conference* (New York: National Association of Social Workers, 1974), p. 11. (Original work published in 1929.)
3. Harriet M. Bartlett, "Towards Clarification and Improvement of Social Work Practice," *Social Work* 3 (April 1958): 5–7.
4. See *Social Work* 19 (September 1974), *Social Work* 22 (September 1977), and *Social Work* 26 (January 1981).
5. National Association of Social Workers, *Standards for Social Service Manpower* (Washington, D.C.: NASW, 1973), pp. 4–5.
6. Mary E. Richmond, *Social Diagnosis* (New York: Russell Sage Foundation, 1917).
7. Edith Abbott, "The Social Caseworker and the Enforcement of Industrial Legislation," in *Proceedings of the National Conference on Social Work, 1918* (Chicago: Rogers and Hall, 1919), p. 313.
8. Ernest V. Hollis and Alice L. Taylor, *Social Work Education in the United States* (New York: Columbia University Press, 1951).
9. Rosalie Balinsky, "Generic Practice in Graduate Social Work Curricula: A Study of Educators' Experiences and Attitudes," *Journal of Education for Social Work* 18 (Fall 1982): 47.
10. Mona S. Schatz, Lowell E. Jenkins, and Bradford W. Sheafor, "Milford Redefined: A Model of Initial and Advanced Generalist Social Work," *Journal of Social Work Education* 26 (Fall 1990): 217–231.
11. Council on Social Work Education, *Statistics on Social Work Education in the United States: 2006* (Alexandria, VA: Council on Social Work Education, 2007), pp. 4, 16.

12. Ibid., pp. 4, 12.
13. Ibid., pp. 4, 17.
14. *NASW Standards for the Classification of Social Work Practice,* Policy Statement 4 (Silver Spring, MD: National Association of Social Workers, 1981), p. 9.
15. Bradford W. Sheafor, "Three Decades of Baccalaureate Social Work: A Grade Card on How the Professionalization of the BSW has Played Out," *Journal of Baccalaureate Social Work* 6 (Spring 2001): 32.
16. Tracy Whitaker, Toby Weismiller, and Elizabeth Clark, *Assuring the Sufficiency of a Frontline Workforce: A National Study of Licensed Social Workers, Executive Summary* (Washington, D.C.: NASW Center for Workforce Studies, 2006), p. 9.
17. Bureau of Labor Statistics, "Occupational Employment and Wages, November 2007." http://www.bls.gov/opub/mlr/2007/11/art5full.pdf.
18. Whitaker, op. cit., p. 9.
19. "Survey Data Show Earnings Increased," *NASW News* 49 (October 2004): 1.
20. Practice Research Network Report 1–1, *Social Work Income* (Washington, D.C.: National Association of Social Workers, 2000).
21. U.S. Bureau of Labor Statistics, "May 2004 National Occupational Employment and Wage Estimates." http://www.bls.gov/oes/2004/may/oes_21Co.htm.
22. Michael C. Barth, "Social Work Labor Market: A First Look," *Social Work* 48 (January 2003): 9–19.

Social work pioneer Jane Addams visits with young women at Chicago's Hull House in the early 1900s.

The Emergence of Social Work as a Profession

Prefatory Comment

The growth and development of social work were not planned events. The profession evolved from the humanitarian response to human suffering in the late 1800s that led to the creation of a workforce to address social problems and later to the profession of social work. The title of this book, *Social Work: A Profession of Many Faces,* highlights the importance social work has given to becoming a fully recognized profession. This chapter examines social work's emergence in the United States, with emphasis on how the desire to become a profession has shaped its actions. It begins with a review of the nature of professions, particularly the helping professions, and traces the emergence of social work during the past century.

A field of sociological inquiry is devoted to the definition and description of the nature of professions. One of the central figures in this field, Wilbert Moore, concluded that "to have one's occupational status accepted as professional or to have one's occupational conduct judged as professional is highly regarded in all post industrial societies and in at least the modernizing sectors of others."[1] Professions are highly regarded, in part, because they have been granted authority to perform essential services that ensure survival and help people enhance the quality of their lives. The benefit of being considered professional has drawn many occupational groups to claim professional status. The term has sometimes been used to describe persons who are paid for activities that others might perform for recreation or pleasure or is at times applied when a person becomes highly specialized in an area of competence, for example, a real "pro" at finding bargains on the Internet. In this book, however, the term *profession* is used in its more traditional sense of identifying a set of carefully prepared and highly qualified persons who assist people in dealing with complex matters in their lives.

Three elements help to explain the unique characteristics of the occupations that are considered to be professions. First, professionals must be free of constraints that might limit their ability to select what they consider to be the best way to assist people in situations to resolve problems or improve the quality of their lives. The maintenance of this *professional autonomy* has been most successful in the "private professions" that typically contract directly with their clients (e.g., medicine, dentistry), although increasingly constraints imposed by managed care companies are eroding this flexibility. In agency-based or "public professions" such as social work and teaching, organizations employ the professionals and then contract with the clients to provide the needed services. In these situations, it is recognized that the organization's rules and regulations will inevitably limit the autonomy of the professionals to exercise their independent judgment.

Second, society has granted *professional authority* to a few people who have acquired the necessary knowledge and skills to provide the needed services in a given area of professional practice. Society grants this authority because it has, in effect, determined that it is inefficient, if not impossible, for every person to acquire all the knowledge and skill needed to meet complex human needs. Thus, these professionals are given the exclusive right to make judgments and give advice to their clients in their specific service areas. In granting this professional authority, society, in essence, gives up the right to judge these professionals except in extreme cases of incompetent or unethical practice. Society depends on the members of that profession to determine the requisite entrance preparation and to be sure those who are practicing as members of that profession do so competently.

Third, when the right to judge practice is relinquished by granting professional authority, the public becomes vulnerable and rightfully expects the professions to protect them from abuses that may accrue from the professional monopoly. Hughes indicates that the motto of the professions must be *credat emptor* ("buyer trust"), as opposed to the motto of the marketplace, *caveat emptor* ("buyer beware").[2] For example, where the layperson would rarely question the prescription given by a physician, that same person might be very cautious when buying a used car and might have it thoroughly tested by an independent mechanic before making a purchase. To maintain this buyer trust, the professions must be accountable to the public that has granted them the sanction to perform these services. To establish and maintain this *professional responsibility*, professions develop codes that identify the expected ethical behavior of practitioners and establish mechanisms for policing their membership regarding unethical or incompetent practice.

In a sense, the professions and society struck a deal. In exchange for responsible service in sensitive areas of life, the professions were granted exclusive authority, that is, a *professional monopoly,* to offer these services.

How does an occupation achieve recognition as a profession? There is no precise dividing line between occupations and the professions. It is most useful to think of a continuum of occupations, from those that have few characteristics associated with the professions to those that have many such attributes. Ronald Pavalko summarizes the attributes necessary to achieve recognition as a profession.[3]

▶ The profession must possess a body of theory and intellectual understanding about the people to be served, the condition to be addressed, and the intervention approaches to be used.

▶ The services provided by the profession must relate to a need that is highly valued and for which the society is willing to take responsibility if that need is not met by other social institutions. These services are concerned with aspects of people's lives that require specialized knowledge and skill to address highly sensitive issues, such as their health, spirituality, learning, or their interpersonal and sometimes intimate interactions with others.

▶ The work to be done is not routine and cannot be reduced to tightly prescribed steps or procedures; thus, the professional must have the autonomy to use individual discretion about how the work is performed.

▶ The professional must complete an extensive education in which both the general knowledge for informed citizenship is required and the specialized knowledge and skill needed to perform the work are transmitted from the experienced professional to the novice.

▶ The profession maintains its focus on service to the clients, as opposed to responding primarily to the worker's self-interest.

▶ The professionals are drawn to the work by a sense of commitment, a "calling," or a "taste" for the work to be accomplished.

▶ The professionals perceive the profession as a community of persons with common interests and goals with which they identify.

▶ The profession creates and promotes adherence to a code of ethical behavior that informs the members of appropriate worker–client relationships and is used to determine if members have abused the privilege of membership in that profession.

The following process, typically followed by professions when developing the requisite attributes, has been identified by Harold Wilensky:

1. A substantial number of people become engaged on a full-time basis in providing the needed services.
2. Training schools or educational programs are established to prepare new practitioners with the advanced knowledge required for the work to be done.
3. A professional organization is formed to promote the interests of the members of that profession.
4. The professional organization engages in political activities to gain protection of the monopoly of the profession in its area through licensing or other forms of regulation of the profession.
5. The professional organization develops a code of ethical behavior to guide the professional's interactions with clients, other professionals, and the general public.[4]

The pattern identified by Wilensky accurately describes the process of social work's evolution as a profession. As professional organizations emerge, a conflict of interest becomes evident. The purely altruistic expectation of professions begins to be compromised because the professional associations operate primarily to promote the self-interest of the professionals, with the interests of clients or patients too often becoming secondary.

Social Work as a Profession: A Historical Perspective

Social work did not evolve in a vacuum. A series of events affected its development and will continue to shape social work in the future. Some of those events are represented by major factors in the history of the United States such as settlement patterns, wars, international conditions, economic fluctuations, the philosophy of elected political leaders, and others. These events influenced decisions about the extent to which this society would respond to its members' social needs and, subsequently, to the social programs that would be supported.

Table 4.1 identifies some of the important events that affected the evolution of U.S. society's approach to the human services and shows selected mileposts in the development of social work. In columns 1 and 2, the table lists dates and events that identify a historical event that may be familiar to the reader, such as the U.S. Civil War or the Great Depression. Column 3 identifies important events that shaped social programs (e.g., the Pierce Veto), and column 4 lists some critical events in the development of the social work profession—for example, publication of *Social Diagnosis* in 1917.

From Volunteers to an Occupation (Prior to 1915)

The roots of social work may be found in the extensive volunteer movement during the formative years of the United States. In the colonial period, for example, it was assumed that individuals and families would care for themselves, but if further difficulties existed, one could depend on *mutual aid*. Friends, neighbors, or other representatives of the community could be counted on to help out when needed. Volunteer activities involved interaction with the poor, the ill, and those experiencing other social problems. As social agencies began to develop, they soon learned how to train volunteers in constructive ways to relate to clients and improved their ability to be helpful.

Developing out of this background came social work as an occupation. The first paid social work–type positions in the country were jobs in the Special Relief Department of the United States Sanitary (i.e., public health) Commission. Beginning as a voluntary agency and then receiving public support as the Civil War progressed, the Special Relief Department and its agents served Union soldiers and their families experiencing social and health problems due to the war. Wartime needs temporarily opened the door to providing social services, and the outstanding performance of these workers helped pave the way for other positions in social work. Several women involved in the war effort performed important leadership roles in the development of human services. For example, Dorothea Dix (Superintendent of Nurses in the U.S. Sanitary Commission) previously had provided leadership in an attempt to secure federal government support for mental hospitals; Clara Barton later founded the American Red Cross; Josephine Shaw Lowell helped start the Charity Organization Society in New York City and also headed the Consumers' League, which worked to protect shopgirls from exploitation; Sojourner Truth gave leadership to the National Freedman's Relief Association; and Harriet Tubman, a central figure in the Underground Railroad, subsequently established a home for elderly African Americans. Following the war, the Special Relief Department was closed.

A short time later, paid social work also appeared when the Massachusetts Board of Charities was established. Founded under the leadership of Samuel Gridley Howe, an advocate for persons who are physically and mentally disabled, this agency coordinated services in almshouses, hospitals, and other institutions of the state. Although its powers were limited to inspection and advice, the Board gained wide acceptance. The concept of boards overseeing state services spread to other states in the 1870s and became the forerunners to today's state departments of human services.

Table 4.1

Timetable of Selected Events in Social Welfare and Social Work History

Approximate Date	U.S. History Event	Social Welfare Event	Social Work Event
Founding of United States	Agriculture-based society	Family responsibility	
	Open frontier	Mutual aid	
	Slavery prevalent	Puritan ethic	
	Open immigration	Town meetings	
		Orphan homes and first charitable societies	
		Poorhouses	
1776	Declaration of Independence Revolutionary War	Growth of voluntary social agencies	
	Act for the Gradual Abolition of Slavery (Pennsylvania)	Society for Alleviating the Miseries of Public Prisons	
	Era of merchant philanthropy		
1789	George Washington inaugurated		
1800	United States prohibits importation of slaves	Elizabeth Seton founds Sisters of Charity	
	War of 1812	Mass. General Hospital	
		Child labor laws	
		Gallaudet School for Deaf	
	Anti-Slavery Movement	Society for the Prevention of Pauperism	
	Chinese immigration began	NY House of Refuge (for juveniles)	Dorothea Dix begins crusade for improved conditions in "insane asylums"
1850	Emergence of industrial society	Pierce Veto	
		Children's Aid Societies	
	Rise of cities and urbanization	Orphan Trains	
1860	U.S. Civil War	YMCA movement	
		Freedman's aid societies	U.S. Sanitary Commission
		Mass. Board of Charities	(first paid social workers)

(Continued)

Table 4.1

(Continued)

Approximate Date	U.S. History Event	Social Welfare Event	Social Work Event
1877	Reconstruction Era	Buffalo Charity Aid Society	Friendly visitors
		Hull House founded	Settlement workers
			National Conference on Charities and Correction
1898	Spanish-American War	First Juvenile Court	NY School of Philanthropy
1910		White House Conference on Children	Medical social work
		U.S. Children's Bureau	Psychiatric social work
		Community Chest (federated fund raising)	School social work
1915	Progressive Era		Flexner, "Is Social Work a Profession?"
			Richmond, *Social Diagnosis*
			National Social Workers Exchange
		NAACP	
		National Urban League	Association of Training Schools for Prof. SW
1920	Women's Suffrage (19th Amendment)	County and state relief agencies	American Association of Social Workers
			American Association of Schools of Social Work
1929	Stock Market Crash The Great Depression	Civilian Conservation Corps (CCC)	
1935		Social Security Act Works Progress Administration (WPA)	
1941	United States enters World War II	U.S.O. organized National Social Welfare Assembly	American Association of Group Workers
			National Association of Schools of Social Administration
	End of WW II		
1945	Postwar recovery period	U.S. Department of Health, Education, and Welfare	Association for the Study of Community Organization

Table 4.1

(Continued)

Approximate Date	U.S. History Event	Social Welfare Event	Social Work Event
			Social Work Research Group
1952			Council on Social Work Education (merger of AASSW and NASSW)
1955	Korean Conflict Civil Rights Movement		National Association of Social Workers (merger of six professional specialization groups and Am. Assn. of Social Workers)
	Women's Movement	Indian Health Service	Greenwood, "Attributes of a Profession" NASW
			"Working Definition of Social Work Practice"
1960		Juvenile Delinquency Act	
	Kennedy administration	Herrington, *The Other America*	NASW "Code of Ethics" Academy of Certified Social Workers (ACSW)
		Equal Pay Act	
		Community Mental Health Act	
1963	Johnson administration Vietnam War	Food Stamp Act	
	Black Power Movement	Civil Rights Act of 1964	
		Economic Opportunity Act	
		Older American Act	
		Indian Civil Rights Act	
1965	Welfare Rights Movement Martin Luther King, Jr., assassination	Immigration Act of 1965	
		Medicare Act	
1968		Medicaid	
	Nixon administration Gay Liberation Movement		

(Continued)

Table 4.1

(Continued)

Approximate Date	U.S. History Event	Social Welfare Event	Social Work Event
		Supplemental Security Income (SSI) approved	
1970			NASW recognition of baccalaureate social worker as professional
1972		Child Abuse Prevention & Treatment Act	
1974	Ford administration	Education of All Handicapped Children Act	NASW "Conceptual Frameworks" series
			CSWE begins BSW accreditation process (generalist emphasis)
			CSWE approves advanced standing for BSWs
			Expansion of doctoral social work education
	Carter administration	Social Security Block Grant Act (decentralize some programs to states)	(GADE)
	AIDS epidemic		
1978		Indian Child Welfare Act	Association of Social Work (licensing) Boards
	Reagan administration	Privatization of human services expanded	
1982		Tax Equity and Fiscal Responsibility Act of 1982 (cutbacks in human service provisions by federal government)	
	Equal Rights Amendment (ratification fails)		
1988	George H. W. Bush administration		
1990			Academy of Certified Baccalaureate Social Workers (ACBSW)

Table 4.1

(Continued)

Approximate Date	U.S. History Event	Social Welfare Event	Social Work Event
	Persian Gulf War	Americans with Disabilities Act	Social workers licensed in all states, D.C., and some territories
1993	Clinton administration	Individuals with Disabilities Education Act	
1996	Oklahoma City federal building bombing	Health care reform fails	ACBSW discontinued "Code of Ethics" revised
	Columbine High School massacre	Family and Medical Leave Act	
		Personal Responsibility and Work Opportunity Reconciliation Act	
2001	George W. Bush administration		ACSW examination discontinued
	September 11 terrorist attacks		
	Invasion of Afghanistan		
	War on Iraq initiated		
2004			NASW Workforce Center Social Work Congress Wingspread Conference on Social Work Unity Social Work Reinvestment Act introduced
2009	Obama administration		

The Massachusetts Board of Charities also introduced social research into human service delivery. An 1893 report, for example, identified the causes of poverty as "first, physical degradation and inferiority; second, moral perversity; third, mental incapacity; fourth, accidents and infirmities; fifth, unjust and unwise laws, and the customs of society."[5] Although the approach was perhaps more moralistic than would be found in social work today, the report reflected the understanding that both personal and societal factors contribute to poverty.

Another significant development leading to the emergence of social work was the establishment of the Charity Organization Society (COS) of Buffalo, New York, in 1877. Modeled after an organization in London, charity organization societies sprang up in a number of communities with the dual purposes of finding means to help the poor and preventing the poor from taking advantage of the numerous uncoordinated social agencies that provided financial assistance. Leaders in social work from the COS movement included Mary Richmond, who helped identify a theory of practice in her books *Friendly Visiting Among the Poor* (1899) and *Social Diagnosis* (1917); Edward T. Devine, a founder of the New York School of Philanthropy in 1898; and Porter Lee, who was instrumental in founding the American Association of Schools of Social Work in 1919.

Another important development that contributed to the emergence of social work was the Settlement House Movement initiated in 1886. Patterning settlement houses after London's Toynbee Hall, settlements were established in New York and Chicago. Within fifteen years, about one hundred settlement houses were operating in the United States. The settlements helped the poor learn skills required for urban living and simultaneously provided leadership in political action efforts to improve the social environment. Robert Bremner sums up the impact of the settlement movement:

> Where others thought of the people of the slums as miserable wretches deserving either pity or correction, settlement residents knew them as much entitled to respect as any other members of the community. Numerous young men and women who lived and worked in the settlements during the 1890s carried this attitude with them into later careers in social work, business, government service, and the arts.[6]

The residents of Chicago's Hull House are a good example. Its founder, Jane Addams, won the Nobel Peace Prize in 1931; Julia Lathrop became the first director of the U.S. Children's Bureau and was succeeded by other Hull House alumnae Katherine Lenroot and Grace Abbott, thus contributing to the protection of children and youth for several decades.

The efforts to integrate the African American population into the mainstream of U.S. society following the Civil War also contributed to the development of social work. George Haynes, the first African American graduate of the New York School of Philanthropy, for example, helped found the National Urban League, while Mary McLeod Bethune, who gave leadership to the education of African American women, was a founder of the National Council of Negro Women and was influential in making New Deal policies more equitable for the African American population.

Social work expanded into another setting in the early 1900s when Richard Cabot and Ida Cannon opened a social work program at the Massachusetts General Hospital. There social workers provided services for patients experiencing health-related social problems and simultaneously worked to strengthen the services of related health and welfare agencies throughout the community. Roy Lubove identifies the significance of this development for the professionalization of social work:

> The enlistment of medical social workers marked an important stage in the development of professional social work. (An occupation) limited to the charity organization and child welfare societies provided too narrow a base for professional development, associated as it was with problems of relief and economic dependency. Medical social work added an entirely new institutional setting in which to explore the implications of casework theory and practice.[7]

Medical social workers became interested in professional education as a means of moving beyond social work's "warm heart" image and into a more disciplined understanding of psychological or social conditions as the base of patient distress. In 1912, the hospital's one-year training program in medical social work was established in the Boston School of Social Work.

Through these years, social work jobs were also springing up in other practice areas such as mental hygiene (mental health), prisons, employment and labor relations, and schools. Beginning in 1873, an organization designed to draw together members of this diverse occupation was formed, the National Conference on Charities. Later renamed the National Conference on Charities and Correction, this organization brought volunteer and professional staff members of social agencies together to exchange ideas about the provision of services, discuss social problems, and study the characteristics of effective practice. By the time World War I began, social work was an established occupation clearly distinguishable from the many volunteer groups and other occupations concerned with the well-being of members of U.S. society.

Professional Emergence (1915–1950)

With social work firmly established as an occupation, attention then turned to its development as a profession. At the 1915 meeting of the National Conference on Charities and Correction, Abraham Flexner addressed the subject, "Is Social Work a Profession?" Dr. Flexner, an authority on graduate education, had previously done a penetrating study that led to major changes in medical education. The organizers of this session of the National Conference apparently hoped Flexner would assure them that social work was, or was about to become, a full-fledged profession. However, that was not in the cards. Flexner spelled out six criteria that an occupation must meet to be considered a profession:

1. Professions are essentially intellectual operations with large individual responsibility.
2. They derive their raw material from science and learning.
3. This material is worked up to a practical and clear-cut end.
4. Professions possess an educationally communicable technique.
5. They tend to self-organization.
6. They become increasingly altruistic in motivation.[8]

Based on these criteria, Flexner concluded that social work had not yet made it into the professional elite. Following Flexner's admonition to "go forth and build thyself a profession," social workers busily attended to these functions over the next thirty-five years.

One effort was to develop a code of ethics. In 1921 Mary Richmond indicated that, "we need a code; something to abide by, or else we will have low social standing."[9] One code, the "Experimental Draft of a Code of Ethics for Social Case Workers," was discussed at the 1923 meeting of the National Conference on Social Welfare. Although this proposed code was never acted on, it represented a beginning effort at formulating a statement of professional ethics.

Probably the greatest amount of effort was devoted to self-organization. The National Social Workers Exchange opened in 1917 to provide vocational counseling and job placement for social workers and later became actively involved in the identification and definition of professional standards. In 1921 its functions were taken over by the broader American Association of Social Workers, which made significant efforts to develop a comprehensive professional association. This effort was later weakened by the attempts of some specialized practice areas to develop their own professional organizations. A chronology of the development of these specialized groups follows:[10]

▶ 1918 American Association of Hospital Social Workers
▶ 1919 National Association of Visiting Teachers
▶ 1926 American Association of Psychiatric Social Workers
▶ 1936 American Association for the Study of Group Work
▶ 1946 Association for the Study of Community Organization
▶ 1949 Social Work Research Group

At this point, it was not clear whether social work was one or many professions.

Another development during this period concerned the required preparation to enter the social work profession. Social work education had begun as agency-based training, but a concerted effort was made during this period to transfer it to colleges and universities, where other professions had located their professional education. In 1919 the Association of Training Schools for Professional Social Workers was established with seventeen charter members—both agency and university affiliated schools. The purpose of that organization was to develop standards for all social work education. By 1927 considerable progress toward that purpose had been made, and the Association of Training Schools reorganized into the American Association of Schools of Social Work (AASSW). Although education programs had been offered in agencies, as well as at both undergraduate and graduate levels in colleges and universities, the AASSW determined that by 1939 only university-affiliated programs with two-year graduate programs would be recognized as professional social work education.

That action led to a revolt by schools whose undergraduate programs prepared professionals to meet the staffing needs of the social agencies in their states. A second professional education organization was formed in 1942, the National Association of Schools of Social Administration, made up largely of public universities in the Midwest that offered baccalaureate-level and one-year graduate-level professional education programs. Ernest Harper, a leader in that organization, described this development as "a protest movement against unrealistic and premature insistence upon graduate training and overemphasis upon professional casework as the major social work technique."[11]

With leadership from governmental and voluntary practice agencies, the two organizations were later merged (1952) into the Council on Social Work Education (CSWE) following the landmark Hollis–Taylor study of social work education.[12] The outcome of that decision favored the two-year master's program as the minimum educational requirement for full professional status. Undergraduate social work education temporarily faded from the scene.

Another important area of concern that was given only limited attention during this period was strengthening the knowledge and skill base of social work practice. Richmond's rich contribution, *Social Diagnosis,* was the first effort to formalize a communicable body of techniques applicable to the diverse settings in which social caseworkers were found.[13] Momentum from this thrust, however, was lost as social work slipped into the grasp of the popular psychoanalytic approach. Nathan Cohen comments, "The search for a method occurred just at the time the impact of psychoanalysis was being felt. Did social work, in its haste for professional stature, reach out for a ready-made methodology for treating sick people, thus closing itself off from the influence of developments in the other sciences?"[14] This question must be answered in the affirmative. By adopting the helping methodology that was currently in vogue, social work embraced firmly, but perhaps inappropriately, the private model of professionalism.

Consolidating the Gains (1950–1970)

The move to consolidate the accrediting bodies for the schools of social work into the CSWE set an important precedent for the field and was part of a movement to treat social work as a single and unified profession. In 1950 the several specialized associations and the American Association of Social Workers agreed to form the Temporary Inter-Association Council of Social Work Membership Organizations (TIAC). The purpose behind the formation of TIAC was to bring these specialized groups into one central professional association. After considerable efforts by the specialties to maintain their identities, TIAC proposed a merger of the several groups in 1952. By 1955 this was accomplished, and the National Association of Social Workers (NASW) was formed.

NASW membership rose from 28,000 to 45,000 between 1961 and 1965, largely because of the formation of the Academy of Certified Social Workers (ACSW), which required both NASW membership and a two-year period of supervised experience. Many job descriptions were revised to require membership in the Academy, forcing social workers to join the NASW and obtain certification.

The late 1950s were a time of great introspection, and the professional journal *Social Work* was filled with articles such as "The Nature of Social Work,"[15] "How Social Will Social Work Be?,"[16] and "A Changing Profession in a Changing World."[17] Perhaps the most significant work was Ernest Greenwood's classic article, "Attributes of a Profession," in 1957.[18] Greenwood identified five critical attributes of professions that, depending on the degree to which they have been accomplished, determine the level of professionalism for any occupational group:

1. A systematic body of theory
2. Professional authority
3. Sanction of the community
4. A regulative code of ethics
5. A professional culture

He related the development of social work to each of these five criteria and concluded that social work was now a profession. He observed:

> When we hold up social work against the model of the professions presented above, it does not take long to decide whether to classify it within the professional or nonprofessional occupations. Social work is already a profession; it has too many points of congruence with the model to be classifiable otherwise.[19]

To the credit of social workers, they were as stimulated by Greenwood's declaration that they had become a profession as they were by Flexner's conclusion that they were not yet in the select circle. In 1958 the NASW published the "Working Definition of Social Work Practice," a valuable beginning to the difficult task of identifying professional boundaries.[20] This was followed by Gordon's excellent critique, which helped strengthen and clarify some parts of the working definition, particularly in relation to knowledge, values, and practice methodology.[21] In 1960, the NASW adopted a Code of Ethics to serve as a guide for ethical professional practice,[22] thus completing the steps to become a fully recognized profession.

Turning Away from the Elitist Professional Model (1970–Present)

From the turn of the twentieth century to the late 1960s, social work displayed a pattern typical of an emerging profession. It created a single association to guide professional growth and development; adopted a code of ethical professional behavior; provided for graduate-level university-based professional schools and acquired recognition to accredit those educational programs; successfully obtained licensing for social work practice in some states; conducted public education campaigns to educate the public about social work; achieved recognition for social work among the helping professions; and moved in the direction of other professions by increasing specialization and limiting access to the profession. Indeed, social work was on its way to carving its niche among the helping professions.

However, social work did not vigorously pursue the path that would lead to even greater professional status. Perhaps influenced by a renewed spirit of concern emanating from the Civil Rights, Welfare Rights, and Women's Rights movements, the development of social work as a profession during the 1970s and 1980s was marked by ambivalence over following the more traditional format of the established professions.

First, there was a resurgence of social change activity on the part of social workers. A legacy from Lyndon Johnson's Great Society programs was federal support, in the form of jobs and other resources, toward efforts to eliminate social problems and alleviate human suffering. Social work was already committed to those goals, and social workers were prepared to move away from their clinical orientation and onto the front lines of social action.

For social workers bent on achieving higher professional status, activist social workers were sometimes unpopular. Their somewhat controversial activities created an unwelcome public image of social workers as militant activists on the front lines of social change. This change in the balance of activities performed by social workers, however, helped to bring social work back to its roots and reestablish the "change" orientation in its purposes of caring, counseling, and changing the society. The more liberal political climate that supported social work activism was short lived. Federal support for programs encouraging social change dwindled and was nearly nonexistent under the Reagan and George H. W. Bush administrations.

Next, in 1970, NASW made a dramatic move by revising its membership requirements to give full membership privileges to anyone who had completed a baccalaureate degree in social work from an undergraduate program approved by CSWE. In opposition to the pattern of professions becoming more exclusive, social work opened its membership to more people by determining that professional qualifications could be gained through professional education at the undergraduate level. However, social work has been uneasy about operating as a multilevel profession, and, although the NASW classification system is clear about the "basic social worker" being viewed as professional, the social worker at this level has never been fully embraced by many MSW social workers. Some advocates for the baccalaureate social worker contend that NASW did not devote sufficient attention to this practice level and that its program priorities in the 1980s "centered too much on licensing, vendor payments, private practice and other issues that were not sufficiently relevant to the baccalaureate worker."[23] NASW's creation of the Academy of Certified Baccalaureate Social Workers in the early 1990s represented movement away from that overemphasis on the interests of master's level social workers, but the discontinuance of that certification in 1996 was a retreat from that position.

With NASW's formal recognition of baccalaureate social work as fully professional, in 1974 the Council on Social Work Education began accrediting baccalaureate social work education (BSW) programs. Initially, 135 schools met the undergraduate accreditation requirements, and by 2008 that number had increased to 464 schools in the United States and Puerto Rico, with another 16 schools in candidacy for accreditation. With 190 MSW programs and an additional 19 in candidacy status, social work has developed a substantial place in higher education.[24]

In 2007 and 2008 a surge of interest in strengthening social work as a single, somewhat unified profession developed. Underpinning this effort was the creation of the Center for Workforce Studies by NASW in 2004, where data are collected to document the work of social workers. These data suggest that a large portion of today's social workers, especially males, are age fifty or older and that the profession faces the likelihood of many of its members "aging out" in the next decade. Also, it is estimated that forty to fifty different organizations had been formed around various interests in social work practice and education, with no unified voice of the profession articulating the needs and concerns of social workers. In response, NASW and CSWE jointly facilitated a "Social Work Congress," where many of these organizations were represented and that called for greater unity within the profession. Subsequently, representatives of several of these organizations met at the Wingspread conference facility in Wisconsin to begin mapping ways to strengthen unity—through mergers of organizations or greater collaboration among existing professional associations. Finally, with the sponsorship of two social workers who were U.S. senators, along with a companion bill in the House of Representatives, the Social Work Reinvestment Act containing several provisions that would strengthen social work and social work services, was introduced in the federal legislature in 2008.

Social Work Confronts a Disaster: Evidence of a Maturing Profession

In the mid-1950s, Marion K. Sanders published a highly critical article on the social work profession titled "Social Work: A Profession Chasing Its Tail." Although some of his criticism was no doubt accurate, Sanders essentially cast social work as an ill-defined occupation that had compromised too much of its original concern for the vulnerable members of society to achieve professional status. Illustrating the intangible nature of social work practice and the poor definition of the profession at that time, Sanders created the following story to illustrate his point.

The day after the bomb fell, the doctor was out binding up radiation burns. The minister prayed and set up a soup kitchen in the ruined chapel. The policeman herded stray children to the rubble heap where the teacher had improvised a classroom. And the social worker wrote a report: since two had survived, they held a conference on Interpersonal Relationships in a Time of Intensified Anxiety States.

Of course the bomb hasn't fallen. And the social workers have not yet abdicated all the hard and daring tasks to the other benevolent callings. But it could happen. Despite their shortcomings, the doctors, teachers, and reverend clergy at least know what is expected of them.... In contrast the social workers—though specialists in good deeds—seem to have lost track of what particular good needs doing by them.[25]

Contrast Sanders' depiction of social work in the 1950s with the reports of the activities social workers performed when terrorists crashed airplanes into several critical locations in the United States. On September 11, 2001, social workers were immediately on the front lines—in New York; Washington, D.C.; and elsewhere. A few representative stories confirm that today social workers are prepared to effectively apply their knowledge and skills in a time of crisis.

▶ Already in place was an agreement with the American Red Cross that the National Association of Social Workers (NASW) would facilitate the delivery of mental health services to victims of disaster, rescue workers, military personnel, and their families. NASW, through its national and chapter offices, immediately coordinated efforts to make social work services available, and more than 1,000 social workers were contacted to provide services through this mechanism.

▶ In New York City, the NASW Chapter's eighty-five-member Disaster/Trauma Working Group immediately made itself available to provide a variety of mental health and other services.[26]

▶ Ilia Rivera-Sanchez was on the scene at the Pentagon by 6:00 P.M. the afternoon of the attacks, comforting and counseling firefighters and military personnel engaged in the rescue work. She later worked at the morgue offering counseling to those bringing in the bodies recovered from the Pentagon.[27]

▶ Social workers at Bellevue Hospital in New York City operated two support centers—one for staff members who were working around the clock with victims and another for families of victims. They also prepared lists of missing persons, handled emotional telephone calls from people searching for missing family members, coordinated with other human services agencies, provided clothing for persons unable to reach their homes, and so on.[28]

▶ In airports, train stations, and bus stations around the world, social workers provided services to people whose travel was interrupted by the attacks. Housing was often needed, funds for meals were provided, alternate transportation arrangements had to be made, and loved ones were contacted regarding the whereabouts of stranded travelers. Social workers were there to assist.

Indeed, social work has matured in its capacity to contribute to the society and was prepared to respond to this emergency, and the society recognized and made use of the competencies of many social workers.

Concluding Comment

In the past century, social work has developed in a manner that meets the criteria for professions. Consensus about its unique purpose among the professions has been reached, and social work has achieved sanction as the appropriate profession to help people resolve problems in their interaction with their environments. Social workers have been granted the professional authority to provide the necessary helping services for people in need and have taken their authority to provide these professional services seriously. The National Association of Social Workers and the Council on Social Work Education have worked through the decades to clarify social work's knowledge, value, and skill base. Social work has developed educational programs that prepare new people to enter this profession and has established a process for accrediting the programs that meet qualitative educational standards at both the baccalaureate and master's levels. Social work has also adopted and regularly updated a Code of Ethics and has established procedures for dealing with violations of that code, which allows the profession to carry out its professional responsibility to protect clients and the general public from abuses that might arise from the monopoly it has achieved.

We can observe the subtle but important influence that professional recognition, educational preparation, and practical training have had on Demetria (see Box 4.1) as she carries out her investigation and initiates services in the suspected child abuse case found in Chapter 1.

Box 4.1

Demetria's Functioning as a Professional Social Worker

Demetria's work with the Miles family (see Chapter 1) illustrates professional social work activity. What made her work "professional"? First, Demetria had the recognized educational preparation (a BSW degree from an accredited social work education program) for a beginning social worker. It appears that, at least partially because of that status, she was granted adequate professional autonomy to exercise her professional judgment about the case; she had sufficient professional authority, which allowed Mrs. Miles to trust her with quite a bit of information about family problems; and Demetria reflected professional responsibility in the discrete way she handled client information and her willingness to extend beyond the minimum job expectations to initiate discussion of needed social change.

Second, if one ticks through the criteria for being a professional, Demetria and her work exemplify a number of ways social work practice is professional. For example, she was prepared from her social work education with enough knowledge about people and programs to be able to immediately work constructively in this case; the child welfare services she provided were highly valued by the society, as the protection of children is one of the most strongly supported human services; Demetria functioned in a highly ethical manner throughout the interactions around this case, and so on. These factors, largely unseen by Joseph and Mrs. Miles, were instrumental in the agency hiring Demetria in the first place, the school personnel working with her to identify Joseph's issues, Mrs. Miles' openness to Demetria's offer to help, and Demetria's competence in carrying out the work. This preparation for social work practice and the sanction from the community facilitated Demetria's ability to quickly establish rapport and successfully begin the helping process.

KEY WORDS AND CONCEPTS

Profession
Attributes of professions
Professional autonomy, authority, and
  responsibility
Public vs. private professions

State boards of charities
Charity organization societies
Settlement houses
Council on Social Work Education
National Association of Social Workers

SUGGESTED INFORMATION SOURCES

Greenwood, Ernest. "Attributes of a Profession," *Social Work* 2 (July 1957): 45–55.
Leighninger, Leslie. *Social Work: Search for Identity.* Westport, CT: Greenwood, 1987.
———. *Creating a New Profession: The Beginnings of Social Work Education.* Alexandria, VA: Council on Social Work Education, 2000.
Lubove, Roy. *The Professional Altruist.* Cambridge, MA: Harvard University Press, 1989.

ENDNOTES

1. Wilbert E. Moore, *The Professions: Roles and Rules* (New York: Russell Sage Foundation, 1970), p. 3.
2. Everett C. Hughes, "Professions," *Daedalus* (Fall 1963): 657.
3. Ronald M. Pavalko, *Sociology of Occupations and Professions,* 2nd ed. (Itasca, IL: F. E. Peacock, 1988), pp. 19–29.
4. Harold Wilensky, "The Professionalization of Everyone?" *American Journal of Sociology* 70 (September 1964): 137–158.
5. Cited in Ralph E. Pumphrey and Muriel W. Pumphrey, eds., *The Heritage of American Social Work* (New York: Columbia University Press, 1961), p. 12.
6. Robert H. Bremner, *From the Depths* (New York: New York University Press, 1956), 66.
7. Roy Lubove, *The Professional Altruist* (Cambridge, MA: Harvard University Press, 1965), 32.
8. Abraham Flexner, "Is Social Work a Profession?" in *Proceedings of the National Conference on Charities and Correction, 1915* (Chicago: National Conference on Charities and Correction, 1916): 576–590.
9. Pumphrey and Pumphrey, *Heritage,* p. 310.
10. John C. Kidneigh, "History of American Social Work," in Harry L. Lurie, ed., *Encyclopedia of Social Work,* 15th ed. (New York: National Association of Social Workers, 1965), pp. 13–14.
11. Herbert Bisno, "The Place of Undergraduate Curriculum in Social Work Education," in Werner W. Boehm, ed., *A Report of the Curriculum Study* Vol. II (New York: Council on Social Work Education, 1959), p. 8.
12. Ernest V. Hollis and Alice L. Taylor, *Social Work Education in the United States* (New York: Columbia University Press, 1951).
13. Mary E. Richmond, *Social Diagnosis* (New York: Russell Sage Foundation, 1917).
14. Nathan E. Cohen, *Social Work in the American Tradition* (New York: Holt, Rinehart, & Winston, 1958), pp. 120–121.

15. Werner W. Boehm, "The Nature of Social Work," *Social Work* 3 (April 1958): 10–18.
16. Herbert Bisno, "How Social Will Social Work Be?" *Social Work* 1 (April 1956): 12–18.
17. Nathan E. Cohen, "A Changing Profession in a Changing World," *Social Work* 1 (October 1956): 12–19.
18. Ernest Greenwood, "Attributes of a Profession," *Social Work* 2 (July 1957): 45–55.
19. Ibid., p. 54.
20. Harriet M. Bartlett, "Towards Clarification and Improvement of Social Work Practice," *Social Work* 3 (April 1958): 5–7.
21. William E. Gordon, "Critique of the Working Definition," *Social Work* 7 (October 1962): 3–13; "Knowledge and Values: Their Distinction and Relationship in Clarifying Social Work Practice," *Social Work* 10 (July 1965): 32–39.
22. National Association of Social Workers, *Code of Ethics* (Washington, D.C.: The Association, 1960).
23. Bradford W. Sheafor and Barbara W. Shank, *Undergraduate Social Work Education: A Survivor in a Changing Profession* (Austin: University of Texas School of Social Work, 1986), Social Work Education Monograph Series 3, p. 25.
24. "Archive of COA Decisions, February 2008." http://www.cswe.org.
25. Marion K. Sanders, "Social Work: A Profession Chasing Its Tail," *Harper's* Monthly 214 (March 1957): 56.
26. John V. O'Neill, "Social Workers Heed Call After Attacks," *NASW News* 46 (November 2001), p. 8.
27. Ibid., p. 1.
28. Ibid., p. 8.

part three

Social Work Career Options

The payoff in social work is in the services rendered to clients and the improvements made to problematic social conditions affecting the quality of life for people. After all, these are the primary motivations for entering this profession. Nevertheless, if one is to be satisfied in his or her work, that social worker must find a niche in the profession where the work is fulfilling. Although one can change directions during the course of a social work career, it is helpful to make at least preliminary decisions about level of education one will need, type of client issues to be addressed (i.e., field of practice), kind of organization in which to work (i.e., practice setting), providing services compatible with one's basic values, and identifying the specific knowledge and skills to begin acquiring. The five chapters in this part of *Social Work: A Profession of Many Faces* introduce the elements included in these career choices.

Each social worker must make certain decisions that will affect his or her career path. One important decision concerns one's level of educational preparation. Chapter 5 summarizes a considerable amount of data about social workers at different educational levels and highlights the employment opportunities at each. In essence, the baccalaureate-level social worker works primarily in direct services with clients and is more likely than master's-level social

workers to serve either children and youth or older adults. The master's-level social worker may also hold administrative and supervisory positions, and those in direct service positions are most likely to address medical, mental health, and school-related issues with the adult population. Some doctoral-level social workers can be found in complex administrative and direct practice jobs, but the majority is concentrated in research and teaching positions.

A second decision concerns the practice area one chooses to enter. Chapter 6 surveys thirteen unique fields in which social workers apply their trade. Despite the differences in these fields of practice, a basic pattern emerges of the social workers helping people address their issues and interact more effectively with the world around them.

A social worker must decide if he or she is to work in a human service organization or engage in private practice. Chapter 7 examines those organizations where most social workers are employed. Factors affecting agency structure and functioning are discussed. Private practice presents a different set of problems than are experienced by those social workers employed in human service organizations, and these differences are examined.

Chapter 8 examines the basic values that have shaped social work's approach to practice. Examples of these values are beliefs that all people are worthy of being treated with respect, that people should be helped to have meaningful interactions with others, that people should be guided toward becoming independent and taking responsibility for themselves, and that society has a responsibility for helping people lead fulfilling lives. In addition, we examine the ethical guidelines imbedded in the NASW Code of Ethics that guide social workers in the way they conduct their work on a day-to-day basis.

Finally, Chapter 9 describes the basic knowledge and skills required of social workers. Based on research about the tasks social workers perform, this chapter then identifies what a social worker needs to know and be able to do in order to carry out those tasks. Although this is not an exhaustive list of competencies, it suggests the content that one would expect to find in a social work education program and the activities social workers will be expected to perform in working with clients.

Entry to the Social Work Profession

Prefatory Comment

Selecting a career is one of the most important decisions a person must make. Whether that decision is to become a homemaker, physician, salesperson, teacher, chemist, or social worker, it should be based on a thorough understanding of the physical, emotional, and intellectual demands of the field and a close look at one's own suitability for that type of work. Whatever the choice, it will dictate how a person spends a major part of each day. It will also spill over into other aspects of life, including lifestyle, general satisfaction with self, and quality of life.

The decision to enter a particular profession does not lock a person into that occupation for a lifetime, but it does represent a substantial commitment of time, energy, and resources to prepare for professional practice and to obtain the requisite credentials. If it is a good career choice, one's job can be an exhilarating and stimulating experience. However, if there is a poor fit between a person and his or her chosen occupation, work can be frustrating and unrewarding. Further, the complexity of human situations requiring professional assistance and the growing knowledge about effective helping, obligate the professional to a career of continued learning and skill development. Unless a person is willing to make such a commitment, a professional career should not be pursued.

For the person considering the social work profession, it is useful to have a clear perception of the career opportunities this profession affords. Social work has evolved a four-level career ladder that has two entry points (i.e., the basic and specialized social worker) and two additional levels based on more advanced experience and education. This chapter describes the educational preparation and practice experience required for each practice level and identifies factors that shaped the evolution of social work practice at those levels.

Making a career choice is difficult because of the wide range of careers to choose from but, more importantly, because of the problems an outsider experiences in gaining an adequate and accurate understanding of a career. Too often, only after a person has made substantial commitments in time, energy, and money or has cut off other opportunities by taking steps to enter a career does he or she find that it is not what was expected or wanted. Another difficulty lies in having a clear perception of one's own needs, interests, and abilities. Personal introspection, occupational preference testing, guidance counseling, and experience in activities related to the career are all resources for making this choice.

The person contemplating a career in social work must consider a number of factors. It is evident that social work is extremely broad in scope—ranging from social action to individual therapy—with a knowledge base that is far from stable or well developed. Thus, explicit guidelines for social work practice do not exist, leaving the social worker with the responsibility for exercising a great deal of individual judgment. Furthermore, the skills demanded of the social worker vary widely and require a flexible, creative, and introspective person to practice them. The pressures of a social work job create a degree of stress because the outcome of the work is critically important to the clients. In addition, social workers are regularly criticized by both clients and the general public, frequently in regard to programs over which they have little policy-making influence. If a person can tolerate the ambiguity, responsibility, pressures, and criticism that are a part of social work; if the values, skills, and interests required of social workers are compatible; and if it is rewarding to work constructively to help people improve their level of social functioning, social work offers a very satisfying career.

Issues in Social Work Preparation and Employment

Membership in any profession requires that its members acquire specified qualifications. The very act of defining professional membership inherently excludes some persons who operate with similar knowledge and values but lack the identified qualifications. In social work, for example, completion of the education and practice experience specified by the National Association of Social Workers (NASW) in its membership qualifications is necessary to gain professional recognition. However, social workers are cognizant that many other helping people with different educations and experiences also make important contributions to the delivery of human services. For the person entering social work, it is important to be aware of several issues that relate to professional qualifications.

Education and Accreditation

The social work profession requires that a person must have a formal social work education; that is, either a baccalaureate degree with a major in social work (BSW) or a master's degree in social work (MSW) from an accredited social work education program, as a minimum for professional recognition. The *accreditation* process is administered by the Council on Social Work Education (CSWE) and has become a significant factor in social work because the graduate of the accredited program is assumed to be prepared to enter practice ready to apply the appropriate knowledge, values, and skills in the service of clients. For all practical purposes, education is the gatekeeper of the profession. This does not mean that all graduates are equally prepared to enter practice, that some people who do not have all the required social work courses are unable to perform some tasks expected of the social worker, or even that all schools offer the same opportunity for learning the essentials of social work. Rather, accreditation attests to the fact that the public can have confidence that graduates are at least minimally prepared for beginning-level social work practice because they have completed an instructional program that is soundly designed and taught by competent faculty.

Professional Certification

The National Association of Social Workers provides confirmation to clientele and employing human services agencies that some social workers have demonstrated the requisite knowledge and competence to engage in practice, that is, *professional certification*. Where accreditation is testimony to the quality of an educational program, certification is the profession's testimony regarding the individual's knowledge, values, and skills.

Following it's formation in 1955, the NASW created two professional certification programs that were based on the social worker's practice level. In 1960, the Academy of Certified Social Workers (ACSW) was created. The ACSW was the profession's nationally accepted mechanism for designating those social workers who were qualified at the "independent social worker" level and was often a requirement for social work jobs. It required the MSW degree, two years' post–master's experience, a sufficient score on a national exam, and favorable evaluation of the worker's competence by peers. With exam-based licensing of social workers implemented in every state, the exam portion of the ACSW became redundant and in 2005 was discontinued as a requirement for membership in the Academy. In 1990, NASW also created the Academy of Certified Baccalaureate Social Workers (ACBSW), but this credential did not catch on as a job credential and was discontinued in 1996.

In addition to the ACSW, for many years NASW also maintained two professional recognition programs for advanced social workers engaged in clinical practice: the Qualified Clinical Social Worker (QCSW) and the Diplomate in Clinical Social Work (DCSW). More recently, the demand to recognize qualified social workers in specialty areas has led NASW to create credentialing programs in several practice areas. At the MSW level are the Certified School Social Work Specialist; Certified Social Worker in Health Care; Certified Clinical Alcohol, Tobacco, and Other Drugs Social Worker; Certified Advanced Social Work Case Manager; Certified Advanced Children, Youth, and Family Social Worker; Advanced Social Worker in Gerontology; and Clinical Social Worker in Gerontology certificate programs. At the BSW level are the Certified Social Work Case Manager; Certified Children, Youth, and Family Social Worker; and the Social Worker in Gerontology certificates. All of these certificates require NASW membership, graduation from a CSWE-accredited educational program, practice experience after graduation, and adherence to the NASW Code of Ethics. Usually a state license to practice social work or a passing score on the appropriate social work exam offered by the Association of Social Work (licensing) Boards is required, as well as a favorable evaluation by the worker's supervisor and a professional colleague. These credentials are designed to serve as indicators of competency by the profession of social work to clients and employers, as well as to the insurance companies that offer reimbursement for social workers' services.

Licensing or State Regulation of Social Work Practice

The social work profession has shaped its educational programs through accreditation requirements and, through NASW, has sought to identify its competent and experienced practitioners by creating its certification programs. However, over the past two decades, perhaps the most dominant issue on NASW's agenda has been to encourage the licensing of social workers throughout the United States. As described by the Association of Social Work Boards, *licensing* is:

> ...a process by which an agency of state government or other jurisdiction acting upon legislative mandate grants permission to individuals to engage in the practice of a particular profession or vocation and prohibits all others from legally doing so. By ensuring a level of safe practice, the licensure process protects the general public. Those who are licensed are permitted by the state to use a specific title and perform activities because they have demonstrated to the state's satisfaction that they have reached an acceptable level of practice.[1]

The intent of licensing is to have state governments identify those social workers who are properly prepared through professional education and experience to provide client services. Both consumers of service (particularly in private practice settings) and health insurance companies that reimburse for the cost of social work services have looked to licensing as a desirable way to determine a social worker's practice competence.

As opposed to the uniform national requirements for professional certification used by NASW, each state controls whether there will be licensing of social workers, the levels of practice it will license, and the requirements to be licensed. Thus there is substantial variability among the states. After many years of effort by NASW and the Canadian Association of Social Workers to achieve legal regulation of social work, all fifty states, the District of Columbia, Puerto Rico, the U.S. Virgin Islands, and ten Canadian provinces license (register or certify) social workers. Approximately two-thirds of the states provide for licensing or registration of social workers at the basic level, and most have more than one level requiring the MSW as the educational preparation.[2] The Association of Social Work Boards serves as the coordinating agency for the state boards and offers testing at the following levels:

▶ **Basic:**   BSW degree on graduation
▶ **Intermediate:**   MSW with no post-degree experience
▶ **Advanced Generalist:**   MSW with two years' post-master's supervised experience
▶ **Clinical:**   MSW with two years' post-master's direct clinical social work experience

The individual states then determine whether they want to use these test results for licensing of social workers and whether they want to grant *reciprocity* (i.e., accept the licenses of social workers from other states) when social workers move from state to state.

Professional Standards

A profession is expected by society to protect the public from those members who abuse the professional monopoly. To conduct this self-policing, professions must establish standards and develop procedures for evaluating complaints and imposing negative sanctions if a member engages in incompetent or unethical practice. State licensing, too, performs this client protection function by withdrawing the legal right to practice as a social worker if such violations occur.

NASW establishs appropriate standards of conduct through its Code of Ethics and maintains a process to ensure the public that recognized professional social workers meet those standards. The Code spells out in some detail the social worker's ethical responsibilities to clients, colleagues, practice settings, other professionals, the profession of social work, and the broader society.[3] When a social worker becomes a member of NASW, he or she must profess willingness to practice within the guidelines prescribed by the Code of Ethics, and the Code, in turn, becomes the baseline for evaluating the professional behavior of social workers.

The process established for reviewing complaints begins with the local chapter of NASW when an individual or organization lodges a formal complaint about the practice of a social worker. A committee of the chapter will then conduct an investigation of the complaint and make a determination that the complaint is or is not substantiated. Either party has the right to appeal to the NASW National Committee on Inquiry, which reviews the charges and makes a final judgment. If the Committee on Inquiry concludes that ethical standards have been violated, a plan to correct the behavior through training or treatment may be developed, or the individual's membership in NASW may be suspended. The sanctions remain in effect until the terms established by the Committee on Inquiry are satisfied.

Options for Human Service Practice

Addressing complex human needs requires providers equipped with a variety of knowledge and skills. The human services, therefore, are made up of many people—from volunteers to highly trained professionals—who provide many different forms of helping. The person considering a career in a helping profession should carefully compare social work with other human service providers to determine if serving as a social worker would be the most satisfying way to spend one's work life.

Volunteers

One cannot fully examine the human services without recognizing the important role played by volunteers. For many people who have other vocations, one way to be involved with human services is to volunteer. The willingness to give of oneself, without monetary reward, in order to help others is expressed in the activity of millions of people who give their time, energy, and talents to make this a better world. It was from efforts to prepare volunteers to provide more effective human services that social work became an occupation and, later, a significant helping profession.

Today, social workers work closely with volunteers in many agencies. Their jobs often include the recruitment, selection, training, and supervision of volunteers. The qualifications of volunteers vary from activity to activity. At times professionals volunteer their services beyond their jobs in their own agencies. These volunteer activities may use their professional abilities but may also require skills unrelated to professional training. Like any other good citizen, the social worker has an obligation to donate his or her talents to improve social conditions.

Nonprofessional Service Providers

Not all human service practice requires the competencies of a social worker or someone with related professional skills. These providers have been referred to in the literature as *indigenous workers*. They may be clients, former clients, or others who have rapport with low-income or other client groups based on having similar experiences to the client population. At times indigenous workers can build relationships with clients when professionals have difficulty establishing rapport. Their life experience and knowledge of the individuals or groups being served are the most important qualifications.

Another important source of nonprofessional personnel for human service agencies are *graduates of community colleges*. These Associate of Arts (AA) degree programs vary considerably from school to school but focus on preparing for very specific human service jobs with titles such as mental health technician, community service aide, case aide, or social work technician. The AA degree programs usually include the study of human growth and behavior, social problems, the social service delivery system, personal values and self-awareness, and basic communication skills. These programs may provide field experiences so students have an opportunity to apply knowledge acquired in the classroom. The tasks the AA graduate can be expected to perform are typically very concrete and supervised by experienced workers.

Other Baccalaureate-Level Disciplines

Several disciplines offer majors in colleges and universities that are closely related to social work. Completing these degrees can serve as helpful preparation for some human service jobs and can also be good preparation for a subsequent degree in social work. However, these programs of study should not be confused with social work degree programs that, if accredited, carry professional recognition.

Social Science Disciplines.   Social work has traditionally had a close relationship with the social science disciplines for two reasons. First, social work has drawn on basic knowledge from the disciplines of psychology, sociology, anthropology, economics, and political science, while developing its theoretical base for understanding the individual, family, group, organization, community, and the impact of culture on all of these. Second, in higher education, social work has had close administrative ties with these disciplines at the baccalaureate level. It is not uncommon to find a baccalaureate-level social work education program housed in a department that includes one or more social science disciplines.

Most positions for social scientists involve research or teaching in a college or university, and, thus, a Ph.D. is necessary to be competitive in the job market. With the exception of specialized areas of clinical psychology and the small branch of applied sociology, social scientists do not typically engage in the provision of human services. Their purpose is to develop and test theories that will increase understanding of the people or places they study, but they do not intend to intervene to help people or social institutions change.

Related Helping Professions. When making a career choice within the human services, a person should examine a range of helping professions that might fit his or her individual talents and interests. The more established professions are medicine, law, nursing, teaching, and psychology. Other helping professions, such as physical therapy, music therapy, occupational therapy, marriage and family therapy, urban planning, and school counseling, also offer challenging and rewarding careers.

Each of these is an established profession, and there are accredited educational programs a person must complete to be recognized as a member of that profession. Like social work, these professions identify standards for competent and ethical practice and take responsibility for policing the membership for compliance with these standards. The clientele of these professions, then, have some protection from the possible misuse of professional authority. Employment opportunities in these professions vary considerably, but most jobs are defined as requiring professional education for entry.

It is instructive to compare estimates of the demand for social workers with that of other helping professions. Table 5.1 provides a comparison of selected helping professions based on the projections of the U.S. Bureau of Labor Statistics (BLS). The BLS estimates of annual growth indicate that social work is already one of the largest professions and is expected to be a moderately fast-growing occupation. Table 5.1 also reveals that the average annual earnings of social workers is on the low end of the helping professions. For comparison purposes, the table identifies the expected terminal professional degree for each discipline.

Emerging Human Service Occupations. During the 1970s a new occupational group began to emerge, known generally as *human services* or *human development*. The human services occupations differ from the helping professions we have reviewed because they intend to be nonprofessional. Most people giving leadership to these occupations are professionally trained in other disciplines and have been largely involved in corrections and mental health services—although they branch into every aspect of the social services.

The development of the human services field was stimulated by dissatisfaction with the service delivery system. Fundamental to the philosophy behind this field are two viewpoints.[4] First, the human services have been fragmented into problem areas

Table 5.1

Estimated Employment, Earnings, and Training Requirements for Related Professions: 2006–2016

Profession	Total Employment 2006	Estimated Employment 2016	Est. Annual Growth (%)*	Annual Job Openings (Attrition and Job Growth)	Estimated Annual Earnings 2004	Expected Professional Degree
Registered Nurse	2,505,000	3,092,000	2.35	100,100	$62,480	Assoc. or Bachelor's
Elem./Middle School Teacher	2,214,000	2,496,000	1.27	76,600	50,040	Bachelor's + License
Social Worker	595,000	727,000	2.22	25,800	47,170	Bachelor's or Master's
Special Ed. Teacher	459,000	530,000	1.55	17,300	51,230	Bachelor's + License
School Counselor	260,000	292,000	1.26	8,400	51,690	Bachelor's or Master's
Clinical/Counseling/ School Psychologist	152,000	176,000	1.58	5,100	68,150	Master's or Ph.D.
Rehabilitation Counselor	141,000	173,000	2.30	6,000	33,350	Bachelor's or Master's
Mental Health Counselor	100,000	137,000	3.00	5,000	39,450	Bachelor's or Master's

(Continued)

Profession	Total Employment 2006	Estimated Employment 2016	Est. Annual Growth (%)*	Annual Job Openings (Attrition and Job Growth)	Estimated Annual Earnings 2004	Expected Professional Degree
Occupational Therapist	99,000	122,000	2.31	3,700	$ 65,540	Master's
Marriage/Family Therapist	25,000	32,000	2.98	1,200	45,310	Master's

*Annual Growth Rate: Bureau of Labor Statistics projections are based on the assumption of an average growth rate of 0.80 between 2006 and 2016. Social work, for example, is in the highest projected growth category with a 2.22 per year projected growth.

- (Employment Projections) U.S. Bureau of Labor Statistics. http://www.bls.gov.emp/cmptabapp.htm.
- (Mean Wage Estimates) U. S. Bureau of Labor Statistics. http://data.bls.gov/oes/search.jsp.
- (Expected Professional Degree) U. S. Bureau of Labor Statistics. http://www.bls.gov/oco/home.htm.

(e.g., child welfare, corrections, mental health) that create barriers to good service because many clients experience complex problems and must deal with multiple agencies, programs, and service providers. Second, the integration of services into "umbrella agencies" and the creation of a broad discipline that can provide a wide range of services is preferable to the more focused professional orientation.

Social workers would agree that the fragmented methods of delivering social services often make it difficult for clients to locate help. However, the profession does not regard service integration as a solution (division lines can exist just as rigidly within one large agency as in several smaller ones) and believes that the professional model, with all its limitations, continues to be the most valid means of identifying the people who are prepared with the knowledge, values, and skills to respond to specific human needs. Social work would argue that clients are better served through greater efforts at *interdisciplinary practice,* rather than the emergence of new human service disciplines that have no clear service focus or practice approach, no established standards for ethical conduct, no professional responsibility for quality control, and no standardized educational preparation subject to professional accreditation.

Levels of Professional Social Work Practice

Social work's evolution as a profession has been uneven, and the career paths one might follow as a social worker can be confusing. Figure 5.1 portrays the various career options available to the professional social worker. It recognizes that, before a person decides to begin the educational preparation required to become a professional social worker, he or she will typically have had some positive experiences that have motivated this decision. This future social worker will typically have been a good natural helper or volunteer, the client of a social worker who received useful services, or perhaps a human services provider who did not have professional preparation. If he or she has not already completed a bachelor's degree, the most likely place to begin would be in a BSW program. However, if this is a person who has a degree in another discipline, a second entry point is available— an MSW program.

To make appropriate career development decisions, it is useful for the potential social worker to understand what is expected of a social worker at each of the four practice levels and how that practice level has emerged historically. The following materials, based on NASW's classification system,[5] briefly describe each level, identify the qualifications, and trace the manner in which its central characteristics have emerged.

The Basic Professional

Description: Practice as a basic social worker requires professional practice skills, theoretical knowledge, and values not normally obtainable in day-to-day experience but that are obtainable through formal social work education. This knowledge is distinguished from experiential learning by being based on conceptual and theoretical

Figure 5.1

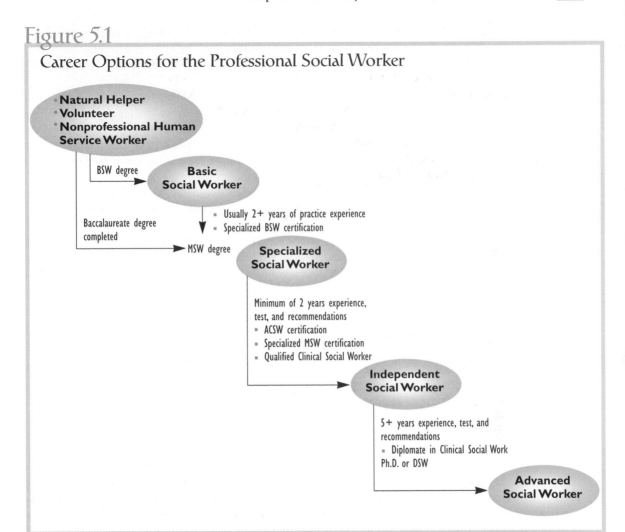

Career Options for the Professional Social Worker

knowledge of personal and social interaction and by training in the disciplined use of self in relationship with clients.

Qualifications: Requires a baccalaureate degree from a social work program accredited by the Council on Social Work Education.

Characteristics: Practice at this first level has been formally recognized as professional only since 1970, when the NASW first admitted to full membership persons with a degree from a social work program approved by the Council on Social Work Education. This recognition substantially increased the quantity and quality of undergraduate social work programs.

A few schools offered baccalaureate-level social work courses as early as the 1920s.[6] However, the thrust of social work was toward graduate education. In 1932 the American Association of Schools of Social Work (AASSW) declared that, to be recognized as professional, a social worker must graduate from a four-year college and complete at least one year of graduate education. In 1937 this requirement was revised to establish two years of graduate education as the minimum level for professional practice.

In response to the AASSW policy, in 1942 several schools created a competing organization, the National Association of Schools of Social Administration (NASSA), for the purpose of having undergraduate programs recognized as professional preparation. After several years of conflict over the legitimacy of undergraduate professional education, thirteen organizations interested in the resolution of this issue and in the overall enhancement of social work education formed the National Council on Social Work Education. In 1952 these organizations morphed into the single accrediting body for social work education: the Council on Social Work Education (CSWE).

The CSWE offered membership to both undergraduate and graduate schools and undertook a thirteen-volume curriculum study of social work education at both levels. One volume of this study recommended establishment of professional social work education at the undergraduate level with a continuum developed from undergraduate to graduate programs.[7] This recommendation was initially rejected by the CSWE. During most of the 1960s, undergraduate programs operated under CSWE guidelines that might best be described as a traditional liberal arts education oriented toward social welfare.[8] They were usually taught in departments of psychology or sociology, offered no more than three or four social work courses, and sometimes had no social workers as faculty. These programs were not professional education, and neither employers nor graduate social work education programs gave credit for this background or preference in admissions to applicants who had completed this major.

Disenchantment of students, employers, and professional social workers with undergraduate education contributed to the establishment of a joint CSWE–NASW Ad Hoc Committee on Manpower Issues in 1968. The Committee's recommendations contributed to concurrent actions in 1970 by NASW members to grant full membership to graduates of approved undergraduate programs and by the CSWE to establish standards for approval of these programs. The first standards adopted were essentially structural: they contributed to the visibility of social work programs, required that social workers be included in faculty, and demanded specification of educational objectives.[9] CSWE "approval" was granted to 220 schools by 1973 but was at best a limited and informal type of accreditation. Specification of curriculum content was slower to develop because a workable division between baccalaureate- and master's-level education had not yet evolved.

In 1973 CSWE took the second step to complete formal accreditation: it adopted much more substantial standards for baccalaureate degree programs, placing the primary focus on preparation for professional social work practice. Some previously "approved" programs could not meet the new standards, but most were able to secure the necessary resources to upgrade their programs and achieve accredited status. In 1984 another significant step to upgrade the quality of baccalaureate social work education was taken when the CSWE operationalized a new set of accreditation standards and a much more substantive Curriculum Policy Statement. Rigorous application of the accreditation standards did not deter colleges and universities of all sizes in all states from building and maintaining undergraduate social work education programs. As of 2006, 458 colleges and universities had BSW programs that were fully accredited and enrolled more than 27,000 junior- and senior-level students.[10]

With NASW recognition came the gradual acceptance of baccalaureate-level social work, both by employers as preparation for practice and by the graduate programs as preparation for advanced education. Increasingly, jobs were defined to recognize the competence and abilities of social workers who had completed this type of educational program, and salary and work assignments were differentiated from those without this preparation. Furthermore, in 1972 CSWE granted approval for graduate schools to accept up to one year's credit for special groups of students. Today, approximately 85 percent of the graduate programs offer some form of *advanced standing* to graduates of accredited programs that typically amount to waiving one to two terms of graduate work.[11]

Clearly, the developments since the 1970s enhance the conclusion that the social worker who has completed an accredited undergraduate social work program should be prepared with the competencies for that level of professional practice. Perhaps the most valid test of the acceptance of baccalaureate or basic social workers is whether they find employment as social workers. One study of 5,228 graduates of BSW programs found that 71.4 percent found their first job in social work, and 86.8 percent of these graduates secured employment within six months after graduation. Over time, 84.3 percent of the BSW graduates were employed as social workers. These data suggest that the human service agencies found baccalaureate-level social workers attractive, especially in direct service positions, in which 90.2 percent were employed in their first social work job.[12]

The basic social worker is now well established in the United States as the first level of professional practice. The demand for social workers is increasing, and agencies readily employ these graduates. A niche has developed for BSW graduates that involves working largely with children and youth, with the aged, in the traditional nonprofit social service agencies and residential centers, and primarily on the front lines of social work practice providing services directly to clients.

The Specialized Professional

Description: Practice at this level requires the specific and demonstrated mastery of therapeutic techniques in at least one knowledge and skill method, as well as general knowledge of human personality as influenced by social factors. Specialized practice also requires the disciplined use of self in treatment relationships with individuals or groups, or a broad conceptual knowledge of research, administration, or planning methods and social problems.

Qualifications: Requires a master's degree (MSW) from a social work program accredited by the CSWE.

Characteristics: Prior to the reemergence of baccalaureate-level social work education and the basic social worker, the generally accepted level of preparation for social work practice was that of the specialized social worker. It is expected that the MSW social worker will have sufficient competence to function effectively in at least one area of specialized practice.

Historically, master's-level social work education began much like the more sophisticated in-service training programs of today. The first formal education program, known as the New York School of Philanthropy (now the Columbia University School of Social Work), was a six-week course offered under the auspices of the New York Charity Organization Society in 1898. The early curricula of the evolving schools incorporated preparation for a range of services, from individual helping approaches to economic and reform theory. They included a heavy investment in internships or field experiences as tools for learning practice skills and tended to be organized around practice settings, such as hospital social work and school social work. The MSW programs' greatest emphasis was on preparation for the services offered by private social agencies, and they tended to neglect the growing demand for social workers in the public social services.

By the 1940s the two-year MSW had become the minimum requirement for professional practice. The two-year programs were typically organized around what was known as the "Basic Eight," in reference to what at that time were considered the eight primary divisions of social work practice: public welfare, social casework, social group work, community organization, medical information, social research, psychiatry, and social welfare administration. By 1965 the schools had largely abandoned programs structured on the basis of practice setting and instead organized curricula around the practice methods of casework, group work, community organization, administration, and research.

Two factors have significantly influenced social work education at the master's level in the past quarter-century. First, the emergence of baccalaureate-level social work forced a reorientation of master's education; it was necessary to adapt to the student who entered the MSW program with a substantial social work education already completed. For this student, provision was made for advanced standing in the graduate-level program that typically has meant waiving out of up to one year of graduate work, usually with a few summer courses designed to help students for different BSW programs balance out differences between their programs and the initial year of the school's MSW program.

Second, the Council on Social Work Education's Standards for Accreditation and Curriculum Policy Statement allowed individual schools increased flexibility in determining curriculum content. As the typical two-year MSW program evolved, it offered a general orientation to social work practice during the first year and then provided more specialized content based on population served, social problem addressed, practice intervention approach, or client group served during the second year. Prior to that development, students attending MSW programs could expect pretty much the same basic curriculum regardless of which school they attended. Today, because of the breadth of social work practice, the accreditation standards require that during the introductory or "foundation" part of the program the student must be prepared to practice from a generalist perspective. Thus, the first year of master's-level social work education is relatively similar from school to school. However, after that base is developed, the final year (or its equivalent) prepares the student for a specific area of concentration, and at this level the schools differ widely. The dominant specializations increasingly have been related to the clinical aspects of social work practice. In the 2006 academic year, for example, the concentrations MSW students chose were mental health (18.6 percent), child welfare (14.3 percent), family services (12.8 percent), school social work (7.2 percent), and health and aging (both 7.0 percent) as their specialized practice areas.[13]

For the 2006 academic year, 24,910 full-time and 14,656 part-time students were enrolled in the 173 reporting master's-level programs. About two-thirds of the applicants were accepted for admission, and about 40 percent actually enrolled—often because students apply to several schools and end up enrolling in only one. The reporting master's programs graduated 17,207 new MSWs that year.[14]

As opposed to the basic social worker, this specialized worker is expected to possess advanced knowledge and skill in specific areas of social work practice. The worker at this level has been awarded the highest professional social work practice degree (i.e., the terminal professional degree).* Yet, he or she is not yet expected to work independently, that is, outside the structure and supervision provided in a human services agency.

The Independent Professional

Description: The independent practice level is based on appropriate specialized training beyond the MSW plus continued professional development under supervision that is sufficient to ensure dependable, regular use of professional skills in independent private practice. A minimum of two years of post-master's experience is required to demonstrate this direct practice, administration, or training competence.

Qualifications: Requires an accredited MSW and at least two years of post-master's experience under appropriate professional supervision.

Characteristics: The independent social worker is expected to have acquired and integrated the knowledge, values, and skills of social work in at least one practice area. From this experience, he or she should be able to develop sufficient expertise in that field to function independently and skillfully in sensitive situations and should be prepared to practice outside the auspices of a social agency. Furthermore, the independent social worker should be able to provide leadership in at least one practice arena and to supervise and consult with other social workers.

----

*Advanced degrees such as the DSW or the Ph.D. are not subject to accreditation standards established by the profession and are not considered to be professional practice degrees. Most doctorates in social work are academic degrees intended to prepare students for positions in teaching and research rather than in the more typical practice methods.

One indicator of reaching the independent professional level is membership in the *Academy of Certified Social Workers* (ACSW). The ACSW was established in 1960 to establish a more favorable public image, to obtain societal sanction, and to increase confidence and understanding in social work. Requirements for becoming a member of the Academy include maintaining membership in NASW, having a minimum of two years of full-time practice experience, and providing reference letters from professional peers.

As Figure 5.1 indicates, NASW has also developed a credential to recognize the social worker with additional clinical practice experience who has demonstrated knowledge and competence above that expected of the new master's-level worker, that is, the *Qualified Clinical Social Worker* (QCSW) credential. As an additional means of recognizing practice areas where the worker has increased capability, NASW has developed additional areas where specialized certification is possible—school social work; case management; health care; children, youth, and families; gerontology; and alcohol, tobacco, and other drug abuse. Although many social workers employed in human services agencies have attained greater skill and experience than required at the "specialized" social worker level, those engaged in private practice are expected by the profession to have attained this "independent" practice level. The assumption is that the social worker at this level is prepared to function independent of the monitoring typically provided by other staff members in a human services agency. Therefore, credentials become an important means of verifying that the worker is prepared to perform high-quality and ethical services without the need for additional professional oversight.

The Advanced Professional

Description: Practice at the advanced level is that which carries major social and organizational responsibility for professional development, analysis, research, or policy implementation, or is achieved by personal professional growth demonstrated through advanced conceptual contributions to professional knowledge.

Qualifications: This level requires proficiency in a special theoretical, practice, administration, or policy area, or the ability to conduct advanced research studies in social welfare; this is usually demonstrated through a doctoral degree in social work or another discipline—in addition to the MSW.

Characteristics: This classification is reserved for the most highly experienced practitioners as well as for social workers who have obtained a doctorate in social work or a related field. In contrast to many professions, relatively few social workers seek or achieve the advanced professional level.

For direct service or clinical practitioners who aspire to the advanced level, NASW has developed the *Diplomate in Clinical Social Work* (DCSW). To be recognized as a diplomate in clinical social work, a person must have completed an accredited MSW program, possess an advanced or clinical state license, have a minimum of five years of post-master's clinical experience, perform satisfactorily on an advanced-level examination, and receive a favorable comprehensive supervisory evaluation.

Doctoral education represents the second route to the advanced social work level. The curricula for doctoral degrees (DSW or Ph.D.) in social work do not reflect a uniform pattern. Most programs devote their efforts to preparing the researcher and teacher, but increasingly there has been some focus on preparation for the advanced practitioner. Because the doctorate is not viewed as an entry practice degree for the social work profession and it is not accredited by the profession, the doctoral programs receive their sanction only from their universities. Therefore, the schools have considerable flexibility to determine the focus of their curricula and thus have developed unique identities. By 2006, sixty-nine doctoral programs in social work were available throughout the United States, enrolling 1,637 full-time and 917 part-time students, yet only 293 doctoral degrees in social work were awarded.[15] These numbers do not, however, reflect the total number of social workers completing doctoral degrees because some complete doctoral work in related fields such as sociology, psychology, public health, higher education, and public administration.

Concluding Comment

Through the years of its emergence, social work has gradually evolved four distinct practice levels. The National Association of Social Workers has codified these levels into a classification system with expectations for the practitioner at each level defined and education and experience qualifications specified. This classification system encomposses two problems in terminology—both created by the acceptance of the concept of an advanced generalist social worker. First, the MSW graduate prepared as an advanced generalist is qualified under the classification system as a "Specialized Social Worker." Can one be a specialized generalist? Also, an advanced generalist social worker is not the same as an Advanced Social Worker in NASW's classification system. Persons new to social work should be aware of this confusing terminology.

Nevertheless, the NASW classification of social work practice levels is a useful tool for both social agencies wanting to match workers with job demands and for persons considering a career in social work. For the latter, the selection of a particular practice level as a career goal requires that one assess his or her desire to provide the particular types of service and then consider the necessary preparation and the ability to arrange one's personal life to acquire the requisite professional education. In social work, in contrast to some of the other helping professions, one can change directions after entering the profession. A person might enter social work in a particular field of practice, such as providing services to the aged or developmentally disabled, and later transfer the skills used in that job to employment in mental health or corrections. Box 5.1, for example, depicts several factors our social worker, Demetria (see Chapter 1) may have considered as she thought about what her BSW degree represented and what options she might have in the future. Or the direct service worker (usually with a master's degree) might transfer into a job involving agency administration or move away from agency-based practice and into private practice.

Box 5.1

Demetria's Career in Social Work

Demetria, the social worker investigating the report received from Joseph's school of possible child abuse or neglect (Chapter 1), was employed in her first social work job after completing her BSW degree. What did it mean for her future that she had completed the degree, had joined the National Association of Social Workers (NASW), and was now considered a professional social worker?

First, to achieve professional recognition, Demetria's educational program must have met the *accreditation standards* established by the Council on Social Work Education. Her school, then, had required courses and field experiences that included the content specified in national curriculum requirements and were taught by faculty members meeting national standards, making her education comparable to the education students would receive at other accredited schools. Already receiving professional supervision, Demetria was likely to be in the process of applying for the *Basic Social Worker license* in her state (if her state was one that offered a license at this level) and would soon start preparing for the examination she would need to pass to become a licensed social worker. To become an NASW member, Demetria signed a pledge to uphold the *Code of Ethics* and would be deepening her knowledge of the meaning of those guidelines to ethical practice as she periodically examines them to inform her practice decisions.

Second, Demetria was just beginning her career as a social worker. She knew that one positive feature of this profession was that the social work career ladder provided the opportunity for a social worker to make changes in the work he or she does in the future. For now it would take all Demetria could manage to perform her entry-level social work job in an effective manner, but later she might want to change to work with older people, in corrections, or in some other field of practice. For some changes, such as a move to more clinical work or agency administration, she would need an MSW degree and would transition to the next practice level, the *specialized professional*.

KEY WORDS AND CONCEPTS

Accreditation (of educational programs)
Professional certification
Licensing (state regulation of practice)
Indigenous workers
Advanced standing

Basic social worker
Specialized social worker
Independent social worker
Advanced social worker

SUGGESTED INFORMATION SOURCES

Gibelman, Margaret, and Phillip H. Schervish. *Who We Are: A Second Look*. Washington, D.C.: NASW Press, 1996.

National Association of Social Workers. "NASW Credentials Specialty Certification." http://www.naswdc.org.

Randal, Amanda Duffy, and Donna DeAngelis. "Licensing," in Terry Mizrahi, ed., *Encyclopedia of Social Work*, 20th ed. New York: Oxford University Press, 2008.

Whitaker, Tracy, Toby Weismiller, and Elizabeth Clark. *Assuring the Sufficiency of a Frontline Workforce: A National Study of Licensed Social Workers.* Washington, DC: National Association of Social Workers. http://workforce.socialworkers.org/studies/natstudy.asp.

ENDNOTES

1. Robert R. Wohlgemuth and Thomas Samph, *Summary Report: Content Validity Study in Support of the Licensure Examination Program of the American Association of State Social Work Boards* (Oak Park, IL: The Association, 1983), p. 2.
2. Association of Social Work Boards, "Social Work Laws and Regulations: Online Comparison Guide." http://www.aswb.org.
3. National Association of Social Workers, "Code of Ethics." May be downloaded from http://www.socialworkers.org/pubs/code/code.asp.
4. Joseph Mehr, *Human Services: Concepts and Intervention Strategies,* 8th ed. (Boston: Allyn & Bacon, 2001), pp. 11–20.
5. National Association of Social Workers, *NASW Standards for the Classification of Social Work Practice* (Washington, D.C.: The Association, 1981).
6. A comprehensive analysis of the evolution of baccalaureate-level social work can be found in Bradford W. Sheafor and Barbara W. Shank, *Undergraduate Social Work Education: A Survivor in a Changing Profession* (Austin: University of Texas at Austin School of Social Work, 1986).
7. Herbert Bisno, *The Place of Undergraduate Curriculum in Social Work Education, Social Work Curriculum Study* Vol. 2 (New York: Council on Social Work Education, 1959).
8. Council on Social Work Education, *Social Welfare Content in Undergraduate Education* (New York: The Council, 1962), pp. 3–4.
9. Council on Social Work Education, *Undergraduate Programs in Social Work* (New York: The Council, 1971).
10. Council on Social Work Education, *2006 Statistics on Social Work Education: A Summary* (Alexandria, VA: CSWE, 2007) pp. 4, 10, 12.
11. Council on Social Work Education, *Summary of Information on Master of Social Work Programs: 2001–02.* (Alexandria, VA: Council on Social Work Education, 2002).
12. Bradford W. Sheafor, "Three Decades of Baccalaureate Social Work: A Grade Card on How the Professionalization of the BSW Has Played Out." *Journal of Baccalaureate Social Work* 6 (Spring 2001): 25–43.
13. Council on Social Work Education, *Statistics,* op. cit., pp. 4, 15.
14. Ibid., pp. 4, 14.
15. Ibid., pp. 4, 18.

Fields of Social Work Practice

Prefatory Comment

One factor that makes social work different from many other professions is the opportunity to help people deal with a wide range of human problems without needing to obtain specialized professional credentials for each area of practice. During his or her lifetime, for example, one social worker might organize and lead self-help groups in a hospital, deal with cases of abuse and neglect, develop release plans for persons in a correctional facility, plan demonstrations protesting social injustices, arrange for foster homes and adoptions for children, secure nursing home placements for older people, supervise new social workers, and serve as director of a human service agency. Regardless of the type of work performed, the social worker always has the same fundamental purpose—to draw on basic knowledge, values, and skills in order to help achieve desired change to improve the quality of life for the persons involved.

Although there are similarities in the tasks performed by social workers regardless of the nature of the services provided, there are also unique aspects of their practice with each population group. For example, services to a single mother differ from services to a frail older adult, the needs of an adult with a disability differ from those of a person about to be released from a correctional facility, and the assistance required by a pregnant teenager differs from that needed by a teenager engaged in gang activity. Each of these fields of practice typically uses some specialized language, emphasizes specific helping approaches and techniques, or may be affected by different laws or social programs. Therefore, what a social worker does and needs to know will vary to some extent from field to field.

The human services system is indeed complex, and the layperson cannot be expected to negotiate this system alone. As the profession with the primary responsibility for helping people to gain access to the services in a community, the social worker must not only know what services are available but must also be prepared to interpret them to their clients and help these clients gain access to the resources they need. To reduce the client's sense of "getting the runaround" in securing services, and perhaps reduce the chance of the client becoming discouraged and not getting the needed help, the social worker must be sure that the referral is to an appropriate resource. In addition, the professional, at times, may need to provide a variety of supports, such as encouragement, telephone numbers, names of individuals to contact, or even transportation to facilitate the client's getting to the correct resources. Thus, the social worker must not only work within a single practice field but should also be prepared to help clients negotiate services among practice fields.

This chapter identifies some of the features of the primary fields of social work practice. *Field of social work practice* is a phrase used to describe a group of practice settings that deal with similar client problems. Each field may include a number of different agencies or other organized ways of providing services. For example, in any community, the social agencies concerned with crime and delinquency might include a juvenile court, a residential center or halfway house, a community corrections agency, a probation office for adult offenders, and/or a correctional facility where offenders are incarcerated. All of these agencies work with people who have come to the attention of the legal system and would be considered part of the practice field of corrections. Although the fields discussed in the remainder of this chapter do not exhaust the full range where social workers might practice, those identified suggest the great variety of settings in which social workers provide services.

Aging

> Sara May is a social worker with the Senior Center, a community recreation program offering programs geared to the needs and interests of the community's older citizens. The center's hot lunch program draws many older people daily, and Sara interacts informally with the "Lunch Crowd" as a means of building relationships and encouraging the participants to ask her for advice and counseling, if needed. Today Mrs. Jackson, a widow in her early 80s, asked if she could visit with Sara for a few minutes after lunch to talk over a difficult decision she needed to think through. Quickly Mrs. Jackson summarized her issues. It was getting much more difficult for her to manage living alone, and she was considering moving to a retirement center or possibly moving to another state to be near her daughter. The following are some questions Sara anticipated Mrs. Jackson should be helped to consider: If she stayed in this community, could she afford to live in an independent living center? What could she do with her long-time companion, her dog Sidney? Mrs. Jackson had lived in the community most of her life and in her home for 25 years. How difficult would it be to make friends somewhere else? What implications might there be for her daughter's family if she moved to be near them?

In 2006, nearly 38 million people in the United States were age 65 and over, making up 12.6 percent of the total population. This part of the population is expected to double over the next thirty years, partially as a result of the large number of baby boomers (those born between 1946 and 1965) reaching this age level and partially as a result of better health care that is increasing life expectancy. Of particular significance is the fact that the group aged 85 and older is expanding substantially and is becoming much more ethnically diverse. At age 85, the population is already 70 percent female, and, as age increases, the percentage of women living alone increases even more.[1]

The aging population is served by a substantial number of social workers. Sometimes the services are provided directly to the older persons and at other times through their families. Most of the direct work with older people is provided by "basic" social workers, with the "specialized" and "independent" workers more likely to work with families around the health and mental health problems of their older parents. Progress has been made in reducing the poverty rate for older people, although in 2006 a total of nearly 3.4 million older people (9.4 percent) had incomes at or below the poverty line.[2] Thanks to Medicare coverage, 99.3 percent of older people have health insurance, minimizing some of their financial worries over health care,[3] and assistance with expensive prescriptions makes the economic position of older people less precarious. This population group is projected to be the fastest growing of all age groups at least into the mid-2000s and is a substantially expanding area of specialization for social workers.

A number of programs are available to help older people remain in their own homes as long as doing so is a safe and satisfying experience. Social workers help older people make links to community programs that bring health care, meals, and home-maker services into their homes; provide transportation services; and offer daycare or recreation programs. Increasingly, when older people are faced with a terminal illness, social workers help them deal with their impending death through counseling or referral to a hospice program.

For approximately 4 percent of the older population, some form of long-term care in a nursing home or other group living facility becomes a necessity. Social workers frequently help the individual and/or family select the facility and make moving arrangements; some are even staff members of the facility.

While much attention in a long-term care facility is directed toward meeting the basic physical and medical needs of the residents, social workers in these facilities contribute to the quality of life for residents by helping them maintain contact with their families and friends when possible, develop meaningful relationships with other people within the facility, and engage in a variety of activities within the facility. They also facilitate access to other social services when needed and help residents secure arrangements that protect their personal rights and ensure quality care while living in the long-term care facility.

Alcohol and Substance Abuse

Andrew Richards is a social worker in an outpatient drug and alcohol center. Each Tuesday evening Andrew facilitates a group of parents who have a high school-age child experiencing a drug and/or alcohol problem. The topic of discussion tonight concerns peer influence and ways that parents might help their child deal with peers who pressure them to use drugs or alcohol. One parent argues for a get-tough, "just say no" stance, another believes getting the child to therapy is the only solution, and still another contends that giving a child room to make mistakes is the only way the child can learn to make mature judgments. Andrew knows his skills in group work will help him be sure that everyone has a chance to share his or her views and have the pros and cons of each position carefully considered. Ultimately, each parent must decide how he or she will address this matter.

Although some social workers are employed in agencies that exclusively treat drug and alcohol problems, social workers in virtually every type of human services agency deal with problems that are associated with this social problem. It is estimated that each individual experiencing a drug or alcohol problem affects at least four other persons in some negative, unhealthy, or destructive manner.[4] The social implications of alcohol and substance abuse are significant since they are highly correlated with murders, suicides, accidents, health problems, and domestic violence.

Using current scientific understanding of these problems, Lawson and Lawson have identified three primary factors that should be considered in treating and preventing alcoholism and substance abuse. First, they recognize that physiological factors such as physical addiction, disease or physical disorders, medical problems, inherited risk, and/or mental disorders with physiological causes may contribute to the problem. Second, they identify several sociological factors, such as ethnic and cultural differences, family background, education, employment, and peer relationships, as also related to alcoholism and substance abuse. Finally, they note that psychological factors, including social skills, emotional level, self-image, attitude toward life, defense mechanisms, mental obsessions, judgment, and decision-making skills, can be contributors to this disease.[5] Growing understanding of these associated and interrelated factors has provided the helping professions with an opportunity to apply their knowledge and skills to helping clients prevent and resolve their problems. Social work plays a particularly important role, as the addictions inevitably have a significant effect on family, friends, coworkers, and others who are in contact with the person experiencing the addiction. Both the person and the environment must be helped to change when this disease is treated.

Child Welfare

Megan Messer, a social worker with the County Division of Child Welfare, has a difficult recommendation to make to the judge. Her job is to evaluate the conditions in the Benjamin Bradford home to determine whether Kate, the Bradford's new baby, is getting proper care. Neighbors reported that the house is always dirty, food and unwashed clothing are left around, and the baby can be heard crying at almost any time of the day or night. When Megan called Mr. Bradford to schedule an interview, he told her it was none of her damn business and to butt out of his life. Megan had to be very persistent to get an appointment scheduled. She wasn't looking forward to the interview.

The U.S. society has entrusted the family with full responsibility for the care and nurturing of children. Law and custom mandate that other social institutions must not interfere with the rights and responsibilities of the family to care for its children. Historically, it has been assumed that parents would make choices that were in the best interest of both themselves and their children. For example, if parents thought it more important for children to contribute to the family's income by working in a factory or helping with farm work than attending school or having time for play, that decision was honored. That authority, however, left children vulnerable. Legislation permitting other social institutions (e.g., child protective services, police, and courts) to intervene in family situations that were potentially harmful to children was reluctantly adopted. Today, children and youth continue to be somewhat hidden within families with only limited protection when abusive situations are present.

In most situations, social workers seek to work with both the parents and the children by providing support services in order to keep children in their own homes. These services might involve one-to-one counseling with a parent, child–parent counseling to resolve a particular problem, or family counseling to resolve issues affecting some aspect of the family's functioning. Family members may also participate in group counseling with other parents of children experiencing similar problems where a social worker guides the group to address issues relevant to their problems. Finally, the social worker may assist the families to use outside resources such as day care and homemaker services. The following services are typically provided by social workers employed in child welfare.

Protective Services

More than 825,000 cases of child maltreatment occur in the United States each year. Of these cases, 56 percent are classified as neglect, 21 percent are related to physical abuse, 11 percent involve sexual abuse, 8 percent are psychological or emotional abuse, and the remainder are unclassified or related to other forms of abuse or neglect.[6] *Abuse*, whether it is physical, sexual, or emotional, is an active mistreatment or exploitation of the child. *Neglect* is a more passive mistreatment but can be just as damaging. It can take the form of inadequate food and shelter, unwholesome conditions, failure to have the child attend school, or inadequate provision of medical care.

The social worker, as an agent of society, seeks to protect the child without infringing on the rights of the parents. When a referral is received, the social worker must determine if the child is in immediate danger, assess the ability of the parents to resolve the problem, and make a judgment about the risks of working with the family while keeping the child in the home. If the child is removed from the home (with approval of the courts), the social worker continues to work with the family in an effort to eliminate the difficulties that led to the referral. This process may involve individual, family, or group counseling; the provision of support services; or education of family members in the areas of their incompetence.

Foster Care

At times children may need to be removed from their own homes, but it is not possible, or desirable, to permanently sever their relationship with their natural parents. In these cases, temporary (and sometimes long-term) foster care is required, and the social worker must work with the parents, the child, and the courts to obtain a decision to remove a child from his or her own home and make a foster home placement. The process involves a careful assessment and a plan whereby the child can return home if conditions improve. Although both federal and state laws discourage removing children from their families, a total of 513,000 children were living in foster care in 2005.[7]

The social worker is also responsible for developing a pool of good quality foster homes. He or she must recruit, select, train, and monitor those families that are entrusted with the care of foster children. The placement of a child in a foster home often creates severe stress on the child, the natural parents, and the foster parents. Considerable practice skill by the social worker is required if he or she is to help resolve these problems.

Residential Care

At times the appropriate placement for a child is a residential care facility, that is, a group home or residential treatment center. These facilities are most likely to be chosen when the child exhibits antisocial behavior or requires intensive treatment to change behaviors that may create problems for him- or herself or for others.

In these situations, one role of the social worker is to select an appropriate residential care facility, which involves working with the child, the family, and, often, the courts. In addition, other social workers are usually staff members of such a facility, providing care and treatment for the children who are placed there. They are especially involved in helping maintain positive contact between the child and the family and in making plans for the child to return home when appropriate. The fact that these residential care facilities require licensing creates another role for the social worker—evaluating facilities for the purpose of licensing.

Adoption and Services to Unmarried Parents

Child welfare work also involves assisting expectant mothers, often unmarried, address the difficult decision of whether to keep the baby or place the child for adoption. Nearly 36 percent of all children born in the United States in 2004 were born to unmarried parents, a factor that substantially increases the likelihood that the child will grow up in a household with income below the poverty line.[8] A few of the factors to be considered in this decision include the mother's plans for the future, such as attending school or securing employment and child care, the attitudes of the mother's family about the pregnancy, the feelings of the father's and the mother's relationship with him, and where the mother will live while pregnant and after the baby arrives. Social workers use both individual and group counseling to help women consider the implications of their decisions. They also, at times, offer counseling to unmarried fathers to help them deal with this situation.

If the decision is made to place the child for adoption, the social worker must screen and select adoptive parents carefully. Matching parents and children is a task that requires considerable knowledge and skill. To gain the best information possible on which to base these decisions, the social worker might conduct group orientation meetings and develop social histories of the prospective adoptive parents. Detailed information on the child's background and even special interests of the natural mother for the child's future (religious affiliation, for example) become part of the basis for final adoptive placement. It continues to be difficult to secure satisfactory adoptive homes for older children or those who experience a physical or mental disability. An important function of the social worker is to recruit parents for these hard-to-place children.

Community/Neighborhood Work

Luis Garcia is a social worker at a storefront neighborhood center in a large city. His job is to help residents rectify substandard housing conditions in the area. Tonight Mr. Garcia is helping a group from the neighborhood plan a strategy for pressuring some of the landlords to improve the quality of housing and to demand that the city increase traffic safety in the neighborhood.

From their beginning, social workers have clearly seen the need both to coordinate the multiple human services that exist in a community and to stimulate change in communities to make them more responsive to the needs of people or change patterns of operation that have negative effects on people. When social workers provide neighborhood or community services, three approaches characterize this work: community organization, community planning, and community development.

Community Organization

The primary job of some social workers is to work within the network of human services to increase their effectiveness in meeting human needs. This activity involves collecting and analyzing data related to the delivery of services, matching that information with data on population distribution, securing funds to maintain and enhance the quality of services, coordinating the efforts of existing agencies, and educating the general public about these services. The principal agencies in which social workers are employed to do this type of work are community planning councils, United Way agencies, and other federations of agencies under the auspices of religious groups, such as the Jewish Welfare Federation.

Community Planning

Social workers sometimes have the specialized training to join physical, economic, and health planners in creating long-range plans for communities. This work requires the ability to apply planning technology, with the special contribution of the social worker to analyze the needs for human services as towns, cities, or regions undergo change. These contributions might mean anticipating the demands that result from, for example, creating a new ski area in rural Colorado or helping an urban neighborhood plan for changes in the demand for human services when a factory shuts down, leaving the community with an eroding tax base.

Community or Neighborhood Development

Social work joins a number of disciplines in giving assistance to people in communities as they seek to improve conditions. This approach is based on a self-help philosophy that encourages members of the community to mobilize their resources in order to study their problems and seek solutions. In rural areas, the social worker contributes to this "grass roots" approach by guiding those involved toward a process that maximizes the participation of many concerned citizens. The social worker or other professional also serves as a resource for obtaining technical consultation in areas where there is not expertise among the community members. In urban areas this process, sometimes known as an "asphalt roots" approach, is used to help neighborhoods or special population groups (such as the poor, minorities, or older people) work together to improve the quality of their lives.

Corrections/Criminal Justice

Jean Drobek, a social worker employed as a juvenile probation officer, is preparing her testimony for a court hearing regarding one of her clients, Miranda Herman. Following an intense argument with her mother over her increasingly frequent use of "recreational drugs" when hanging out with her friends, Miranda impulsively decided to run away. She stole a neighbor's automobile and wrecked it when entering a nearby highway. Luckily no other vehicles were involved, and Miranda sustained no serious injuries. Since Miranda had not been using drugs when the accident occurred, she was assigned community service and placed on probation. At the start of probation, Miranda frequently failed to show up for community service assignments, although more recently she and her mother had actively participated in counseling with Ms. Drobek and were just beginning to deal with their conflicts. Should Ms. Drobek recommend that probation be continued until more progress is made?

Another important expression of social work practice occurs in the area of corrections and criminal justice. Correctional social workers are employed in courts, parole and probation offices, and correctional facilities. Social workers often find corrections a perplexing field of practice because the structure of services is usually based on punishment and taking custody of the lives of offenders, which conflicts with many social work values and principles. Yet, because the problems experienced by persons who come to the attention of professionals in this field are basically those of social functioning, the social worker has a valuable contribution to make.

The corrections field embraces offenders from all aspects of society—youth and adults, males and females, rich and poor, members of dominant population groups and minorities, and even well-known celebrities. In correctional settings, the poor, especially minorities, are very much overrepresented. The social worker's involvement with the criminal justice system can begin at the time of arrest and terminate at the person's release. Some social workers serve as, or work with, juvenile officers in diversionary programs, where they provide crisis intervention or referral services at the time of arrest. These programs divert people from the criminal justice system and into more appropriate community services. Social workers also prepare social histories and make psychosocial assessments of individuals charged with crimes as part of the data a judge uses in making decisions about a case. If the person is placed on probation, a social worker might be the probation officer providing individual, family, or group counseling and helping the convicted person make changes in behavior that will satisfy the terms of probation and hopefully prevent additional problems from developing.

Social workers are also found in correctional facilities. In these facilities, they provide counseling and serve as a link to the outside world, which encompasses the family, potential employers, and the community service network that will provide support to that person at the time of release. If parole is granted, a social worker might serve as the parole officer or work in a halfway house where the person may live prior to a completely independent re-entry to the community.

Disabilities (Physical and Mental)

K. G. Murder is executive director of the Council on Disabled Persons. This council identifies and seeks solutions to problems experienced by persons with disabling conditions, including mental retardation; physical deformity; or hearing, visual, or speech impairments. As executive director, Mr. Murder provides leadership to the citizen board as it develops programs to meet the needs of its clientele. Tonight the board will work on designing a plan for evacuating handicapped persons throughout the community should there be a disaster that requires removing people from their homes or residential care settings.

Assisting persons with physical, mental, and developmental disabilities is a field of practice in which basic social workers are most likely to be the primary service providers. Yet helping people deal with disabling conditions affects most fields of social work. Social workers are concerned with such disabling conditions as mental retardation, visual and hearing impairment, communication disability, learning disability, and cerebral palsy, which affect not only the person's physical and intellectual functioning but also interaction with others, that is, social functioning. The special role of social work is to help these persons and their families learn to live as successfully as possible in a society structured for the more fully functioning individual.

The U.S. Centers for Disease Control and Prevention estimates that, in 2007, 36 million people (12 percent of the population) experienced one or more chronic conditions that limited their activities. About 4 million people experienced such a severe condition that they needed help with daily living activities such as eating, dressing, or bathing. Another 9 million people could not do household chores or shopping without help. Health-related conditions prevented another 6 percent of the adult working-age population from employment, and another 3 percent were limited in the kind of work they could perform. Further, 6 percent of the school-age children were receiving special education services. Indeed, a substantial part of the U.S. population experiences some form of disability, and these disabilities are experienced to a greater extent among people who have the least education and the lowest income.[9] In addition to the physical disabilities, many more people experience mental or emotional conditions (or both) that are disabling.

The term *developmental disability* has evolved to include a broad range of disabling conditions that affect the physical, social, and intellectual development of a person. The Developmental Disabilities Assistance and Bill of Rights Act (Public Law 95-602) includes the following definition of a developmental disability:

. . . a severe chronic disability of a person which: a) is attributable to a mental or physical impairment or combination of mental or physical impairments; b) is manifested before the person attains age 22; c) is likely to continue indefinitely; d) results in substantial functional limitations in three or more of the following areas of major life activity, including self-care, receptive/expressive language, learning, mobility, self-direction, capacity for independent living, and economic self-sufficiency; and e) reflects the person's need for a combination and sequence of special, interdisciplinary, or generic care, treatment, or other services which are individually planned and coordinated.[10]

While the definition of a disabled person contained in PL 95-602 does not include all people who are physically and intellectually disabled, it does encompass a large share of the most seriously disabled. In an effort to enhance the quality of life for all people, social workers serve clients who experience both mild and severe disabilities. To accomplish this goal, social workers help people find suitable living arrangements (either with their families or in community facilities), assist in the alleviation of problems associated with the disability, contribute to public education efforts about the causes and society's responses to these disabilities, and help individuals gain access to needed services.

Family Services

Nadine Harrison is a specialized social worker and an expert in family casework. She has just begun working with the Machin family to help each member change his or her patterns of interacting with other family members to reduce conflict and make each a more productive member of the family. Ms. Harrison has asked that all family members come to the family counseling session and will encourage each to identify the behaviors of others that make him or her feel unsupported by the family. Then they will collectively look for ways to prevent or modify those behaviors, as well as identify ways to reinforce improved behaviors. Ms. Harrison hopes that all members of the Machin family arrive on time as there is much to be done in the next hour.

Social workers at all levels are likely to be involved in helping families address issues in their social functioning. Changing marital arrangements, child-rearing practices, and patterns of employment in the United States have placed considerable strain on the nuclear family. A growing number of single-parent families, reconstituted families (often involving her children, his children, and their children), duo-breadwinner families, and gay/lesbian households, for example, have dramatically affected previously established family patterns. Social workers have a key role in helping society address these changes and in assisting individual families and households to adapt to these newer conditions or resolve problems associated with them.

Three broad service areas capture the bulk of family services provided by social workers. First, much of the activity involves providing various forms of counseling or therapy to families. Patterns of interaction may develop that are dysfunctional for the individual members; membership may change through marriage or death, requiring new ways of relating to each other; or one member experiencing a severe social or emotional problem may create strain among the family members. Family life is often difficult and taxing for members, and issues sometimes cannot be resolved without professional help. Thus social workers working with troubled families must be skilled at providing family casework, family therapy, and other forms of family services.

Second, as opposed to working to solve family problems, social workers also work proactively to strengthen families through activities that fall under the label of *family life education*. This social work practice activity recognizes that all families face certain kinds of stress and seeks to prevent family breakdown by educating family members to cope with anticipated problems. It teaches about interpersonal, family, and sex relationships to help people to have more satisfactory and fulfilling lives.

Finally, social workers have long been sensitive to the fact that both an unwanted child and his or her parents often experience problems. Adequately carrying out the responsibilities of raising a child is difficult under the best of circumstances, and an unwanted pregnancy makes it even more difficult. Thus, helping families plan the number, spacing, and timing of the births of children to fit with the family's capacities improves the quality of life for all family members.

Income Maintenance

> Dorothy Simmons, a social worker in the local public human services agency, has an appointment with Mrs. Sang Woo. She knows from a telephone call arranging the appointment that Mrs. Woo is terribly worried about her future and that of her two small children. Her husband was killed two months ago in a robbery at the neighborhood market where he worked. In addition, Mrs. Woo found that, after paying funeral expenses, little money was left for raising the children. She hopes that Ms. Simmons can help her find a way to secure the financial resources to get by temporarily and to obtain job training and daycare so that she can support the family in the long run.

Once income maintenance was a primary practice activity engaged in by social workers, but today relatively few professionally prepared workers are employed in income maintenance positions. However, social workers in many fields of practice regularly deal with clients for whom financial matters are a primary factor in the situations they bring for help. Therefore, the social worker's knowledge of the various programs that can be accessed for financial assistance is a valuable resource for their clients.

On an emergency or short-term basis, there are usually many local agencies that provide support in the form of used clothing outlets, food banks and food kitchens, shelters for homeless individuals and families, emergency child care facilities, transportation vouchers, subsidized housing, and other resources where the poor can obtain social provisions for meeting basic needs. These resources are so unique to local areas that few people have a good understanding of what resources are available. Knowledge of these resources and how to gain access to them is therefore a special responsibility of the social worker.

In addition to locally developed services, a number of government-sponsored programs exist to meet basic needs or provide a minimum level of support in order to prevent more serious health or income problems from developing. Among the income maintenance programs are "safety net" programs that require that the recipients experience serious social or economic problems before the resource can become available to them. Examples of these programs are *Food Stamps, Temporary Assistance for Needy Families (TANF), Social Security Income (SSI),* and *Medicaid.* In addition, several social insurance programs anticipate the needs of special populations that have been designed in the "social utilities" philosophy and are available as a right for the designated client situations without the stigma of demeaning eligibility tests. These programs include *Old Age Survivors, Disability, and Health Insurance (OASDHI); Medicare; Unemployment Insurance;* and *Worker's Compensation Insurance.* Social workers practicing in most settings need to be familiar with these programs and skilled at helping clients access them.

Medical and Health Care

Ahmed Al Awam is a social worker employed in a large community hospital. For the past two years, he was assigned to the emergency room (ER), assisting individuals and families as they dealt with or adapted to the traumatic situations that brought them to the ER. Mr. Al Awam's crisis intervention skills were of primary importance in this work. Now, he has moved to the rehabilitation unit, where he is engaged in much more long-term work with patients who have experienced a substantial disabling injury. Today he is having his first session with Ted Barker, a bricklayer who sustained an injury in a construction accident that resulted in the amputation of his right arm. Mr. Barker is understandably depressed as he recognizes that he will undergo a substantial change in his life. He will no longer be able to practice his trade, and therefore he has lost his source of income to support his family, his social group of fellow bricklayers will no longer be part of his life, and he believes his wife will no longer view him as the "man" she once did. Mr. Al Awam and Mr. Barker have many issues to address.

Medical social work was initiated in the early 1900s, with social workers playing a peripheral role to physicians and nurses in health and medical settings. With increased understanding that illnesses can be caused or exacerbated by social factors, social workers gained a more central role in providing medical and health care. Today, social work in hospitals, outpatient clinics, and other health-related organizations is one of the largest practice fields for both basic and specialist/independent social workers.

A primary place for social work practice in this field is in hospitals. In these settings, for example, social workers address social and psychological factors that are either contributing causes of medical ailments or are side effects of a medical condition that must be dealt with to facilitate recovery and prevent excessive dependence on others. Social workers help to link patients experiencing changed levels of functioning due to a medical problem with their environments by providing individual, group, and family counseling; serving as patient advocates; and working with self-help groups of patients experiencing similar medical or social problems. Social workers also might be engaged in counseling terminally ill patients and their families.

In addition, social workers are involved in other health and medical care facilities besides hospitals. They work in public health clinics and private physicians' offices providing counseling and referral services to people who have sought medical treatment related to family planning, prenatal care, child growth and development, venereal disease, and physical disability, for example. They have also taken an active role in health maintenance and disease prevention programs in local communities. With the skyrocketing costs of medical care, it is even more important that these efforts be continued by the social work profession.

Mental Health and Illness

> Kirsten Laurali is a social worker in the adolescent unit of a large psychiatric hospital. Although she counsels some patients individually, this afternoon she will meet with a group of adolescent girls who are expected to be released from the hospital in a few weeks. Ms. Laurali plans to facilitate the girls in expressing any concerns they feel about leaving the security of the hospital and to discuss any family, school, and peer interaction problems they anticipate experiencing when returning to home and school. She will also help to connect them and their parents with a local mental health clinic where they can receive ongoing support after their hospitalization has ended.

It has long been recognized that one's mental health and capacity for healthy social functioning are highly correlated. A person who is depressed, hyperactive, hallucinating, or experiencing any of the other symptoms of mental illness is likely at some time to become the client of the social worker. It is estimated that 15 percent of the general population experience some form of emotional disturbance at any one time, creating a high demand for social workers, who are twice as prevalent as psychologists and psychiatrists in the mental health field. In the field of mental health and illness, the specialized social worker (with an MSW degree as preparation) is the usual practice level—although social workers in other settings, at all practice levels, regularly work with clients for whom emotional illness is at least a contributing factor to their problems.

Social workers in mental health settings work with people experiencing these difficulties by treating those who have the potential to improve the quality of their lives. They help them learn to cope with problems in their social functioning and, at the same time, work to change factors in their environment to promote better mental health or eliminate social conditions that have a negative effect on their functioning.

There are three practice settings where social workers are most likely to engage in psychiatric social work: outpatient mental health clinics, inpatient psychiatric hospitals, and private practice. In an outpatient clinic, social workers provide clinical or therapeutic services to individuals and families or to small groups of clients. They may also consult or work with a variety of organizations, such as group homes or the mass media, in an effort to create an environment that is conducive to the healthy growth and development of all people. When employed in a psychiatric hospital, social workers may provide a variety of treatment activities to the patients themselves, but they also serve as a liaison to the patient's outside world and help family or friends maintain contact while the person is hospitalized. The social worker might also assess the impact of family, friends, an employer, school, and so forth on the client's situation and offer assistance in helping these significant others change in ways that will benefit the client. When patients are ready to return home, social workers help to arrange appropriate living situations, ranging from housing accommodations (if needed) to ongoing service from a community mental health center. Finally, the social worker in private practice is most likely to focus on treatment for individuals and families, although small group intervention approaches may be used on occasion.

Occupational or Industrial Social Work

Working for a large manufacturing firm was a new experience for Doug Perry, an experienced clinical social worker. The CEO of the company was concerned that the employees increasingly are experiencing social problems such as marital conflict, alcohol dependence, and issues related to their children that interfere with their ability to perform their work in the company's plant. Mr. Perry's first assignment was to prepare a plan to increase worker productivity by reducing these social problems. Next week a report is due to the Board of Directors, and Mr. Perry is outlining a plan that includes (1) establishing a case-finding and referral service on the premises, staffed by social workers; (2) outsourcing the most serious cases to community agencies and private practitioners; and (3) strengthening prevention efforts by creating a company foundation with sufficient funding to support research into the factors contributing to these problems.

Social work has been practiced in business and industrial settings since the late 1800s. Social workers have been employed both by management and labor unions to offer services and provide consultation through employee assistance programs. In recent years, with businesses increasingly realizing that worker productivity is closely related to the workers' general satisfaction with the quality of their lives, an investment in helping employees resolve problems in social functioning is seen as simply good business. This perspective has created a small but growing field of practice known as occupational or industrial social work. With more than 154.5 million people in the civilian labor force in 2008,[11] the workplace is an opportune setting in which to identify social problems and provide needed services. Often, early intervention at the location of one's employment can prevent more serious problems from developing later.

Shank and Jorve identify three models of social work practice in business and industry: the employee service model, the consumer service model, and the corporate social responsibility model.[12] An explanation of each follows.

The *employee service model* of occupational social work focuses on activities that provide direct service to the employees of a business or industry. The social worker using this model might develop and implement employee assistance programs and various supervisory training programs. In addition, the social worker might provide counseling to individuals or families in relation to marital, family, substance abuse, aging, health, and retirement problems, and offer referral to other community agencies or self-help groups. Typical problems the social worker might also address would be the identification of job-related factors such as boredom or stress, an employee's desire to find resources to upgrade his or her job skills, or the need for preretirement planning.

The occupational social worker following the *consumer service model* might serve as the company's representative to various consumer groups and focus on identifying consumer needs and methods of meeting them. Typically found in banks, public utilities, and government agencies, these social workers help to provide a liaison between consumer groups and social service agencies, develop outreach programs, and provide counseling to customers to meet unique needs.

The third model of practice, the *corporate social responsibility model,* places the social worker in the role of assisting corporations and businesses to make a commitment to the social and economic well-being of the communities in which they are located. The social workers consult with management on their policies concerning human resources, their donations to nonprofit organizations, and social legislation they may wish to support. In addition, social workers may administer health and welfare benefit programs for employees; represent the company in research and community development activities; and provide linkage between social service, social policy, and corporate interests.

Schools

The death of a loved one seems to be epidemic in Cesar Chavez Elementary School this year, and Bruni Baez, the school social worker, is aware that five children in the fifth and sixth grades have experienced the deaths of grandparents or siblings in the few months since the school year began. For all of these children, performance in the classroom has deteriorated, and they show little interest in extracurricular activities. With the support of their teachers, Mrs. Baez has arranged for a 30-minute group session once each week in which these children can work on their grief and loss issues. Each week they will talk about a different issue, such as normal grief reactions, healthy and unhealthy coping patterns, the effect of grief on social relationships, understanding physical and mental reactions to grief, talking about the person who died, and so on. She wonders which of these topics might be best for the first session with the students.

Just as places of employment are important locations for identifying and addressing problems of social functioning for the employed population, schools are an important place to serve children and youth. It is known that individual and family problems directly affect a child's ability to learn, and school social workers are employed to help parents, teachers, and children address these complex issues.

The traditional approach of social workers in schools has been to counsel the child and confer with the family. They have depended on the cooperation of teachers to make referrals when problems are evident and have had varying degrees of effectiveness, depending on the willingness of teachers and school systems to use them as a resource. Problems of truancy, suspected child abuse, inadequate nutrition, substance abuse, parental neglect, and inappropriate behavior are often referred to the social worker.

Social workers serve as a link between school, family, and community. Some activities that school social workers typically perform include offering counseling to children, their families, and teachers related to factors that affect the child's performance at school; serving as an advocate for children with school administrators and community agencies when specialized services are needed; organizing parent and community groups to strengthen school and community relationships; and coordinating teams that draw on different disciplines' expertise and parents' interests to assess a child and develop a plan to assist a child's development.

Youth Services

Diversion programs have become a hot item in human services agencies designed to work with youth. At the Michael Jordan Recreation Center, Bob Jackson draws on his social work skills to involve members of several neighborhood gangs in activities at the center. He knows that the traditional approach of attempting to engage these youths in competitive sports has not been successful, and he is seeking new forms of activities that might capture the interest of these gang members and help divert them from the more harmful activities in which they are now engaged. Mr. Jackson had decided to create an advisory board of former gang members and is preparing for a focus group session in which he hopes to draw out information that will assist in his planning.

Very early in U.S. history a number of human service programs were developed to provide educational and recreational opportunities for people of all social classes. These services were aimed at character building among youth, with organizations such as the YMCA, YWCA, Boys and Girls Clubs, and various scouting groups developing. Later, with the growth of settlement houses, programs were broadened to serve other age groups. Although other disciplines also provide staff for these organizations, this field of practice continues to be a small but important area of social work.

These services seek to enhance the growth and development of all interested participants, from the poor to the well-to-do. Through the use of such activities as crafts, sports, camping, friendship groups, drama, music, informal counseling, and other forms of group participation, the members are guided toward personal development. The role of the social worker might be to administer these agencies, to lead the group process, or to provide individual counseling.

Concluding Comment

For the person considering a career in social work, it is important to have an understanding of the many different fields of practice open to the social worker. It is evident that the attention social workers give to helping people and their environments interact more favorably makes an important contribution to resolving social problems or enhancing social functioning in many areas.

The most current data about social work practitioners indicate there are some practice areas where substantial numbers of both basic and specialist/independent social workers are employed, and this includes such areas as work with children and youth, families, and health care. BSW-level workers are much more likely than their MSW counterparts to be engaged in providing services to the aged and working in the disabilities area, while the primary practice area for the MSWs, by a substantial margin, is mental health.

A clear picture of client needs addressed by social workers emerges from data presented in this chapter. Helping clients resolve problems in family functioning stands well above all others. A second and often interrelated tier of issues are those of client functioning that have been affected by mental illness or retardation, character disorders or behavior problems, health-related matters, anxiety or depression, difficulties in interpersonal relations, and problems associated with alcohol and substance abuse.

The knowledge and skills acquired when obtaining a baccalaureate or master's degree in social work are intended to prepare one to engage in social work practice in any of these practice fields. The social work practice performed by Demetria (Chapter 1) is located in the field of child welfare practice, i.e., working with children and youth. However, the discussion presented in Box 6.1 also highlights the fact that a practicing social worker must be knowledgeable about the work performed in other fields to serve clients effectively, should he or she someday transition to a different field. The ability to transfer these competencies from field to field gives the social worker considerable flexibility in selecting where he or she will work and what type of client issues will be the focus of practice. This job flexibility has long been an attractive feature of social work.

Box 6.1

Demetria's Field of Practice

In the case presented in Chapter 1, the primary field of practice for our social worker, Demetria, was *child welfare*. In this case she was employed by a county human services department, although child welfare work is performed in virtually any type of agency setting—public, private nonprofit, private for-profit, and even in private practice. Demetria's work was related to one of several child welfare programs, *protective services,* with the mission of protecting children and youth from various forms of abuse and maltreatment.

In this field of practice, Demetria might also have had responsibility for placing a child with severe emotional or behavioral problems in a *residential care* facility, placing children who can benefit from a different home environment in a *foster care* home, or arranging for the legal *adoption* of children who cannot reside with their natural parents for a variety of reasons but who do not have such serious problems that they cannot become part of another family permanently.

Demetria's work in this case touched other fields of practice where social workers might be employed. The case was initiated from a school in which there might have been a *school social worker,* her colleague in the Boys and Girls Club was employed in a *youth services* agency, and the root of the Miles family's issues appeared to be related to unemployment and the subsequent financial problems that would be addressed by social workers in the field of *income maintenance*. Should the issues experienced by Joseph diminish and Mr. Miles return home, a helpful referral might be to a *family services* agency where in-depth counseling could occur to help this family get its life back in order. In short, although Demetria was employed in child welfare, she needed knowledge of the work that occurs in several other fields of social work practice to do her job adequately.

KEY WORDS AND CONCEPTS

Field of social work practice
Developmental disability

Occupational or industrial social work

SUGGESTED INFORMATION SOURCES

Literally hundreds of books and articles are published each year on the various fields of practice described in this chapter. The four books listed below are recommended as resources for beginning the process of acquiring additional information about the various fields of social work practice.

Mizrahi, Terry, and Larry E. Davis, eds. *Encyclopedia of Social Work*, 20th ed. Washington, D.C.: NASW Press and Oxford University Press, 2008. The four-volume *Encyclopedia of Social Work* is a valuable resource for investigating most topics relevant to social workers. The author(s) of each chapter is selected by the *Encyclopedia's* editorial board as a highly respected expert on the subject matter. Each author provides a "state-of-the-art" summary of the topic and a bibliography of the seminal literature on that subject. Its availability as an electronic document makes searching for specific topics efficient.

Gibelman, Margaret. *What Social Workers Do*, 2nd ed. Washington, D.C.: NASW Press, 2004. This book is packed with short chapters describing more than fifty different examples of social work practice. Each contains a short case vignette that helps the reader gain insight into what the social worker does while serving clients.

Grobman, Linda May, ed. *Days in the Lives of Social Workers*. Harrisburg, PA: White Hat Communications, 1996. Forty-one practitioners tell their stories about what they do in a typical day as a social worker. The sections are organized around fields of practice (for example, health care, school social work, mental health, and so on) with several examples of social work in each field.

LeCroy, Craig Winston. *The Call to Social Work: Life Stories*. Thousand Oaks, CA: Sage, 2002. Thirty-four social workers share the experiences that led them to select social work as a career, and in the process they provide insight into why they selected a particular field of practice.

Ritter, Jessica A., Havaevalu F. O. Vakalahi, and Mary Kiernan-Stern. *101 Careers in Social Work*. New York: Springer, 2009. Helpful for exploration of the many career possibilities in social work.

ENDNOTES

1. U.S. Census Bureau, "National Population Estimates: Characteristics." http://www.census.gov/popest/national/asrh/NC-EST2007-sa.html.
2. U.S. Census Bureau, "Historical Poverty Tables, Table 3": Poverty Status of People, by Age, Race, and Hispanic Origin: 1959 to 2006." http://www.census.gov/hhes/www/poverty/histpov/hstpov3.html.
3. U.S. Department of Commerce News, "More People Have Health Insurance, Census Bureau Reports." http://www.census.gov/Press-Release/www/2001/cb01-162.html.
4. Ronald E. Herrington, George R. Jacobson, and David G. Benzer, eds., *Alcohol and Drug Abuse Handbook* (St. Louis: Warren H. Green, 1987), p. xiii.
5. Gary W. Lawson and Ann W. Lawson, *Alcoholism and Substance Abuse in Special Populations* (Rockville, MD: Aspen Publishers, 1989), pp. 5–7.

6. U.S. Department of Health and Human Services, *Trends in the Well-Being of Children and Youth, 2001*. Washington, D.C.: U.S. Government Printing Office, 2001, p. 143.
7. Child Trends Data Bank, "Foster Care." http://www.childtrendsdatabank.org/indicators/12FosterCare.cfm.
8. Federal Interagency Forum on Child and Family Statistics, *America's Children in Brief: Key National Indicators of Well-Being, 2007*. http://www.childstats.gov/americaschildren06/pop.asp.
9. *Summary of Health Statistics for the U.S. Population: National Health Interview Survey, 20037*. National Center for Health Statistics, Series 10, Number 238. http://www.cdc.gov/nchs/data/series/sr_10/sr10_238.pdf.
10. Robert L. Schalock, *Services for Developmentally Disabled Adults* (Baltimore: University Park Press, 1982), p. 12.
11. U.S. Bureau of Labor Statistics, "Civilian Labor Force and Unemployment." http://data.bls.gov/cgi-bin/surveymost?bls.
12. Barbara W. Shank and Beth K. Jorve, "Industrial Social Work: A New Arena for the BSW." Paper presented at the National Symposium of Social Workers, Washington, D.C., 1983, p. 14.

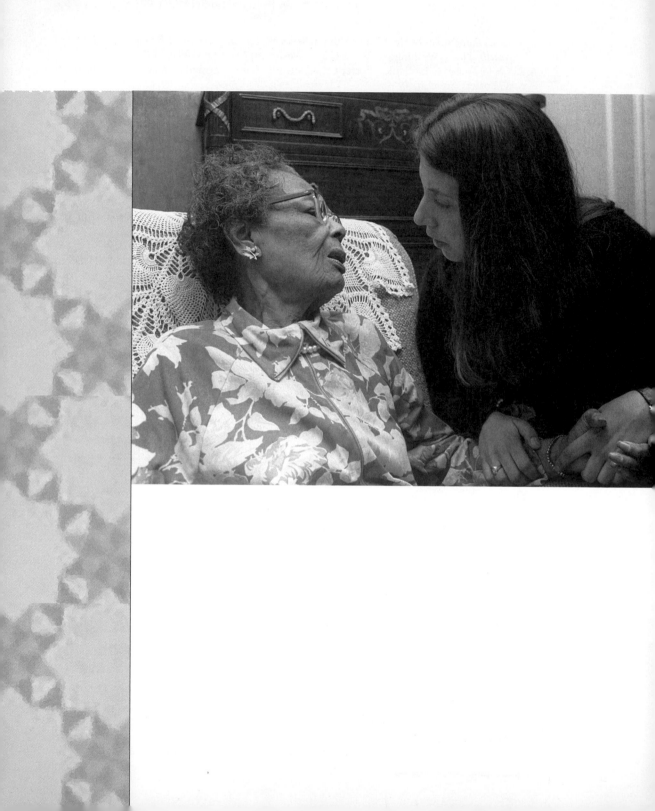

7

Settings for Social Work Practice

Prefatory Comment

Our society's commitment to the welfare of its members is played out through an extensive array of social programs that are delivered by several different helping professions—including social work. For people to gain access to these programs and the professionals who deliver them, there must be some form of organizational structure that serves as a vehicle for delivering the services. Usually that is a formal organization that operates under the auspices of a federal, state, or local government; a nonprofit community agency; or a for-profit organization operated as a business. The latter setting includes social workers who are private practitioners; that is, they create their own business in the same manner as the private physician or attorney who maintains an office where clients receive the services.

These differing practice settings influence the nature of client problems a social worker addresses, the clients served, the amount of paperwork required, the salary earned, and many other factors that affect one's work activity and job satisfaction. This chapter examines the advantages and disadvantages for both social workers and their clients in the different practice settings.

Throughout its history, social work has been primarily an agency-based profession. Like teaching, nursing, and the clergy, social work practice emerged primarily within organizations, and today, as in the past, most social workers are employed in some form of human service organization. In recent years there has been a shift in the employment patterns of social workers into the for-profit sector. Nevertheless, today the nonprofit sector employs the largest percentage of today's social workers (37 percent), followed closely by the government sector (34 percent), with the remaining 29 percent employed in the business or for-profit sector.[1]

Characteristics of Practice Settings

When social programs are created, a decision must be made about whether the program will be delivered under the auspices of a human service organization or by an independent practitioner. When programs are provided by human service organizations, the agencies establish the necessary policies and supply the administrative structure to make the program available to recipients. Clients then contract with that agency for the needed service, and the agency employs staff to deliver the program. The organization is responsible for determining who is eligible for service and how that service will be performed, for screening and selecting its staff, for assigning the work to various staff members, for monitoring the quality of the work, and for securing funds to pay the costs of providing the service.

When the service is delivered by a social worker in private practice, the client contracts directly with the social worker or the private practice group with which the worker is associated. The client then pays directly for the service or draws on insurance, Medicare, or other funds to pay for the service. Licensing helps the clients or companies paying for this service determine if the practitioner is qualified to perform this service.

Government Sector Settings

Government organizations are established and funded by the general public with the intent to provide services that preserve and protect the well-being of people in the community. These agencies must operate within the provisions of the laws under which they were established. The largest government sector social programs are created by lawmakers in Washington, D.C., or a state capital. These policy makers are usually geographically distant from the clients and service providers alike and, too often, are unfamiliar with the day-to-day issues that arise when these laws are implemented by local agencies. For this reason, social workers often find their practice in government agencies frustrating. There is inherent inflexibility in these settings because laws are difficult to change, budgeting and auditing systems are highly structured, and cumbersome civil service or personnel systems are mandated. Further, these organizations are subject to political manipulation, and financial support and program development can be significantly influenced by a changing political climate. Except through substantial political action efforts, those who must carry out these programs have limited opportunity to influence their structure and funding.

On the positive side, although sometimes client fees are required, public agencies are financed largely by taxes, and the regular flow of tax money offers some stability to the programs. Legislative bodies are authorized to levy taxes so human needs can be met, and, in times of economic difficulty when voluntary contributions may be reduced, legislators have the power to tax and, therefore, maintain the services.

It should be recognized that government sector agencies provide services that are likely to meet the most basic human needs such as food, clothing, and shelter. It simply has not been possible to adequately respond to the fundamental needs of the poor, homeless, disabled, aged, and others through voluntary and for-profit human services.

Nonprofit (Voluntary) Sector Settings

Out of the history of providing assistance for persons needing help, a number of *mutual aid organizations* have been created to facilitate members of a group providing services for other members of that group. Churches and labor unions, for example, support some human service programs for their members, yet they rarely employ professional staff.

Some religious groups have created *sectarian* or *faith-based programs* for the general public that are sometimes staffed by social workers. A substantial number of human services, from counseling to social provisions, are provided to members by synagogues and various denomination groups. Other religious groups believe it is part of their mission to serve all persons in need, whether members of their faith or not, and they have a long history of providing services for the benefit of the general public. These *nonsectarian programs* include the sponsorship of hospitals, group homes, retirement centers, and family counseling agencies.

Labor unions represent another mutual aid setting where social workers might be found. Unions historically have been successful in organizing workers who are underpaid and undervalued by management and advocating for their rights. Today, the labor union setting presents an exceptional opportunity to intervene with people at the place they work and therefore improve the likelihood of resolving problems before they reach a crisis level. Social workers in these settings typically help union members with such work-related problems as finding child care, dealing with family problems related to work schedules, and addressing stress created by changed family roles when both spouses are employed.

A second type of practice setting in the voluntary sector of human services is the *private nonprofit agency.* Private agencies traditionally have depended on voluntary individual and corporate support for their operation. Their sources of funds have included gifts and bequests, membership dues, fees for service, and participation in federated campaigns such as a United Way or a Jewish Welfare Federation. More recently, however, private agencies have begun receiving a substantial share of their funding through contracts with government agencies to provide specific services, conduct research and demonstration projects, or to support their programs through block grants or revenue sharing. Government agencies have increasingly found this a desirable arrangement because it has allowed them to bypass much of the rigidity of the large bureaucratic organizations in favor of the more flexible private agency structures.

Although there has been an intermingling of taxes and donated funds in the budgets of these private agencies, they are classified as part of the voluntary sector because they operate with policies established by a governing board made up of community volunteers. In their governance, then, nonprofits differ dramatically from government agencies that have elected officials responsible for making basic policy decisions. In most instances, these agencies have the advantage of being small and primarily concerned with the provision of local services. Thus, the board members are able to become directly exposed to the agency and are usually more prepared to respond to changing conditions and needs for services in a local community.

The term *nonprofit* indicates that if the agency should end a year with any funds remaining, those resources are allocated to enhance the agency's operation and not paid to staff, board, or any other parties. Because no one profits financially from the operation of the agency and it serves the public good, the Internal Revenue Service has created a process to approve agencies [Section 501(c)(3) of the Internal Revenue Code] as nonprofit organizations. With this designation, persons who donate funds to support the agency can deduct the contribution from their income taxes. In this way, the government is underwriting the voluntary sector human services.

Business Sector Settings

The most rapidly growing setting for social work practice is the for-profit or business sector. This category of practice includes both private practice and employment in large organizations that exist to earn a profit for their owners. The term *private practice* is used to indicate a practice situation where a contract for the provision of service is made directly between the worker and the clients. Usually this term is applied in reference to social workers who provide clinical services, but sometimes private practice involves nonclinical activities such as consulting, conducting workshops or training programs, or contracting to perform research or other professional service for a fee.

With direct client–worker contracts, the practitioners have considerable autonomy in determining how the practice situation will be addressed and what intervention approaches will be used. However, without the monitoring of services that human services agencies provide, clients are more vulnerable to incompetent or unethical practitioners. It is fundamentally for client information and protection that all 50 states license or certify social workers, as well as for NASW's development of the several specialized credentials.

For some social workers, private practice is an attractive alternative to agency-based practice. Usually there is less paperwork to manage, more flexibility in scheduling, and, often, the elimination of unnecessary supervision. In addition, private practice is among the highest-paying settings for social workers. The downside of private practice is that it is a small business and, like many small businesses, is difficult to sustain. A practice must attract a sufficient number of clients who can pay the fees to support the ongoing operating costs (e.g., space, utilities, clerical staff) and also provide a wage for the social worker. For this reason, many social workers engage in private practice on a part-time basis and maintain their primary employment in a human services agency.

Another entrepreneurial setting for social work is in *for-profit organizations*. There has been a transformation in the funding of human service programs. From the 1930s through the 1970s, legislative bodies allocated substantial funds for government agencies to provide services directly to clients. Therefore, a relatively large public sector developed. Later, that pattern shifted to purchase-of-service agreements, with non-profit agencies rather than governmental agencies providing many of these services. A second, and perhaps even more dramatic, shift known as *privatization* is now occurring where governmental agencies invest in the purchase of service from for-profit organizations that are owned and operated as any other business. In fact, many are owned and operated by large corporations.

Several fields of practice have rapidly increased their reliance on these businesses to provide human services. For example, in child welfare, proprietary firms are used extensively as vendors for services for residential treatment, institutional care, and group homes. To a lesser degree, public agencies rely on contracts with for-profit organizations to provide daycare, day treatment services, nursing home care, correctional facilities, and health care.

Social work professionals are uneasy about the growing amount of for-profit practice. The trend toward the privatization of human services threatens to replace the profession's service orientation with the profit motive. Privatization risks making the bottom line the amount of return to the shareholder, rather than the quality of service to the client. When the shareholder is also the service provider, additional ethical issues arise that can erode public trust in the professions.

One development that has affected all social workers in the business sector, whether in private practice or employed by for-profit organizations, is the evolution of *managed care*—or perhaps more accurately, managed costs. Stimulated by the escalating cost of health and mental health services, a variety of plans have been developed to provide health care consumers with needed services at controlled costs. On the positive side, these plans require greater accountability for the quality of services offered, which ultimately should enhance the services clients receive. However, many decisions about the nature and extent of services provided are shifted from the professionals and clients to the managers of the insurance companies. These are not typically people with the qualifications to determine an individual's need for professional services. In relation to mental health services, Stroul, Pires, Armstrong, and Meyers analyzed the effects of managed care and concluded that under managed care programs children and adolescents have had greater access to outpatient services but reduced access to inpatient hospital care—particularly youths with serious emotional disorders or those who are uninsured. In addition, they note that services have become briefer, more problem-oriented, and more focused on behavioral health disorders.[2] The social worker's role with managed care also includes advocating for clients who are not receiving authorization for needed services from these health insurance companies.

Social workers have a central role to play in all three sectors of the human services—government, voluntary, and business. The ability of these professionals to perform their function depends at least partially on their ability to work effectively within a human services organization or manage a private practice. Understanding several issues typically experienced in each of these settings can help future social workers anticipate difficulties they may face and be prepared to deal with them head on.

Issues Affecting Agency-Based Practice

When considering a social work job, potential employing agencies should be examined in relation to their relative compatibility with professional values and standards and the autonomy workers have to exercise their professional judgment in performing the job tasks. Also, the manner in which a human service organization deals with the following issues will affect the work of its professional staff.

Accommodating Horizontal and Vertical Influences

Social workers employed in most human service organizations, as well as those in private practice, often find they cannot successfully work in isolation from other agencies. At the local level, social workers often lead efforts to coordinate the services provided to clients by several social agencies in that community. This coordination sometimes requires that interagency networks, or *horizontal affiliations,* are developed among the agencies. The form of these horizontal networks may range from informal discussions among agency representatives regarding human service programs to the formal creation of human resources planning organizations that study the local service network, encouraging efforts to fill gaps in the services, and facilitating cooperation among the agencies. Decisions made through these horizontal affiliations will influence the choices the social worker can make in serving his or her clients.

Social agencies and social workers are also influenced by *vertical affiliations,* that is, those organizations external to the community that have the authority at least partially to shape the services or operating procedures of a local agency. Voluntary agencies, for example, might affiliate with a national organization, which can give the agency name recognition, provide the community with some assurance that at least minimum standards acceptable in that practice field are being met, make staff development opportunities available through national meetings, and sometimes help secure financial resources. At the same time, these agencies give up some local autonomy as they are committed to operate within the guidelines of the national organization. Vertical affiliation with the American Red Cross, Child Welfare League of America, YWCA or YMCA, and the Family Service Association of America are typical examples of such affiliations. Further, many local voluntary agencies must meet state licensing requirements or other state standards if they are vendors of services to public agencies. This also limits their discretion.

Public agencies typically have more formal vertical relationships. A local governmental agency may be implementing programs that have been created and partially funded at the federal level, further defined and partially funded at the state level, and finally modified and also funded by county government. Thus, a county human services department, for example, is constrained by requirements imposed by federal, state, and county governments. Although these vertical affiliations add to the complexity of tailoring service programs to local needs, they have the advantage of fostering greater equality in the services provided to people throughout a region and the nation. In addition, vertical affiliation creates a larger geographic area for securing funds to support the services, making it possible to more adequately meet needs in a local or regional area that lacks its own resources.

Balancing Efficiency and Effectiveness

A fundamental goal of all human service agencies, whether they are public or private, is to use the scarce resources available to provide the most and best service possible. To achieve this goal, agencies must operate both efficiently and effectively. An agency that leans too far in favoring one over the other ultimately creates problems for the staff members employed in that agency.

Efficiency represents the efforts of the agency to achieve the maximum output of services with a minimum input of resources. The goal of efficiency places the emphasis on the quantity of services provided and often attracts most of the attention of lawmakers, governing boards, and local media. Yet, quantity must be related to quality if an agency is to find a balance that represents the maximum level of service. The qualitative aspects of service are represented in an agency's *effectiveness,* or the degree to which the agency achieves its goals.

The governance of most social agencies has been dominated, in both the public and voluntary sectors, by people who have experience in business and industrial enterprises. They often bring a strong bias toward efficiency, and, although some degree of effectiveness in producing goods was necessary for their success, low cost-per-unit production was clearly their most valued goal. That orientation is especially evident in managed care and the for-profit human service organizations. Thus, the social worker considering agency employment should carefully examine the agency's effectiveness orientation lest the quality of his or her work be seriously compromised in favor of overemphasis on efficiency.

How can efficiency be attained in human service organizations? One management tool used successfully in business and industry and transferred to the human services is bureaucratic structure. Bureaucracy worked to build automobiles and appliances at a fraction of the cost of handmade products. Weber created the clearest statement of bureaucratic theory. His "ideal-type" description of the characteristics of a bureaucratic organization was intended to reflect the fundamental elements of a bureaucracy. The following is a synthesis of Weber's extensive work on this topic.[3]

1. *Division of Labor.* Each person in the organization has a clearly defined and specialized assignment in the organization.
2. *Hierarchy.* Specific lines of authority exist in which every person is not only responsible for his or her own assignments but is also responsible for the performance of subordinates.
3. *Consistent System of Rules.* Every task in the organization is governed by an explicit set of rules that specify the standards of performance and the relationships among tasks.
4. *Spirit of Impersonality.* Work is to be performed without favoritism or prejudice entering official decisions.
5. *Employment Constitutes a Career.* Persons are employed on the basis of qualifications required by the organization, with rewards provided to encourage loyalty and to offer opportunity for a career in that organization.

With some modifications, when applied to the assembly line that produces automobiles in Detroit or toasters in New Jersey, bureaucratic principles led to a high degree of organizational efficiency. This model yielded good results when the product was made from standardized parts. In fact, the greater the standardization, the more effective the bureaucratic organization becomes. A person could quickly be trained to perform a very specific function, for example, installing a fuel pump as an automobile passes on the assembly line. With a line supervisor to provide quality control and enforce the rules established for efficiency (the worker cannot be taking a break when the engine arrives for a fuel pump), the company usually produced a good-quality product. Under this system, there could be no allowance for the worker's personal problems, nor could the boss play favorites. Bureaucratic theory assumes that the rewards of job security, salary increases, and retirement benefits are sufficient to keep the successful employee satisfied with the organization—although some of these companies have recently reneged on providing these promised benefits.

When these principles are applied to human services agencies, social workers and other professionals often find that bureaucratization has both positive and negative consequences. Indeed, the application of bureaucratic principles can ensure equity for both clients and workers, facilitate efficiency in operation, and enhance public support of the organization. Rigid application of bureaucratic principles, however, is in direct conflict with the very nature of professions. As opposed to manufacturing products, in human services the parts being worked with are people who are constantly changing, and the product (attaining maximum client well-being) differs to some degree in each situation. It is simply not realistic to provide narrow technical training, to create highly specialized assignments, or to establish an inflexible system of rules that a staff must follow without adjusting for the uniqueness of the client or practice situation.

Accommodating the Professional Model in Bureaucratic Organizations

When the professional model is compared with the bureaucratic model of conducting work, inherent conflicts emerge that are likely to result in some level of tension for professionals employed in bureaucratic organizations. Scott suggests the following conflicts almost always exist between these two models:[4]

▶ *Resistance to bureaucratic rules.* When a division of labor exists, each person provides only a narrowly defined part of the work. Procedures are then established to coordinate the activities among workers, and these procedures often make it difficult for professionals to individualize services and respond to the unique needs of each client.

▶ *Rejection of bureaucratic standards.* Standards of client eligibility for services and procedures that determine the extent of the services a worker can provide are designed to respond to the "typical client." In reality, clients represent great variability, and professionals in bureaucratic agencies often feel frustrated in their ability to fulfill their obligation to provide the best services possible to their clients.

▶ *Objection to bureaucratic supervision.* In bureaucratic organizations, authority is assigned to a position (e.g., a supervisor or foreman) who is primarily charged with responsibility to monitor the work of the line workers for compliance with agency rules and regulations. Conversely, professional authority is generated from practice competence as judged by one's peers. Professionals, then, object to assigned supervision where the supervisor may or may not possess sufficient practice competence to consult about the worker's practice.

▶ *Conditional loyalty to the organization.* Employees in bureaucratic organizations are trained in the specific job tasks needed by that organization and their success is judged by movement up the organizational ladder, that is, from line worker, to supervisor, to foreman, and so on. Thus, the workers usually have few skills that can be transferred to another organization and are therefore somewhat locked in to their companies. Professionals, however, tend to be primarily committed to careers in their professions and are prepared with competencies that are transferable from one organization to another, making it relatively easy to change their work environment.

How does a professional social worker address these areas of incompatibility? Clearly, an employee is obligated to work within the legitimate requirements of his or her employer, and a social worker cannot ethically ignore the rules and regulations of the agency. However, it is not sufficient to be merely a passive employee who unquestioningly accepts and carries out the rules and regulations of the agency. Client services can be compromised if social workers do not actively work to promote agency flexibility in service provision and, when warranted, be willing to challenge the agency's methods of operating. At times, this may mean taking some risks that may affect one's evaluations, pay increases, or even employment in the agency. Thus the successful agency-based social worker must be smart about organizational change efforts.

Many times constricting agency rules and regulations do not need to be changed. Creative interpretations that stretch the rules to fit client needs are often possible and frequently can be applied with the full support of one's supervisor. Some regulations, however, may not lend themselves to this flexibility, and it may be necessary to attempt to initiate a process to change these rules. Change, especially in large public agencies, takes considerable time and effort. With skill, patience, and perseverance, such change can be accomplished and the professional obligation of the worker to provide the best services possible fulfilled. If this effort fails, however, the worker must either learn to live with the existing regulations or make the decision to seek employment elsewhere.

Assuming that satisfactory conditions exist in an agency for performing social work practice, it becomes important for the worker to discover ways to be responsible to the agency and at the same time maximize the ability to provide services to clients. Pruger suggests four helpful tactics that a worker might employ.[5] First, it is important to understand the agency's (or supervisor's) legitimate authority. Within the guidelines of responsible behavior, one should discover the limits of the discretion a worker has in providing services to clients. Second, because organizations often present demands (e.g., paperwork, staff meetings) that divert the worker's time and energy from the work of providing services, the worker should be cautious about overcommitting to these activities that are of secondary importance. Third, the worker should develop supplemental competencies that are needed by the agency. Professional work involves more than carrying out the routine job duties. It involves making a commitment to expand one's contributions by learning, for example, new practice techniques, skills in grant writing, knowledge of computer applications in practice, or methods of interpreting the agency and its services to the public. Finally, the worker should not yield unnecessarily to agency requirements established for administrative convenience. For instance, it may be convenient to have clients come to the worker's office to receive services so that back-to-back interviews can be scheduled and the worker's time used efficiently. However, for some clients, the requirement of arranging transportation, leaving work, or the unfamiliarity with the agency may discourage them from keeping the appointment. In such a case, a home visit by the worker may be far more successful. Although challenging unproductive regulations may not help the social worker win popularity contests, this action can be a valuable contribution to the organization's effectiveness.

Another contribution that a social worker can make to an employing agency is to prepare to move into a supervisory role or assume an executive or high-level administrative position in the agency. Making such a transition is difficult. As compared to direct service practitioners, the social workers who are administrators are much more involved in activities such as making staff assignments and conducting evaluations of their work, representing the agency and helping to build the service delivery system in the community, engaging in program development, and carrying out various tasks (e.g., budget development, expense approval, staff coordination) that help to maintain the organization's daily operations.

Finally, a worker should be prepared to engage in teamwork and interprofessional practice. Agency practice typically draws together volunteers, persons from varying professions, and other staff members in an effort to respond to human needs. In theory the unique roles and capacities of each discipline appear clear and workers need only coordinate their efforts. In reality, however, there is considerable blurring of lines between the various helping disciplines. Turf problems inevitably emerge that, if not resolved, can jeopardize good client service. Thus, interprofessional collaboration and teamwork are essential.

Human service agencies continue to seek means of improving interprofessional cooperation through various administrative structures, team approaches to case situations, the development of protocols that spell out the functions to be performed by each discipline, and the use of case managers charged with coordinating the services an individual or family might require. Social workers, with their mission to facilitate the interface of clients with their environments, have a particularly important leadership role to perform in facilitating interprofessional collaboration.

Determining the Centrality of Social Work

One final factor to consider when selecting a place of employment is the centrality of social work to the mission of that particular setting. The status of social work in an agency influences the manner in which a social worker spends much of his or her time and affects the opportunity of clients to have the full benefit of the perspective that social work brings to the helping situation. When the policies and procedures of the organization are designed to maximize social work services, social workers can most effectively serve their clientele. However, in a practice setting where another discipline is dominant, social workers often spend considerable effort educating others about the contributions social work can make to the agency's clientele.

In some practice settings, social work is the *primary (or host) discipline.* The primary services provided call for social work expertise, most key jobs require social work training, and social workers hold the major administrative jobs. In practice fields such as child welfare, family services, and income maintenance, social work has traditionally been the primary discipline. In these settings, other disciplines may be involved to provide specialized expertise or consultation, but the services are organized to maximize the contributions of the social worker.

In other practice settings, the social worker is an *equal partner* along with members of one or more other disciplines. The services are organized to maximize interdisciplinary cooperation, and a member of any of the disciplines might provide administrative leadership to the agency. The fields of aging, mental health and retardation, and community and neighborhood services are examples of practice fields that are shared by several disciplines.

In still other settings, social work might provide supporting services to another profession. As the *secondary discipline* in these agencies, social work is, in one sense, a guest of the primary discipline. The agency is organized to allow the primary discipline to work as effectively as possible, and the needs of social work or other professions receive lower priority. The role of the social worker in a medical setting illustrates social work as a secondary discipline. Hospitals, a setting for medical practice, are geared to the needs of the physician. Social services are provided at the physician's referral and are organized so they do not compete with the schedule and work of the medical profession. A similar role would be assumed by the social worker in corrections, schools, and industrial settings.

Advantages of Agency-Based Practice

Given the complexities of agency practice, why does social work continue to function as an agency-based profession? Why not adopt the private practice model of other successful professions?

First, services offered through an agency are more visible and, therefore, more accessible to all persons in need. The existence of agencies in a community over time and the attendant publicity about their operations typically make both their programs and their locations familiar to members of the community. As opposed to nonagency practice, which caters to those who can pay the cost of services, public and private human service agencies are more likely to have as clients the most vulnerable members of society. For the social worker committed to serving the part of the population most vulnerable to serious social problems, agency practice provides the preferable setting.

Second, agencies survive because they have received the sanction, or approval, of the community for the services they provide. Clients approach the helping situation with trust in the services they will receive because of the agency's responsibility to ensure that quality services are delivered. In private practice situations, the client must place full trust in the individual practitioner to perform high-quality practice.

Third, clients have the benefit of an extra layer of protection against possible misuse of professional authority in social agencies. Clients in any setting are protected by both the professional ethics of the workers and, in many cases, the legal regulation or licensing of that practice. In agencies, however, they are also protected by the agency's selection of staff and ongoing monitoring of the quality of services.

Fourth, human service agencies tend to have a broad scope and often employ persons from several different professions, which provides clients with ready access to the competencies of multiple professions and gives the worker the opportunity for interdisciplinary practice activities. In addition, as opposed to the more limited service focus found in private practice, agencies typically offer a broad range of services, from direct practice to social action. Thus, they provide the social worker with the stimulation of engaging in a range of different practice activities and make it possible to change the focus of one's practice area or move into supervisory or management positions without changing employers.

Fifth, most agencies offer staff development opportunities that stimulate professional growth among workers. Characteristically, social agencies employ a large enough number of staff members that workers do not feel isolated and, in fact, typically carry out programs that contribute to the continued professional growth and development of other staff members. The rapidly changing knowledge and skill base of the helping professions makes continuing professional development important to the services the clients receive and adds to the intellectual stimulation of the staff.

Last, agencies have the ability to raise funds from the community, whether from taxes or voluntary contributions, and to offer a stable salary to employees. Agencies do not face as great a risk of a fluctuating income as is experienced by persons in private practice settings.

 ## Issues in Private Practice

The principal alternative to agency-based practice for the social worker is private practice, which is the fastest growing sector of social work today. Why is private practice gaining such popularity among social workers? From the vantage point of the social worker, private practice is attractive partially because of the greater opportunity for financial gain but also for the freedom to exercise professional autonomy in how one conducts social work practice. The bureaucratic constraints of many human service agencies have placed restrictions on practice activities that compromise the ability of social workers to fully use their professional competencies for the benefit of clients. Thus, some social workers have actively sought a different practice setting that would not constrain their work.

Although private practice avoids many of the limitations that accrue from practice within a bureaucratic structure, it also places greater responsibility on the social worker to follow the ethical guidelines of the profession. There is no professional monitoring of private practice, although complaints can be filed with a state licensing board or the local NASW chapter.

The Organization of Private Practice

What does a social worker do in private practice? In his study of clinically oriented private practice, Wallace found that the average for these social workers was "63 percent of private practice time in individual treatment, 19 percent devoted to work with marital couples, 8 percent to group therapy, 7 percent to family treatment, and 2 percent to joint interviews with clients other than married couples."[6] For the delivery of these clinical services, three organizational approaches are used.

In the first approach, the social worker engages in multidisciplinary practice. In this arrangement, the social worker participates with members of other disciplines (for example, psychiatry and psychology) to provide a *group practice* that can meet a broad range of client needs. The social worker is an equal partner with the other disciplines and, in fact, is often a co-owner of the business.

In the second form of private practice, the social worker provides a *supportive practice* for a member of another profession. For example, some physicians are hiring social workers to help patients deal with social problems related to specific illnesses. The social worker might also provide more general services in the physician's office such as educating expectant parents about child development, counseling families that need help with child-rearing practices, or referring people to appropriate community resources for help with other problems.

In the third form, social workers are the *sole owners* of their private practice. Sole ownership involves securing office space, hiring staff, advertising services, making contacts to acquire referrals, overseeing the determination and collection of fees, and doing everything related to the management of a small business. Like any other business, private practice is a "sink or swim" proposition with no guarantee of income equivalent to expenses. The main problems for full-time private practitioners are generating sufficient referrals to be able to keep the business solvent, handling the business details including securing payment from third-party vendors, obtaining competent consultation, minimizing the inherent isolation, arranging for backup in managing crisis situations, and protecting practitioners against their vulnerable position if there should be malpractice charges.

It is estimated that 17.5 percent of all social workers are primarily engaged in private practice, yet many agency social workers also maintain a small part-time private practice. Kelley and Alexander identify four groups of social workers who elect to engage in part-time private practice:[7]

1. Agency practitioners who welcome the independence and additional income
2. Social workers in supervisory or administrative positions in agencies who wish to maintain client contact and clinical skills
3. Educators who wish to have sufficient practice activity to remain current with a practice to effectively teach clinical courses
4. Social workers who are parents of young children and need to control their hours of work

Some social workers in private practice provide indirect services such as consultation. Consultation might be provided to another social worker or to a member of another helping profession concerning the handling of a case. For example, a social worker might consult with a lawyer about a divorce or child custody case or might be involved in working with a social agency, such as helping a nursing home with staff–patient relations, administrative procedures, or program development.

Concerns Related to Private Practice

The private practice approach has not been without controversy in the profession, and three issues have emerged concerning this practice mode.

First, private clients do not have an agency monitoring system to provide protection against incompetence or abuses of the professional monopoly. Therefore, social work has been careful to specify more extensive education and experience as minimum preparation for the private practitioner than for the agency-based practitioner.

Second, because many private practitioners work on a part-time basis, some agencies are concerned that private practice will detract from agency practice and may not do justice to his or her agency responsibilities because of the amount of time and energy that may go into maintaining a private practice. On the other side of this issue, it is argued that private practice offers different professional stimulation than is found in agency practice and also provides a supplemental income to agency salaries that keeps workers satisfied with their agency employment.

Finally, some critics have accused private practitioners of diverting social work from its mission of serving the most vulnerable members of society, thus failing to perform the social action responsibilities that are central to social work's mission of facilitating both person and environment change. Teare and Sheafor confirmed this accusation but additionally found that most other direct service practitioners also failed to engage in social change activities.[8]

Advantages of Private Practice

There are also arguments in favor of social work's movement toward private practice. First, in most human service agencies, clients have little opportunity to exercise individual choice in regard to which professionals will provide services. Clients typically cannot select their individual social workers nor can they fire them if unsatisfied with the services received. Clients exercise considerably more control in a private setting.

Second, from the social worker's perspective, agency rules and regulations place constraints on the worker's ability to conduct practice in the manner he or she believes would be most effective. Professional autonomy is inherently compromised. For example, agency-based social workers typically cannot choose their clients; are not completely free to determine the length and type of service to be given; and are almost always supervised, at times by one who interferes with the professional judgment of the worker.

Third, agency salaries tend to be lower than those of the private practitioner. As opposed to the market-driven income of the private practitioner that is, at least theoretically, based on competence, agency salaries are based to a greater degree on seniority and position within the agency.

Last, few agencies avoid the pitfalls that plague most bureaucratic organizations, in which workers find that a disproportionate share of their time is devoted to meetings and paperwork. The less elaborate mechanisms required for accountability in private practice free the worker from much of the less people-oriented activity found in agency practice.

Concluding Comment

Social work practice has permeated U.S. society to the extent that it occurs in every sector of society: government, voluntary, and business. Although the roots of social work are in agency-based practice, social work now is offered through both for-profit and private practice modes.

Most social workers continue to be employed in agency settings; thus, they must be able to work effectively within agency structures if they are to maximize their ability to serve clients. Understanding the principles on which agencies are organized and the problems social workers commonly experience in matching their professional orientation with agency requirements is, therefore, important for providing quality services. Box 7.1 identifies some of the factors related to work in a government sector agency that influenced the work of the child welfare worker, Demetria, in Chapter 1.

An increasing number of social workers have entered private practice to avoid some of the problems experienced by the agency-based practitioner and, at the same time, to increase potential income. However, private practice is certainly not trouble-free. Social work is concerned about important issues related to private practice: adequate preparation for the responsibilities of independent practice, the move away from the social work mission of focusing services on the poor and other vulnerable population groups, and client protection for this relatively new method of service delivery.

Box 7.1

The Influence of Setting on Demetria's Practice

In the case that is the substance of Chapter 1, Demetria is employed in the child welfare division of a county social welfare department where social work would be considered the *primary discipline*. From this information, we know that she works in a *local government setting*. Thus the programs are established through legislation and funded through taxes. At least for the child protection services, it would be likely that fees for the services performed would not be charged to the clients. Even in an agency with *sliding scale fees* based on income, the Miles family would no doubt be well below the threshold for fees.

In a *government or public* agency such as this department, it is often difficult for staff to effectively lobby for a change in the services should they become aware of ways the services could be improved. The *bureaucratic structure* evident in the case (e.g., presence of a supervisor, intake worker, and office administrator) indicates that Demetria would

(Continued)

Box 7.1 (Continued)

need to carefully work up the chain of command, perhaps even to the county commission or legislature, if she was to affect major change in agency functioning. Her colleague in the Boys and Girls Club, a *voluntary nonprofit agency,* however, would have a much less cumbersome structure if she wanted to promote change.

The concept of *horizontal and vertical influences* is evident in Demetria's work. Her activity was affected by the other agencies and resources in the community (i.e., *horizontal influences*). The actions of the local school; the counseling group at the Boys and Girls Club; the limited employment counseling/finding services; and the immediate access to Medicaid, food stamps, and other social programs all supported her work with this family. However, the policies and procedures, as well as the amount of funding available to the Division of Child Welfare, are likely to be affected by *vertical influencers,* i.e., a combination of actions of county commissioners, state legislature/governor/social welfare boards, and even by federal legislation and the executive branch of the government that administers these programs—the U.S. Department of Health and Human Services.

KEY WORDS AND CONCEPTS

Government sector
Nonprofit or voluntary sector
Business (for-profit and private practice)
    sector
Mutual aid organization
Privatization

Horizontal/vertical influences
Efficiency vs. effectiveness
Bureaucratic vs. professional model
Social work as primary discipline, equal
    partner, secondary discipline

SUGGESTED INFORMATION SOURCES

Kamerman, Sheila, and Alfred J. Kahn, eds. *Privatization and the Welfare State.* Princeton, NJ: Princeton University Press, 1989.

Mosley, Jennifer E., David Storz, Ram A. Cnaan, Kelly McNally Koney, and Sandra A. Lopez. "Contexts/Settings," in Terry Mizrahi and Larry E. Davis (eds.). *Encyclopedia of Social Work*, 20th ed. Washington D.C.: National Association of Social Workers and Oxford University Press, 2008.

National Association of Social Workers. "Clinical Social Workers in Practice: A Reference Guide" (brochure). Washington, D.C.: NASW, 2004.

ENDNOTES

1. Tracy Whitaker, Toby Weismiller, and Elizabeth Clark, *Assuring the Sufficiency of a Frontline Workforce: A National Study of Licensed Social Workers, Executive Summary* (Washington, D.C.: NASW Center for Workforce Studies, 2006).
2. B. A. Stroul, S. A. Pires, M. I. Armstrong, and J. C. Meyers, "The Impact of Managed Care on Mental Health Services for Children and Their Families." *The Future of Children* 8 (Summer–Fall 1998): pp. 119–133.

3. Peter M. Blau and Marshall W. Meyer, *Bureaucracy in Modern Society*, 2nd ed. (New York: Random House, 1973), pp. 18–23.
4. W. Richard Scott, "Professionals in Bureaucracies—Areas of Conflict," in Howard M. Vollmer and Donald L. Mills, eds., *Professionalization* (Englewood Cliffs, NJ: Prentice-Hall, 1966), pp. 264–275.
5. Robert Pruger, "The Good Bureaucrat," *Social Work* 18 (July 1973): 26–27.
6. Marquis Earl Wallace, "Private Practice: A Nationwide Study," *Social Work* 27 (May 1983): 265.
7. Patricia Kelly and Paul Alexander, "Part-time Private Practice: Practical and Ethical Considerations," *Social Work* 30 (May–June 1985): 254.
8. Robert J. Teare and Bradford W. Sheafor, *Practice-Sensitive Social Work Education: An Empirical Analysis of Social Work Practice and Practitioners* (Alexandria, VA: Council on Social Work Education, 1995), p. 117.

chapter 8

Values and Ethics in Social Work

Prefatory Comment

At the heart of social work are its values. Values assist the social worker and the social work profession in setting goals related to both clients and society. Of course, like any other population group, every social worker does not have identical values. Yet, there are some common themes in social work that suggest that social workers hold some fundamental beliefs in common. As opposed to many other groups of people, for example, social workers tend to believe that society has the responsibility to assist people in meeting their needs, people should be included in making decisions that affect their lives, positive change in people's lives can be attained through professional help, and so on. This chapter examines these and other values that are central to social work's belief system.

The most concrete expression of social work's ethical guidelines is embodied in the NASW Code of Ethics. This code helps social workers to make the inevitable moral choices that arise in their daily practice. If unethical practice is suspected, the Code also becomes the criteria by which the social worker's ethical behavior is evaluated.

From formulating social programs to helping clients, values affect social work practice. Social programs created to "promote the general welfare" of the people are influenced by the values held by legislators, board members, or owners of for-profit organizations who created or maintain those programs. Beliefs about who should be responsible for meeting human needs, what role government or private charity should play, and how much of the nation's wealth should be invested in meeting people's social needs are just three examples of values that have shaped human services programs.

Also, values affect the manner in which human service organizations operate. Values, at least partially, determine the answers to important questions: Should potential clients be encouraged or discouraged from asking for help? Should clients be required to pay for services? To what extent should an agency attempt to make services readily accessible to clients and assure that the surroundings are comfortable and pleasant? Should a social worker be allowed to terminate services before a client's insurance benefits are exhausted when the agency needs the funds to meet its financial obligations? Should services be terminated just because the client can no longer pay yet continues to need help? In short, the dominant values of an agency can have a direct impact on social work practice.

The values of a social worker's clients, too, affect practice. If a client feels stigmatized, demeaned, or embarrassed to ask for assistance, the client's ability to productively use the service is affected. If the client is unnecessarily demanding of a worker's time and attention or resents being required to use social services (i.e., an involuntary client), that, too, affects the way a social worker assists the client. Further, much of practice involves helping clients identify, clarify, and resolve value issues that are almost always present in human interactions.

As members of a profession that has based many of its practice approaches and principles on certain beliefs about people and how they can best be served, social workers must be cognizant of the profession's values. Further, because social work must protect the public from potential abuses of the professional monopoly, it has adopted a code of ethical practice that prescribes certain professional behaviors related to interactions with clients, colleagues, employers, and the community. Each social worker must be prepared to adhere to the NASW Code of Ethics.

Finally, the social worker must be clear about how the profession's values and ethical standards interact with his or her own belief system. Therefore, understanding one's own values becomes critical for the social worker. Most of us do not typically contemplate our values unless they somehow create problems for us as we address the issues we confront in life. This chapter, however, asks the reader to consider the nature of values, their place in promoting people's welfare through shaping social programs, the values and ethics of social workers, and, finally, the fit between social work's values and one's own. Understanding the central place of values and ethics in social work is another important factor in making a career choice or preparing to enter the social work profession.

 ## The Nature of Values

Unlike knowledge, which explains what is, values express what ought to be. Rokeach more precisely defines a *value* as "a type of belief, centrally located in one's total belief system, about how one ought or ought not to behave, or about some end-state of existence worth or not worth attaining."[1] This definition helps to clarify the two central functions our values perform. The first function, for example, how we should or should not behave, reflects our *instrumental values*. These values provide the moral or ethical guidelines that help determine how we conduct our lives and, as social workers, how we perform our work. The second function performed by our values, known as *terminal values*, reflects the bottom line of what we want to accomplish. Ensuring a safe environment for all people, a sufficient distribution of the world's wealth to eliminate hunger, ensuring strong families that nurture the development of children, and achieving social justice within the society are just a few examples of terminal values.

Values are much more than emotional reactions to situations or doing what feels right. Values are the fundamental criteria that lead us to thoughtful decisions. It is important to recognize, however, that people do not always behave in a manner consistent with their values. Values guide decisions but do not dictate choices.

People can and do make decisions contrary to their values. Such decisions might be made when other factors are given priority ("I know that I shouldn't have done that, but when will I ever get another chance to make that kind of money?"), the person acts on emotion ("I was just so angry, I hit her without thinking"), or when one fails to adequately think through and understand the value issues in a situation ("It just didn't occur to me that my quitting school would make my parents think that they had failed").

Each person values a variety of things in life. Differences in the strength with which one holds any particular value and the priority a particular value will have among the whole constellation of that person's values, that is, the person's *value system,* is a part of what makes individuals unique. For example, for many people, the most important value is feeling secure in their relationships with loved ones. For some, generating income is the driving force in their lives. For others, giving service dominates their value system.

Dealing with values is particularly difficult for several reasons. First, values are such a central part of our thought processes that we often are not consciously aware of them and therefore are unable to identify their influence on our decisions. The social worker should constantly be alert to values in practice situations as these values may subtly influence the thoughts, feelings, attitudes, and behaviors of both the client and the social worker.

Second, a person may be forced to choose among values that are in conflict with one another. Who can avoid wrestling with a *value conflict* when confronted by a person on the street asking for money to buy something to eat? We may value responding to people in need, but we may equally value encouraging people to use the organized system for receiving financial assistance that does not put the person into the degrading position of panhandling.

Third, addressing values in the abstract may be quite different from applying them in a real-life situation. The social worker must recognize, for example, that clients may not act on the basis of value choices selected in a counseling session when they are confronted with the actual people and conditions where this value must be operationalized.

Finally, values are problematic because they change over time. Various events, experiences, and even new information can lead clients to adapt their system of values to more closely fit their current situation. A person whose job is eliminated, for instance, may be much more supportive of a universal health insurance program than when he or she was employed and receiving health insurance benefits from the employer.

The Place of Values in Social Work

Helping people to be clear about their individual values, that is, *values clarification,* and facilitating their understanding of how the particular set of values they hold influences their goals and decisions is an important aspect of social work practice. At times, clients also must be assisted in recognizing and understanding the values of others. Taking into consideration the values of family members, friends, employers, teachers, or others in that person's environment may be prerequisite to making appropriate and workable decisions. The matter becomes more complicated when social work practice involves more than one person, as it is likely that each will potentially have a somewhat different value system. In that case, the social worker may need to help resolve issues that stem from differences in values.

Further, the social worker must be concerned with his or her own values and control for their inappropriate intrusion into practice situations. Value choices that may be viable personally for the social worker may not coincide with the needs, wants, priorities, or realities the client experiences. Ultimately, the client must live with the decisions that are made, and those decisions should be consistent with his or her own value system—not the value system of the social worker. Learning to suspend one's own values (i.e., *value suspension*) to keep the focus of helping on the client or client group is an important, yet difficult, task for every social worker.

With social work practice focused at the interface between person and environment, the social worker must simultaneously address several sets of values. It is no wonder that social work has perhaps devoted more attention to values than has any other helping profession. Yet it has not developed a sufficiently clear and adequately tested statement of its core values to offer a definitive description of its central beliefs. At best, there is only rather general agreement that some values are fundamental to social work practice.

 ## Social Values in U.S. Society

Values differ from *needs*. The latter refers to people's basic biological or psychological urges, while values reflect what people hope to get out of life and how this should be accomplished. The choice of which needs a society will attempt to meet depends on what it values. The most predominant feature of Western values is the central place of the individual; that is, the society exists to help individuals lead satisfying and productive lives. These values have their roots in at least four different sources, all of which are concerned with the responsibilities of the individual toward self and society and/or the society's responsibility to the individual.[2] These sources include:

1. Judaism and Christianity with their doctrine of the inherent worth of humans and their responsibilities for their neighbors
2. The democratic ideals that emphasize the equality of all people and a person's right to "life, liberty, and the pursuit of happiness"
3. The Puritan ethic, which says that character is everything, circumstances nothing; that the moral person is the one who works and is independent; and that pleasure is sinful
4. The tenets of Social Darwinism, which emphasize that the fittest survive and the weak perish in a natural evolutionary process that produces the strong individual and society

It is evident that much of the disagreement in the United States over the provision of human services results from value conflicts inherent in the U.S. public's value system. Brill and Levine point out: "Even the casual reader will see that a dichotomy exists within this value system. We hold that all men are equal, but he who does not work is less equal....We hold that the individual life has worth, but that only the fit should survive. We believe that we are responsible for each other, but those who depend on others for their living are of lesser worth."[3]

In carrying out the society's values to respond to human needs, the social worker becomes an intermediary between people in need and society's value judgments about what needs are to be met. As one saying puts it, the social worker stands "between the demanding recipient and the grudging donor." Therefore, the social worker must be particularly skilled at mediating between these divergent views.

What constellation of values is held by the U.S. population? In this nation of people with widely diverse backgrounds and interests, it is not surprising that there is considerable variation in belief systems. The answer to the question "Am I my brother's (or sister's) keeper?" is not a categorical "yes" or "no." Protecting a woman's "right to choose" in regard to abortion in one person's value system, for example, is viewed as a "license to kill" in another's. Determining the preferred values held by the U.S. public is the basis for considerable political debate, but rarely a clear consensus on such issues exists.

Kahle's study of the social values held by Americans suggests that value preferences differ substantially for different segments of the population.[4] The study asked respondents to indicate which of eight fundamental social values was the most important for a person to achieve in life.* The data reveal that the more vulnerable groups consistently hold two values, security and being respected, at much higher levels than the general population. Perhaps that is not surprising. If one is poor, has a limited education, is a minority group member, or is old, he or she is likely to worry about having basic health insurance, sufficient income, and safety. It is also likely that he or she is regularly disregarded by others or will suffer various forms of discrimination. Under these conditions, one values highly what he or she does not have—security and respect. From the vantage point of social work, these data reinforce the view that it is important to support the development of social programs that increase people's security and to deliver those programs in a manner that treats the recipients with dignity. With those two basic social values achieved, people are then ready to address other areas of need that can enhance their lives.

---

*The eight social values, in order of numbers of times it was selected as most important, were (1) having *self-respect* (feeling good about oneself and what has been accomplished in life); (2) attaining a *sense of security* (feeling safe and comfortable about the future); (3) having *warm personal relationships* (maintaining satisfying interpersonal relations with friends and family); (4) *feeling successful* in life's undertakings; (5) being *respected by others;* (6) *feeling fulfilled* by the quality of life experiences; (7) experiencing *a sense of belonging* to valued groups of people; and (8) finding *fun, enjoyment, and excitement* in life's activities.

Social workers and other professionals must be particularly alert to what the client values because those values are not likely to be held with the same strength by the professionals themselves. The data from the Kahle study indicate that attaining such basic values as security and being respected by others were not of high priority to professionals. After all, they really don't need to worry about those basics. Professionals are highly educated, usually have secure jobs with relatively high income and can feel pretty safe about their futures. Their value preferences are related to items such as achieving self-respect, having a sense of accomplishment, and experiencing fulfillment.[5] It takes discipline and commitment to avoid the trap of seeing the world only through one's own eyes and actively seeking to understand and appreciate the value preferences of others.

Values Held by Social Workers

To avoid imposing personal values on the client or making inappropriate judgments about a client's values, the social worker must have a clear understanding of his or her own personal values. In addition, the social worker must be fully aware of, and guided by, the fundamental values of the social work profession.

What, then, are the values commonly held by social workers? When developing its classification scheme for different levels of practice, the National Association of Social Workers identified ten basic social work values.[6] These statements express the basic values that underpin the profession of social work.

1. *Commitment to the primary importance of the individual in society.* Social work accepts the position that the individual is the center of practice and that every person is of inherent worth because of his or her humanness. The social worker need not approve of what a person does but must treat that person as a valued member of society. Commitment to the centrality of the individual has also led social workers to recognize that each person is unique and that practice activities must be tailored for that person's or group's uniqueness. Such individualization permits the worker to determine where and how to intervene in each helping situation, while at the same time communicating respect for the people being served.

2. *Commitment to social change to meet socially recognized needs.* Giving primacy to the individual does not minimize the commitment of the social worker to achieve societal change. Rather, it suggests that the social worker recognizes that the outcome of change activities in the larger society must ultimately benefit individuals. Social workers, then, are committed to the belief that the society has a responsibility to provide resources and services to help people avoid such problems as hunger, insufficient education, discrimination, illness without care, and inadequate housing.

3. *Commitment to social justice and the economic, physical, and mental well-being of all in society.* Social workers believe that social justice will be achieved if each person has the opportunity to develop his or her unique potential and, therefore, make his or her maximum contribution to society. Thus, social workers believe that each person should have the right to participate in molding the social institutions and engage in the

decision-making processes in U.S. society so that programs, policies, and procedures are responsive to the needs and conditions of all. Of course, when resources are limited, choices must be made. Not every person can have all needs met. When social workers are making choices, the values they hold emphasize the importance of responding to the needs of the most vulnerable members of the society. Typically, these vulnerable people are children, the aged, minority group members, persons who are disabled, women, and others who have been victims of institutionalized discrimination.

4. *Respect and appreciation for individual and group differences.* Social workers recognize that there are common needs, goals, aspirations, and wants that are held by all people. In some ways, we are all alike. However, social workers also recognize that, in other ways, each individual's life experience and capacities make him or her unique. Where some may fear differences or resist working with people who are not like themselves, social workers value and respect uniqueness. They believe that the quality of life is enriched by different cultural patterns, different beliefs, and different forms of activity. In contrast to efforts to assimilate persons who are in some way different from the general population, social workers value a pluralistic society that can accommodate a range of beliefs, behaviors, languages, and customs.

5. *Commitment to developing clients' ability to help themselves.* Social workers do not view people as static or unchanging, nor is anyone assumed to be unable to engage in activities that may produce a more satisfying and rewarding life. Rather, social workers view people as adaptable. Although there are conditions that some people face that cannot be changed, the people themselves or the world around them can be helped to adapt to these conditions. Within the individual's or group's capacities, the social worker places high value on helping people take responsibility for their own decisions and actions.

6. *Willingness to transmit knowledge and skills to others.* A significant part of guiding the change process involves helping clients understand the situation they experience from both a personal perspective and the perspectives of others, as well as helping them develop the skills to resolve their problems. Effective helping avoids making clients dependent on helpers and prepares them to address other issues that arise in their lives. Thus, it is important that social workers assist clients in identifying strengths that can be mobilized for solving immediate problems and to help clients learn how to use these strengths in solving problems that may arise in the future.

7. *Willingness to keep personal feelings and needs separate from professional relationships.* It is important for the social worker to recognize that the focus of practice must be maintained on the client—not on the social worker. However, because social workers care about the people they work with, it is easy to become overidentified with clients' lives or even to develop personal relationships with them. If that happens, the client loses the benefit of an objective helper, and the quality of the helping process is diminished because the relationship has changed from professional to personal.

8. *Respect for the confidentiality of relationship with clients.* Although it is rare that the social worker can guarantee "absolute confidentiality," social workers value achieving the maximum possible protection of information received in working with clients. The very nature of a helping relationship suggests that there is sensitive information that must be shared between the person being helped and the helper. In each case, some information typically passes between client and worker that could potentially be emotionally or economically damaging if it is inappropriately revealed to other parties. Also, unless the client can trust the worker to protect this information, he or she is unlikely to reveal this important information, thus limiting the social worker's ability to be of help.

9. *Willingness to persist in efforts on behalf of clients despite frustration.* Situations that require social work intervention typically do not develop quickly and usually cannot be resolved readily. Recognizing the frustration that they experience when change is slow to occur, social workers have come to value tenacity in addressing both individual problems and advocating to address issues that affect groups of people, organizations, communities, and society in general. Social workers must be persistent.

10. *Commitment to a high standard of personal and professional conduct.* The final value on the NASW list directs the worker to use the highest ethical standards in his or her practice. It suggests that the worker must conduct professional activities in a manner that protects the interests of the public, the agency, the clients, and the social worker. This value has been operationalized in the form of the *NASW Code of Ethics,* which is perhaps the single most unifying element among social workers.

Shortly after its founding, the NASW began to formulate a code of ethics that could serve the needs of this profession. First adopted in 1960 as several broad statements to guide ethical practice, the *Code of Ethics* has undergone several major revisions and now is an elaborate document used not only as a practice guide but also as a statement on which to assess allegations against social workers of ethical misconduct.

With a clearly explicated code of ethics in place, NASW members can be clear about expectations for competent and ethical practice, and the profession has a standard against which to assess any complaints that the public trust has been violated. To join NASW, the social worker must sign a statement agreeing to abide by the ethical standards contained in the Code and to participate in the adjudication process if a complaint is made. By renewing one's membership each year, he or she reaffirms the commitment to adhere to NASW's ethical code. NASW has created an elaborate procedure for hearing grievances at the local level with appeal to the national level possible for all parties to the complaint. A member found to have violated the Code of Ethics can be asked to take corrective actions, may be listed on a published report of code violators, or may have his or her NASW membership revoked.

Areas of Practice Addressed by the NASW Code of Ethics

The *NASW Code of Ethics* has evolved from its 1960 format of fourteen general statements to its current format that consumes twenty-seven pages of ethical prescriptions. Mastering the specifics of the Code and interpreting its provisions in actual practice situations is an ongoing challenge for all social workers. This process begins by recognizing the general areas of practice activity that the Code addresses.* The following statements summarize the main sections of NASW's Code of Ethics.

1. Standards related to the social worker's ethical responsibilities to clients. This section of the Code of Ethics is concerned with such factors and principles as the following: the worker's primary responsibility is to the client; respect for client self-determination; securing client's informed consent; the worker's competence to provide needed services; the worker's cultural competence; avoiding conflict of interest; respecting clients' rights to privacy and confidentiality; the prohibition of sexual involvement, sexual harassment, inappropriate physical contact, and abusive or derogatory language; special considerations when clients lack decision-making capacity; avoiding the interruption of services; and the planned termination of services.

2. The social worker's ethical responsibilities to colleagues. Section 2 is concerned with the social workers' responsibility to treat colleagues with respect; concern for maintaining confidentiality among professionals; appropriate collaboration and teamwork; proper handling of disputes and disagreements; developing appropriate consultation relationships; proper referral of clients to colleagues; the prohibition of sexual harassment and sexual involvement with one's supervisees or students; and the requirement for responsible action in relation to a colleague who is impaired, incompetent, or unethical in his or her practice.

3. The social worker's ethical responsibilities in practice settings. This section of the Code of Ethics relates to services performed that only indirectly relate to clients. The items addressed include the competence required for providing supervision, consultation, education, and training; responsible evaluation of the performance of other workers; maintaining proper client records and billing properly; carefully evaluating client needs before accepting transfers; assuring an appropriate working environment and providing ongoing education and training in human services agencies; demonstrating commitment to agency employees; and guidelines for acting responsibly in labor disputes.

4. The social worker's ethical responsibilities as a professional. Section 4 includes items related to the social worker accepting employment and job assignments when he or she may not be competent to perform that work; prohibition from practicing, condoning, or participating in any form of discrimination; engaging in private conduct that compromises the ability to fulfill professional responsibilities; restriction from engaging in dishonesty, fraud, and deception; the responsibility to address one's own problems if impaired; the requirement to be clear in public statements regarding whether acting as a professional or a private citizen; prohibiting uninvited solicitations for business; and properly acknowledging any contributions to one's written or other work made by others.

---

*The full text of the NASW Code of Ethics can be obtained in both English and Spanish from the National Association of Social Workers, 750 First Street, NE, Washington, DC 20002-4241, or it can be downloaded from NASW's web site (http://www.socialworkers.org/pubs/code/code.asp). The Canadian Code of Ethics (which contains similar provisions) can be downloaded by members of the Canadian Association of Social Workers at (http://www.casw-acts.ca/practice/code3_e.html).

5. The social worker's ethical responsibilities to the social work profession. The Code of Ethics is also concerned with issues related to the social worker promoting high standards for social work and contributing time and energy to the profession's growth and development, as well as addressing items related to social workers continuously monitoring and evaluating social policies, programs, and their own practice interventions.

6. The social worker's ethical responsibilities to the broader society. In its final section, the Code of Ethics charges social workers with promoting the general welfare of the society and seeking to ensure social justice for all people, participating in public debate to shape social policies and institutions, providing services in public emergencies, and actively engaging in social and political action.

The Code of Ethics helps to satisfy social work's obligation to be responsible in performing its duties as a recognized profession. It provides guidance to social workers as they make ethical decisions in their day-to-day practice; spells out expected behaviors in areas where ethical compromises may arise; and provides clarity to the general public, employers, and other professionals who may feel that a social worker has violated the principles of ethical practice and wish to have NASW and/or the courts determine if a social worker has violated the public trust granted to professions.

Illustrations of Values and Ethics Operating in Social Work Practice

For most social workers, theoretical or abstract discussion of values and ethical dilemmas is not a daily event. It is usually when these issues are experienced while working with clients that they take on full significance—and they do indeed occur while working with clients. Hokenstad, for example, estimates that "half of professional decision making requires ethical rather than scientific judgment."[7] Thus, examining one's values in the context of a case example helps to translate the value-related issues that regularly arise in practice from the abstract value statements to their more concrete application.

RAGAN ADAMS' VALUE DILEMMA

The interview began as most begin. The school social worker, Ragan Adams, had initiated an interview with the Warring family as a follow-up to a conference she had conducted with the Warring's oldest daughter, Sally Kay. In the conference with Sally Kay regarding her sudden change from being a model student to one who was frequently absent from school, with a sudden burst of tears Sally Kay revealed that she was pretty sure she was pregnant and was afraid to tell her parents. She was sure it would hurt her mother deeply, and she was physically afraid of how her father might react.

Sally Kay indicated that her parents are deeply religious and decidedly "pro-life" in their philosophy about abortion. She felt trapped in the situation as she believed that she was in no way ready to raise a child, knew her parents would not condone her having an abortion, and thought adoption was not a good option because she would need to carry the baby to term and that would ruin her future and bring shame to the family.

When questioned, she indicted that "Yes, she had considered suicide as a way out" but had abandoned that thought because "it would only make things worse." She needed help in figuring out what to do and asked Ms. Adams for help.

Ms. Adams knew that an unintended pregnancy could destabilize a family, especially if the pregnant family member is an unmarried teenager. Also, Sally Kay's fear of possible violence by her father hinted that there could have been violence in the home previously. It would be important to plan helping in a way that would be supportive of Sally Kay's revealing her situation to her parents while minimizing the chances of the father's becoming violent with Sally Kay or others, and then turn the attention to making a decision that would be with Sally Kay for the rest of her life and that, hopefully, the parents would support.

Before taking any action, Ragan Adams needed to do a little soul-searching herself. What were her beliefs about these options, and could she suspend them to allow the family to make the best choice for itself? Might her own values intrude and affect her actions as a social worker? As an agent of the school, was she free to support whatever choice Sally Kay might make? What if the choice should be to help Sally Kay have an abortion, and Sally Kay's parents complain to the principal that Ms. Adams had influenced Sally Kay to make that choice against their will? Who is the client, and to what extent should client self-determination prevail?

Ms. Adams concluded that the safest place for the family interview would be at the school. After introducing herself to the parents, she indicated that she had called the meeting to talk over issues that were interfering with Sally Kay's success in school. As she and Sally Kay had planned and practiced before the interview began, Ms. Adams invited Sally Kay to share her thoughts on the matter. When Sally Kay indicated that she was pregnant, the father went "ballistic," wanting to know "who the hell was the father" and why had Sally Kay let him take advantage of her. The mother burst into tears, mumbling that she had failed as a mother and surely God was punishing them for something she had done wrong. Sally Kay hid her face in her hands and silently sobbed. It was clear that many different emotions and values would have to be reconciled when working with this family.

Where the above case centers around values held by both the clients and the worker, the subset of values related to the conduct of one's professional practice represents the ethical principles that should guide the social worker. Most ethical decisions, unfortunately, are not clear and require the social worker to make choices when, sometimes, none of the alternatives are desirable. The worker must weigh one choice against others and make a decision about which option is best or, too often, which is least harmful. Further, ethical issues sometimes appear relatively easy to resolve in the abstract but are much more difficult in real-life situations. Consider the following case example.

TERRI PERRY'S ETHICAL DECISION

Terri was a good student and was pleased to have discovered social work as a career option. She had always wanted a career helping people, and her friends regularly sought her out in the dormitory to ask advice about problems in relationships with parents, broken love affairs, difficulty in finding a direction in college, and getting through the freshman plague—roommate problems. Her social work professors had described these qualities as those of a good natural helper, and now she is preparing to move her talents to another level, professional helping.

To Terri, the culmination of her social work education was to be her field placement in the county probation office. There she would be able to combine her natural helping skills and the knowledge from her social work classes into her own professional helping style to start down the track of being a social worker. When the placement was planned with the school's field instruction coordinator, Terri had interviewed with the chief probation officer, Mr. DeMiranda, and Ms. Sills, the social worker who was to be her field instructor. She especially liked Ms. Sills, who indicated that she planned to regularly observe Terri working with clients, either directly or through recording, and to meet with her weekly to plan and critique her work so that Terri might improve her competence as a social worker.

At the end of the first month in placement, Terri concluded that the experience had lived up to her expectations—unlike the reports from some of her classmates in other placements. Then it happened! Mr. DeMiranda began to take a special interest in her—too special, she thought. At first he casually brushed against her at the water fountain (it might have been an accident), and then he asked her to sit next to him in a staff meeting where he pressed his leg against hers under the table (maybe he thought her leg was the table leg), making her very nervous. Terri tried to avoid Mr. DeMiranda after that and no longer looked forward to going to her placement.

Terri had learned that avoiding problems did not resolve them. What should she do? Perhaps she should not do anything. What would happen to her field placement if she makes waves? And what if she is just imagining that Mr. DeMiranda is making advances? What would happen to Mr. DeMiranda and his family? What if it is true and yet she has no "proof"? What would happen to her career as a social worker? "Maybe it is wise to just let this one go by," she thought. "After all, I'm just a student."

On the other hand, Terri pondered the implications of letting this pass. What if this happens to others who are in positions where Mr. DeMiranda possesses power over them, for example other interns, staff members, and even probationers? They are just as vulnerable, or perhaps even more vulnerable. If no one speaks up, won't this behavior continue? What policy does the Probation Office have regarding sexual harassment? Will the Department of Social Work at my university stand behind me? What guidance might I find from the NASW Code of Ethics?

The ethical dilemma experienced by Terri Perry, the social worker in the above case, is only one of many a social worker might encounter. The following list gives some examples of the range of decisions a social worker must address that have ethical implications. Fortunately, the Code of Ethics provides the worker with some guidance on each of them, but sometimes, if the worker follows one code guideline, another may be violated.

▶ What should a social worker do if a client announces the decision to return to an abusive spouse when the worker fears for the client's safety?
▶ Is it ethical for a social worker to attempt to provide specialized therapeutic services for which he or she is not trained if the worker doubts the competence of the only credentialed person with that expertise in the area?
▶ Should a social worker accept a personal gift from a client beyond the fee the client pays for the professional service? What about in lieu of a fee for professional service?

▶ Should a social worker report a colleague to NASW or the state licensing board if that colleague reveals that he or she has developed a sexual relationship with one of his or her clients?

▶ What should a social worker do if a grand jury requests a client's file that contains case notes that may be damaging to the client?

▶ Is a social worker obligated to do anything if he or she believes a colleague has developed a substance abuse problem?

▶ What should be done if a client asks a social worker in a probation setting to overlook (and not mention in the case record) a violation of a condition of parole—promising not to repeat the activity?

▶ Is it okay for a social worker not to record information given by a client in confidence in the case file when the agency's administrative procedures require recording all pertinent information to the case? What about if state law requires reporting that information to a central registry or a protective services agency?

▶ If the administrator in a nursing home directs the social work staff to transfer out of the agency all patients who do not have insurance or other benefits because the nursing home is experiencing financial difficulty, should the social workers abide by this directive?

▶ Is it ethical for a social worker who develops a successful helping technique to obtain a patent and market the technique for a profit to other social workers?

▶ Is a social worker obligated to engage in social and political action when his or her job description does not specify such activity?

Concluding Comment

One cannot understand social work without being sensitive to values. Values represent a highly individual and personal view that must be constantly examined during practice. The social worker must be aware of the value system of the client or client group and the values held by society that impinge upon the client. These values, however, are not held equally by all people, and client groups can be expected to vary in the intensity with which they hold particular values. Certainly it would be unrealistic to expect, or even desire, that the helping process occur in a value-free environment. Yet the social worker must attempt to avoid imposing personal beliefs inappropriately on the client or client groups. To practice social work, one must be prepared to accept and understand people who hold values that are different from their own.

The social worker also must be guided by the values and ethics of the social work profession. These beliefs are not held exclusively by social workers. Some overlap with the values of other professions, and there is indication that professionals hold distinctly different values from the general population.[8] Social work's constellation of core values, however, is unique. Roberts, for example, has identified five areas where the values of physicians and those of social workers are quite different, including attitudes about such factors as saving life versus quality of life, the professional's control versus patient autonomy in establishing treatment plans, and so on.[9] Further, Abbott's research identified areas of difference in the values held by social workers, physicians, nurses, teachers, psychologists, and business people. Of these groups, psychologists were most like social workers in their beliefs.[10] A difficulty in addressing values is that they are not usually explicitly stated and must be inferred from people's behaviors. In Box 8.1, some of the values and ethical considerations we can infer from Demetria's work with the Miles family (see Chapter 1) are enumerated.

In many ways, values or beliefs about how things ought to be or how people ought to behave are the cornerstone of social work. Even when the knowledge available to guide practice is limited, the social worker who falls back on the values of the profession cannot go far wrong in guiding the helping process. When the worker is value-sensitive and effectively supplies the competencies of social work practice, clients receive the quality of services they should expect from a professional.

Box 8.1

Values and Ethical Considerations in Demetria's Practice

Although Demetria's values are not directly expressed in the Miles family case (Chapter 1), some values are evident in her actions. It is clear that Demetria valued creating a safe and supportive family environment for Joseph and thus elected to help the family address its issues so that Joseph would not need to be removed from the home and could get help in dealing with his problems with alcohol and gang involvement. Demetria seems to be aware that Mrs. Miles, like other vulnerable people, places a priority on attaining *security* before she could be open to addressing other issues in her life. Thus, attaining food and electricity became a first order of business. Demetria also appeared to recognize that people in vulnerable situations place high priority on *being respected* and politely accepted the offer of a cup of tea (although she couldn't be sure the cup was very clean) and made herself comfortable on the worn couch that might house more of the roaches she had observed in the kitchen.

At least two of the basic social work values were evident in Demetria's performance. One was her *commitment to the primary importance of the individual.* She took Joseph seriously and honored his reluctance to provide her with much information about some of his behaviors by not prying or threatening. She also allowed Mrs. Miles to spill her heart about the issues she faced without judging her as a bad mom or an incapable parent. This would be termed an *instrumental value*, or a value that guided Demetria's actions in her relationship with Mrs. Miles. In her concern about the adequacy of employment counseling for this family, Demetria reflected the basic social work value of *commitment to social change to meet socially recognized needs.* This is a *terminal value* that leads to actions regarding an outcome, better employment services, that she wanted to accomplish.

Demetria seemed not to experience any significant ethical issues in this case. One example of her practice that was in line with the *Code of Ethics* was her commitment to client *self-determination.* She pointed Joseph and Mrs. Miles to certain resources (i.e., the counseling group at the Boys and Girls Club for Joseph and the application for food stamps for Mrs. Miles), but ultimately the decision was left to them to use or not use those resources. Demetria also reflected the Code's commitment to *collegial interaction* as she risked criticism when presenting her case plan for consultation at an agency staffing meeting.

KEY WORDS AND CONCEPTS

Values
Ethics
Value conflict
Value system

U.S. society's values
Social workers' values
NASW Code of Ethics
Value suspension

SUGGESTED INFORMATION SOURCES

Gambill, Eileen, ed. *Social Work Ethics.* Burlington, VT: Ashgate, 2009.

Hultman, Ken, and Bill Gellerman. *Balancing Individual and Organizational Values: Walking the Tightrope to Success.* San Francisco: Jossey-Bass/Pfeiffer, 2002.

Reamer, Frederic G. *Ethical Standards in Social Work: A Review of the NASW Code of Ethics.* Washington, D.C.: NASW Press, 2006.

Reamer, Frederic G. *Social Work Values and Ethics,* 3rd ed. New York: Columbia University Press, 2006.

Rothman, Julie C. *From the Front Lines: Student Cases in Social Work Ethics.* Boston: Allyn & Bacon, 2005.

ENDNOTES

1. Milton Rokeach, *Beliefs, Values, and Attitudes: A Theory of Organization and Change* (San Francisco: Jossey-Bass, 1968), p. 124.
2. Naomi I. Brill and Joanne Levine, *Working with People: The Helping Process,* 7th ed. (Boston: Allyn & Bacon, 2002), p. 29.
3. Ibid., p. 12.
4. Lynn R. Kahle and Susan Groff Timmer, "A Theory and a Method for Studying Values," in Lynn R. Kahle, ed., *Social Values and Social Change: Adaptation to Life in America* (New York: Praeger Publishers, 1983), pp. 47–108.
5. Ibid., p. 110.
6. National Association of Social Workers, *NASW Standards for the Classification of Social Work Practice* (Silver Spring, MD: The Association, September 1981), p. 18.
7. M. C. Hokenstad, "Teaching Practitioners Ethical Judgment," *NASW News* 32 (October 1987): 4.
8. William C. Horner and Les B. Whitebeck, "Personal versus Professional Values in Social Work: A Methodological Note," *Journal of Social Service Research* 14 (Issue 1/2 1991): 21–43.
9. Cleora S. Roberts, "Conflicting Professional Values in Social Work and Medicine," *Health and Social Work* 13 (August 1989): 211–218.
10. Ann A. Abbott, *Professional Choices: Values at Work* (Silver Spring, MD: National Association of Social Workers, 1988), pp. 74–75.

Spirituality in a Secular Profession

Prefatory Comment

In recent years, increasing attention has been given to the role of spirituality and religion in social work. This contemporary dialogue is value-laden and complex. However, the reality that issues of religion and spirituality in social work are here to stay is not in debate. What is debated, however, is whether modern social work curricula should educate and train the professional social worker to handle the intersection of a secular profession in a world with spiritual and religious underpinnings.

To keep pace with the ever-evolving social work profession, it is useful to further the conversation among students, educators, and practitioners about the relevance of this issue for social workers. This chapter addresses religion and spirituality from a historical perspective, as well as the implications spirituality has on today's professional practice. The authors believe these issues have a place in the classroom, if for no other reason than to better equip social work professionals to serve their clients with an expanded level of cultural awareness.

Religion and spirituality are terms often used interchangeably, but that is misleading. To understand the context of this chapter in relation to these two terms, it is critical to define religion and spirituality. For the purposes of this chapter's discussions, *religion*, as articulated by Edward Canda,[1] is "the patterning of spiritual beliefs and practices into social institutions, with community support and traditions maintained over time." Canda further indicates that *spirituality* "relates to the person's search for a sense of meaning and morally fulfilling relationships between oneself, other people, the encompassing universe, and the ontological [metaphysical] ground of existence, whether a person understands this in terms that are theistic, atheistic, non-theistic, or any combination of these."[2] Religion, then, is a term rooted in a narrower cultural and formalized base, with particular experiences, rituals, and value beliefs established by particular religious institutions and governed by their covenants. Spirituality, however, is a much more broad-based concept that may or may not be constrained by a specified religion or denominational affiliation or association.[3] Regardless of which concept one embraces, or neither, the two terms are important realities in the contemporary cultural value composition in the United States and should be recognized and validated as components of human diversity.

Gallup and Lindsay report that an overwhelming majority of U.S. citizens (between 92 percent and 97 percent) believe there is a God or a higher power. In addition, they assert that some 87 percent of American citizens value religion highly and feel it is an important component of their lives.[4] These numbers, perhaps, explain why there is a recent surge in research on the relationship of religion and spirituality in social work practice and increased consideration of its inclusion in curricula in professional schools. Much like the cultural competence discussions that focus on race and ethnicity, sexual orientation, disability, women's issues, socioeconomic diversity, and others, religion and spirituality are poised to take a place among these considerations. To serve clients as effectively as possible, it is increasingly recognized that greater understanding of the impact of spirituality and religion in the practice arena, in social work curricula, and in agency settings must be encouraged and supported.

It is important that we address these issues as the population continues to grow and become more diverse. Our efforts should be to equip practitioners with the knowledge and skills necessary to serve individuals and groups who have varying spiritual and religious cultural beliefs. The tendency to focus on the large organized religions in the United States marginalizes those who fall outside these affiliations. Christianity clearly is the largest organized religion with 160 million members in the United States (76 percent), and those with nonreligious or secular beliefs are a distant second at 13.2 percent.[5] However, Judaism, Islam, Buddhism, Agnostic, Hinduism, Unitarian Universalist, and Wiccan/Pagan/Druid religions are also part of the religious culture of America, not to mention Spiritualists and Native American spiritual traditions and practices.

Clearly, there is heterogeneity among U.S. citizens and their religious, secular, and spiritual beliefs, but the challenge for social workers is that few could become experts in all of them. Rather, the challenge, as formidable as it may be, is to establish ways of honoring and respecting clients' values and beliefs and discovering how these beliefs influence their lives and might serve them in improving their social functioning and well-being.

Spirituality also appears to have a role in the motivations of the persons providing the help. When asked, social work students often assert that they were brought up to be concerned for the welfare of their neighbor. Another common response from students is that their altruistic motives (i.e., placing the needs of others before one's own) are firmly centered in their spiritual or religious beliefs. Whichever the case, persons who enter helping professions tend to find value and personal satisfaction in helping persons in need—and for many that motivation is rooted in spiritual beliefs.

Historical Context of Spirituality in the Human Services

Religion and traditional spiritual practices have had significant influence in the establishment of human services in the United States. From early sectarian and Christian human services to contemporary faith-based church and governmental programs, spiritual values and beliefs, as well as religious doctrines, have played a significant role in the past and current landscape of American social welfare services. According to the *Encyclopedia of Social Work*, the social work profession in North America developed with a strong influence from religious ideologies of service (especially Christianity and Judaism) and humanistic spiritual views.[6] Examples include the Charity Organization Society, the Settlement House Movement, and Jewish Communal Services. Slogans from "it takes a village to raise a child" (African proverb) to "the poor shall not be forgotten" often reverberate in contemporary speeches referencing the struggles of the poor and today's troubled youth.

Perhaps the drifting that has occurred from these historical religious and spiritual foundations through the years has been more in word rhetoric than in the shifting of fundamental values and beliefs guiding the responsibility of the individual to those less fortunate. Canda and Furman, in their book *Spiritual Diversity in Social Work Practice,* assert that spirituality is at the heart of helping.[7] Although there has been a resurgence of discussions on religion and spirituality in the aftermath of terrorist attacks and natural and man-made disasters, many people have increasingly reflected on the meaning of their lives. In historical context, many in the social work profession have been at the center of efforts to care for and help direct society toward becoming more responsive to those suffering from the effects of poverty and disease. How, then, could a profession so guided by religious and spiritual duty evolve to a place that, until recently, seldom mentioned or discussed its historic foundations of religion and spirituality? Perhaps the evolution of social work as a secular profession is to blame. Thus, central to our discussion is the contemporary intersection of a secular profession and its responsibility to both acknowledge and support the reality that many of social work's clients are grounded and guided by their religious and spiritual beliefs, as are many social workers.

The central question, then, becomes "how much personal belief is not professional?" This question rings loudly among social workers of religious and nonreligious affiliations. For example, social workers in the early 1960s, according to Zilboorg, viewed religious and spiritual practices as "an atavism left over (i.e., a throwback) from primitive magic and animism."[8] Such assertions, as simplistic as they were concerning the personal and cultural relevance to the individual, helped to "push or pull" the social work profession away from its historical religious and spiritual roots.

Frank Loewenberg further asserts that many social workers, regardless of their personal religious and spiritual beliefs, do not feel religion and spirituality has any relevance or place in professional practice. "Just as they are committed to the principle of the separation of church and state in government, so have they accepted the principle of separating the sacred and the profane in their own lives."[9] The assertion here is not that the whole of social work endorses such beliefs concerning the role of religion and spirituality in their personal lives and the lives of their clients, but it does echo the diversity of values and beliefs among social work professionals and how such positions have run counter to the profession's historical roots. Loewenberg offers, for further clarity, the following useful typology of social worker's religious beliefs:

> Type 1: These social workers have no formal religious affiliations. They include a wide range of social workers who identify themselves as atheists, agnostics, or humanists.
> Type 2: These social workers have maintained an affiliation with a religious group and accept, more or less, the obligations and rituals of that group, but they do not see any relevance of their religious beliefs for social work practice.
> Type 3: These social workers are affiliated with a religious group and their entire life, including their professional practice, is guided by the tenets of that group.[10]

The influence on the social worker's professional practice found in these varying belief types might be depicted in a graphical representation resembling that of a bell-curve. At one extreme are the Type 1 believers and, at the other, Type 3. For example, a Type 3 social worker who identifies with some fundamentalist religions would find unconscionable the option of abortion under any circumstance and might refuse to counsel a pregnant teenage mother toward this option (personal value conflict). As such, it is not inconceivable then, to have social workers who would adopt a position at the other extreme given this case situation and advocate for abortion with the same client. Given this scenario, what consideration should be given to the clients' religious or spiritual values and beliefs? And in what ways should the culturally aware social worker approach this and similar case situations where religion, spirituality, and culture so boldly intersect?

Social Work Education and Spirituality/Religion

The National Association of Social Workers (NASW) in its Code of Ethics espouses the need for social work practitioners to be sensitive to clients' needs and self-efficacy and to be culturally competent in the delivery of services to clients in need who may have differing values and beliefs from their own.[11] Often in the literature, the focus has primarily been directed toward issues of racism, sexism, classism, heterosexism, and "ableism," all of which present formidable and daunting challenges in their own right to the social work profession in its efforts to assist clients with issues of individual, group, and social functioning. However, one area that has largely been overlooked, or at least underemphasized, is the influence spirituality can have in the helping and healing process. Except in religion-based universities, schools of social work rarely offer courses on spirituality, and only sporadically do professors address the issue in the classroom.

If clients and social workers hold in high regard their personal spiritual and religious values and beliefs, have their worldviews influenced by these beliefs, and make key life decisions directed by these spiritual and religious value positions, should there be place in social work curricula and research for such dialogue? Many social workers and social work educators would conclude, "There certainly should be." However, others would surely reply, "Certainly not." The current literature reflects a growing presence of articles and research with spirituality and religion as their focus. Many contemporary medical and psychology journals, and those more specific to social work (e.g., *Journal of Social Work Education, Social Work,* and *Health and Social Work*), are finding places for articles specifically addressing religion and spirituality. Also, at national meetings and conferences held by social workers, the issues of religion and spirituality have found their place at roundtable discussions and formal presentations. Increasingly, more attention is being given to these issues and to their relevance in the classroom and practice settings. Williams and Smolak, in their article "Integrating Faith Matters in Social Work Education," assert that schools of social work rarely address matters of faith, but that religion and spirituality are significant factors that warrant attention and influence nearly all areas of practice. They further assert that if the profession is to respond competently and sensitively, much less effectively, to clients' multiple layers of culture, we cannot continue to overlook relevant religious and spiritual factors.[12]

In addition to the ideological and philosophical positions of social work professionals engaged in practice and education, what of the value of students' perspectives on spirituality and religion in the social work classroom? Graff, in her exploratory study, found that, among 324 undergraduate social work students from seven Council on Social Work Education (CSWE)-accredited schools, just over 80 percent identified themselves as practicing Christians. In addition, she found that the vast majority desired more social work courses that included content reflecting religious and spiritual diversity, and the overwhelming majority expressed a desire to have content on how to effectively deal with these issues.[13]

Developing understanding of spirituality and religion is troublesome as it relies heavily on individual experiences and interpretation. Both arguments for and against the inclusion of these social and cultural realities in social work education have merit, but the debate continues to polarize social work professionals. Williams and Smolak identify topics that should be considered in the classroom. For example, consider the following benefits identified by proponents of introducing spirituality in the classroom: the value of spirituality as part of culturally competent practice, effective communication with people of faith, the practice of social work in religious settings, and the unnecessary limitations on professional practice imposed by a purely secular view. Those who argue that it is not appropriate to address spirituality in a secular profession contend that the inclusion of faith matters in the social work classroom could compromise the following: the view that social work is a scientific, empirically based profession; the need to maintain clear lines of separation between church and state; opening the door to proselytizing; and contributing to sectarian conflict.[14]

While spirituality and religion, and their inclusion in social work curricula, continue to be a contentious issue among social work professionals, most recent evidence from the literature indicates that the profession's longstanding commitment to creating a social work workforce that is knowledgeable of clients' values may potentially be compromised by the lack of attention to religion and spirituality. The evidence further points to attempts by educators to offer instruction in the form of electives or a more comprehensive approach by the integration of religious and spiritual content in core curriculum courses. Williams and Smolak recommend a more holistic approach that would combine both, rather than either/or, as a plausible strategy. A more comprehensive approach, they argue, would maximize student learning and prove most effective toward adequately preparing future social work practitioners to serve clients with various levels of religious and spiritual beliefs.[15]

Religion and Spirituality in Cultural Competence

The presence of spirituality and religion among U.S. citizens is well documented. Among most developed nations, the United States is one of the most religious, with several studies indicating that some 90 percent of Americans say they believe in God or some higher power. Not so pronounced, however, is the influence these religious beliefs and spiritual practices have on individuals' decision-making. Though most Americans self-identify as "believers," there is substantial variation in the degree and level of individuals' religious and spiritual practices and, ultimately, the impact on their daily lives.

However, social work continues to hold in high regard the responsibility of its workforce to practice with a level and degree of cultural competence and skill. Appreciation of human diversity is embedded in the profession's commitment to helping individuals realize their fullest potential, as set forth in social work's professional code of conduct and the duties, roles, and responsibilities performed by social workers. To this end, as it relates to spirituality and religion, the profession must also include the preparations of new social work practitioners in these areas. It is vital that social workers better understand these influences on clients' actions and how best to access and support religious and spiritual resources to achieve improved client outcomes.

Spirituality and Religion in Professional Practice

The intersection of spirituality and religion in social work has until recent decades been a hidden phenomenon or, at best, a seldom discussed reality. Perhaps, for reasons of discomfort and/or anxiety, the nature and impact of spirituality, religion, and faith seemed out of bounds as a legitimate topic for practice consideration and social work education. However, as history will attest, with the passing of time, change often occurs. Likewise, many professions that serve individuals, families, groups, and communities find themselves confronted with peoples' spiritual and religious cultural values and beliefs.

Bullis asserts that "social work and spirituality are natural allies in personal and social healing." Social work is beginning to seriously consider the inclusion of religious and spiritual influences on the helping and healing process. The resurgence of religion and spirituality in the popular culture and among professional fields of practice (i.e., social work, medicine, psychology, and nursing) suggests that spirituality must be considered when addressing the personal and social challenges people face.[16] For example, one can only wonder how a more inclusive and genuine affirmation of Native peoples' spiritual beliefs and respect for "mother nature" might have affected the nation's current environmental troubles. How might the culture of the United States be different if it had adopted a more cooperative economic approach (interdependence) rather than one more aligned with the notions of rugged individualism (independence)? Spirituality and religion bring to light a perspective that moves beyond the merely concrete and catapults the mind and body into a more subjective dimension of thinking and being. It is to this place that many people are turning to recapture a part of them that they had forgotten existed.

In his book, *Spirituality in Social Work Practice*, Bullis presents four primary rationales for addressing spirituality in clinical practice:

▶ Social work is historically and philosophically connected to spirituality; philosophically, both social work and spirituality promote common interests and self-respect, and social work and spirituality are natural allies.

▶ Social work and spirituality have much to learn from each other. Spirituality offers social work experiences and insights on personal and community levels that promote social and personal transformations.

▶ Knowledge of spirituality helps social workers construct spiritual cosmologies and spiritual anthropologies. Cosmologies are graphic depictions of a person's worldview. A spiritual cosmology is necessary to examine the spiritual sensitivity of the client or the social worker. Likewise, spiritual anthropology is necessary for any examination of healing—whether it be personal or community.

▶ There is no reason why social workers and spiritual leaders cannot collaborate. The historical estrangement notwithstanding, social work and spiritual professionals have no ethical or philosophic barriers to such collaboration.[17]

In essence, a more inclusive view of spirituality in social work practice adds yet another lens to the view of self for the social worker, the client, and the social environment. To lack such a key perspective, may marginalize the impact a practitioner could potentially have in the helping relationship at all levels of social work practice. The seemingly immense gulf that exists philosophically between social work and issues of religion and spirituality can be minimized. Derezotes, for example, asserts that social work practitioners need practical methods that can be used crossculturally and across the vastness of religious and spiritual diversity among differing populations and cultures. What is now needed, he further asserts, are theoretical foundations and research-based methodologies that serve the spiritual and religious dimensions of practice.[18]

The science of social work alone may not be sufficient to address the multiple dimensions of the individual—mind, body, and soul conceptions. Hodge argues that social work oppresses Evangelical Christians by its sanctions and legitimizes discrimination against Evangelicals and other people of faith.[19] Many people of faith, particularly those viewed as radicals, hold hard line positions on issues of homosexuality, lesbianism, abortion, and gay marriage, and they can find strong levels of intolerance from and for a profession that engenders such a strong secular orientation. As the Code of Ethics asserts, social workers should strive to eradicate all forms of discrimination, including racial, gender, age, and religious indifference.

What would a philosophical conception geared more toward the mutually beneficial coexistence of religious and spiritual differences require of social work and social work professionals? Would a more spiritually centered practice orientation be appropriate in the different fields of practice and with different client groups? Consider the following chapter titles from Derezotes' book: Spiritually Oriented Practice with Children, Youth, and Families; Spiritually Oriented Practice with Adult and Aging Clients; Spiritually Oriented Practice in Mental-Health Settings; Spiritually Oriented Practice in Criminal Justice Settings; and Spiritually Oriented Practice in Public Social Service Settings.[20] When examining how spirituality and religion might influence these different expressions of social work, many thoughts, feelings, emotions, and perhaps personal judgments are likely to surface. It is meaningful for social workers and social work students to take some time to personally reflect on why these conceptions might generate such reactions within themselves. Perhaps it is the mind's attempt to struggle with the mingling of a secular professional orientation with the spiritual and religious values and beliefs of social workers and their clients. In social work practice, it stands to reason that the conflict between secular expectations and spiritual feelings and emotions might cause discomfort for the social work practitioner who has not thoughtfully considered these matters.

A CASE VIGNETTE: CHRISTIAN'S SPIRITUAL CHALLENGE

Christian Thomas, a 23-year-old social work intern at the Big Valley Medical Center, found his mind wandering as he headed to work on the light rail into downtown. He was very excited about his field placement at the Medical Center as he hoped for a career in medical social work. He wondered what new and exciting challenges his internship would present during his semester at the hospital.

Christian, the only child of Bill and Kate Thomas, was the joy of his parents' lives. For them, Christian was their "miracle baby" and a precious gift from God they both cherished deeply. As fundamental Christians, Bill and Kate found that their faith and spiritual commitment was strengthened through the five-year struggle to have a child. Both parents felt God had smiled on them—they even named him Christian when their child was born—because their effort to have a child had presented them with the opportunity for spiritual growth.

A dedicated young fundamentalist Christian himself, Christian was committed to his religious beliefs and felt that through these precepts he could offer hope to those with whom he connected. Christian found comfort in his faith and the uncompromising positions regarding the "sins" of abortion, fornication (premarital sex), pornography, and homosexuality that his long-time pastor, John Mitchell, had preached about. Christian had absorbed the teachings of his beloved pastor for many years and had strong convictions regarding the importance of morality in his life and the choices he should make to remain faithful to the principles his parents and others had taught him.

Having arrived at the hospital somewhat early, Christian decided to walk around the hospital before reporting to his MSW field instructor for today's assignments. As he made his way near the emergency room entrance, he heard the blaring siren of an emergency transport vehicle. His heart raced, and his legs gained momentum as he was curious to know what the emergency was all about. Christian followed the emergency medical technicians

(EMTs) into the emergency room. A 45-year-old Caucasian male named Isaac Peterson was in cardiac distress and was barely conscious. The medical team scrambled to stabilize his racing heart before he was in full cardiac arrest. "Phillip, call Phillip," Isaac mumbled through the oxygen mask. The nurse assured him they would contact his family. Isaac fell unconscious and stopped speaking. Christian said a little prayer as they rushed Isaac into emergency surgery. The attending physician asked the nurse to page a social worker to notify the family. "Tell them the situation is life threatening and very serious," she instructed.

Christian's field instructor, Karen, entered the nursing station and asked for an update on the situation with the patient. Christian relayed what he had heard and that the doctor would like the next of kin notified immediately. He continued to inform her that Isaac was only conscious for a short moment after he arrived and then was out, but he mentioned the name "Phillip" several times before he passed out. Karen asked Christian if he felt he could handle assisting with this case. Eager to get more responsibility, Christian jumped at the opportunity to serve as the medical social worker on this case.

Christian contacted the parents and informed them of their son's situation. They lived only about 15 minutes away and said they would be down to the hospital right away. Christian really wanted to be prepared when they arrived. He spoke with his field instructor and shared the progress with her. Karen complimented Christian on his follow-up effort and encouraged him to come and ask any questions he felt necessary. When Mr. and Mrs. Peterson arrived, they both seemed very worried about their son. "Is he alright?" they asked. Christian asked the Petersons to be seated. He told them that Isaac had gone into cardiac arrest and was in emergency surgery, but the doctor would be out to speak with them about his condition as soon as he was out of surgery. Christian asked if he could get them anything while they waited for the doctor. "No, nothing," they both replied in concert. "I will come by a little later to see how you are doing," Christian responded.

Nearly two hours later, Christian was sitting with the parents, but no one was talking. A surgeon dressed in scrubs appeared and reported "Mr. and Mrs. Peterson, Isaac is out of surgery and in the Intensive Care Unit (ICU). His situation is still touch-and-go, and he is in a coma. There has been some damage to the heart muscle, and he is facing a long recovery, if he pulls through the next 72 hours. I will keep you updated on his progress." They both thanked the doctor for his efforts in caring for their son. "Can we see him?" the mother asked. "Yes," the doctor replied, "but I have restricted visitation to immediate family, and you can only stay about five minutes each hour." They understood and agreed to comply with the doctor's wishes.

Christian stood and watched as Isaac's parents walked away with the doctor to see their son. At that moment, in rushed a tall, lean, African-American man, nearly out of breath, asking at the nurses' station about Isaac. Christian introduced himself as the medical social worker and asked how he could help. "My name is Phillip, and I got a call that Isaac was rushed into emergency surgery. How is he?" the man asked. Christian remembered that Isaac was asking for Phillip before he fell unconscious. "How do you know Isaac? Are you a family friend or coworker?" Christian asked politely. "No," Phillip replied strongly, "Isaac is my partner. We have been together for 15 years." At that moment, Christian realized that Isaac and Phillip were in a same-sex relationship and that the two gay men had been a couple for some time.

Mr. and Mrs. Peterson returned to the waiting area. Their eyes locked with Phillip's eyes. Christian felt a huge tension in the room. The parents began to grumble to each other, though not audibly. They turned toward the nurses' station without a word and started to walk away. "Can I see Isaac now?" Phillip pleaded. "He's not family," Mr. Peterson declared. "Only immediate family can visit."

What was Christian to do? Clearly, Isaac had stated before he became unconscious that he wished to have Phillip present. It was also obvious there was tension between Phillip and Isaac's parents, and the parents made it clear they did not want Phillip present. Should Christian advocate for Phillip to be admitted to the ICU as a family member? Should he consult with his field instructor for guidance? Should he call Pastor Mitchell for consultation? How should Christian resolve his own secular–spiritual dilemma, given the conflict of his personal spiritual beliefs versus the patient's clear request?

Concluding Comment

Religion and spirituality are complex personal and cultural issues. The challenge to appropriately consider these powerful forces is particularly great in an increasingly secular society. Indeed, the intersection of religion and spirituality with secularism in American society is real. Social work, as a secular profession, must come to grips with this intersection. As a profession, social work historically has been committed to social, political, and economic justice; the elimination of poverty and discrimination; and social betterment (i.e., the increased social functioning of individuals, groups, and communities that make up the human family). All of these beliefs are compatible with most religious doctrines. To this end, social workers must not only consider the implications of religion and spirituality in the lives of their clients but also must identify and confront personal spiritual and religious beliefs and value orientations that run counter to the overall goals and aspirations of the profession.

KEY WORDS AND CONCEPTS

Spirituality
Religion
Spiritually oriented social work practice
Spiritual diversity in social work

Spirituality in social work curriculum
Integrating spirituality, faith, and social justice in social work practice

SUGGESTED INFORMATION SOURCES

Tirrito, Terry, and Toni Cascio, eds. *Religious Organizations in Community Services: A Social Work Perspective.* New York: Springer Publishing, 2003.

Lee, Daniel, and Robert O'Gorman, eds. *Social Work and Divinity.* Binghamton, NY: Haworth Press, 2005.

Graff, Dorothy L., "A Study of Baccalaureate Social Work Students' Beliefs about the Inclusion of Religious and Spiritual Content in Social Work." *Journal of Social Work Education* 43 (2007): 243–256.

ENDNOTES

1. Edward Canda, "Spirituality in Social Work," in *Encyclopedia of Social Work, Supplement* (Silver Spring, MD: National Association of Social Workers, 1997), pp. 299–309.
2. Ibid.
3. Michael A. Dover, Barbara Hunter, Randall Joseph, Ruth Paris, Ellen R. DeVoe, Toba Schwaber Kerson, Edward R. Canda, and Susan J. Lambert "Human Needs," in Terry Mizrahi and Larry E. Davis, eds., *Encyclopedia of Social Work* (New York: Oxford University Press, 2008).
4. George Gallup and Michael Lindsay, *Surveying the Religious Landscape: Trends in U.S. Beliefs* (Harrisburg, PA: Morehouse Publishing, 1999), pp. 7–41.
5. Adherents.com, *Top Ten Religions in the United States, 2001.* http:// www.urbandharma. org/udharma5/toprelig.html.
6. Canda, op. cit., 1997.
7. Edward Canda and Leola Furman, *Spiritual Diversity in Social Work Practice: The Heart of Helping* (New York: The Free Press, 1999), pp. xv and 1–5.
8. Gregory Zilboorg, *Psychoanalysis and Religion* (London: Farrar Strauss Giroux, 1962), p. 227.
9. Frank, M. Loewenberg, *Religion and Social Work Practice in Contemporary American Society* (New York: Columbia University Press, 1988).
10. Ibid., pp. 3–58.
11. National Association of Social Workers, *Code of Ethics*, 2008. http:// www.socialworkers. org/pubs/code/code.asp.
12. Mark Williams and Alex Smolak, "Integrating Faith Matters in Social Work Education," *Journal of Religion and Spirituality in Social Work* 26 (2007): 25.
13. Dorothy L. Graff, "A Study of Baccalaureate Social Work Students' Beliefs about the Inclusion of Religious and Spiritual Content in Social Work," *Journal of Social Work Education* 43 (2007): 243–256.
14. Williams and Smolak, op. cit.
15. Williams and Smolak, op. cit.
16. Ronald K. Bullis, *Spirituality in Social Work Practice* (Philadelphia: Taylor & Francis, 1996).
17. Ibid., p. 7.
18. David S. Derezotes, *Spiritually Oriented Social Work Practice* (Boston: Allyn & Bacon, 2006).
19. David R. Hodge, "Does Social Work Oppress Evangelical Christians? A New Class Analysis of Society and Social Work," *Social Work* 47: 401–414.
20. Derezotes, op. cit.

Social Work with U.S. Casualties of the Middle East Wars*

Prefatory Comment

Since the beginning of World War II, the United States has been at war nearly 45 percent of the time. In terms of human sacrifice, 379,000 soldiers have been killed in action and another 970,000 severely injured and maimed.[1] These data do not include the uncounted millions of civilian casualties in countries where the fighting occurred. For example, icasualties.org estimates that, in the Iraq War during 2007, nearly 52 Iraqi security forces and civilians were killed every day.[2] And the devastation doesn't end with the death or injury of a soldier. In the Iraq War, many soldiers survived but experienced severe wounds. Meeting the needs of warfare survivors—those who were injured as well as surviving family members—will present a unique challenge for social workers for decades to come.

Social workers in hospitals and veterans' outreach centers play a central role in the recovery process—for both survivors and their loved ones. Social workers in military hospitals help patients and their families maintain communication. They arrange for transitions to other forms of care that might be necessary for rehabilitation or for the development of new job skills. They also address psychological injuries. Social workers in other human service agencies, too, have a role in the aftermath of war. They play a critical role in helping survivors and their families overcome or cope with the often unrecognized long-term consequences of war.

Working with survivors of war is not new for social workers. The first paid social workers in the United States were appointed to help with issues experienced by soldiers and their families in the 1860s, during the Civil War (see Chapter 4). Trattner notes that, "Like all wars, the 'War Between the States' created enormous relief problems, not only for wounded and disabled soldiers but for bereaved families who lost their male breadwinners during the conflict."[3] Social workers continued to provide these important services not only during the seven wars subsequent to the Civil War but also during the intervening years when physical and emotional scars persisted.

---

*This chapter was prepared by Joanne E. Clancy, Clinical Social Worker with the Trauma Recovery Team, Veterans Affairs Medical Center, Houston, Texas, and Bradford W. Sheafor, Professor of Social Work, Colorado State University.

Today and in the foreseeable future, social workers will attend to survivors of wars. Some will serve as social workers in the military. Others will be civilians employed by the Veterans' Administration and other veterans' organizations. Social workers employed in schools, hospitals, courts and prisons, mental health centers, child welfare agencies, drug and alcohol rehabilitation centers, nursing homes, and other practice settings will also serve survivors or families affected by war. Because survivors of warfare access services in many different settings, all social workers should develop skills in grief counseling and management of trauma survivors' complex needs.

As in other areas of the human services, social workers are the professionals most likely to make referrals. They must not only know the general resources available to clients but must also be informed about services specifically designed for veterans and their families. If needed services are not available, social workers must advocate for their creation. Social workers, unlike individuals in the general population, are in a position to observe the far-reaching aftermath of war as it affects members of society for years after the hostilities have ceased. It is from this vantage point that social workers have special insights to contribute regarding the importance of preventing wars.

Social Work with Soldiers and Veterans

The recent wars in Afghanistan and Iraq are the most sustained combat efforts initiated by the United States since the Vietnam War. This new generation of combat veterans requires the focused energies of many service providers (physicians, nurses, psychologists, occupational and physical therapists, and social workers) as the veterans strive to reintegrate into society. The social work profession has a unique opportunity to take the lead in this stabilization and recovery process because the systemic manner through which social workers approach problems, coupled with their ability to provide multiple levels of service in a variety of settings, maximizes their ability to affect the lives of both veterans and their families.

People die in wars—both in battle and increasingly by suicide. An even greater number survive but sustain serious, life-changing injuries on the battlefield. During World War II, one out of every three wounded soldiers died. In Vietnam, one out of four wounded soldiers died. Soldiers serving in Iraq have even better odds of surviving; only one out of every eight wounded soldiers die.[4] Despite this "good news," many surviving soldiers return home with catastrophic injuries that disfigure and emotionally scar them for life. Advances in the field medicine may save their lives but, as one former medic quite eloquently stated: "I'm not sure we did them any favors. These men and women were young, healthy people in the prime of life. They went home with missing arms, legs, and eyes. A lot of them have psychological problems as well. Even the lucky ones, the ones who have people to help and support them, face decades of physical and emotional pain, discrimination, and the challenge of learning to live a life very different from the one they planned. Yeah, I'm not sure we did them any favors."

Adjustment to the traumatic loss of one's physical integrity, especially when functional ability is seriously compromised, is a long and painful process. Simple tasks once taken for granted become impossible or require Herculean effort to accomplish. Depending on the nature and severity of the loss, the affected individual may require months or years of physical therapy to regain even a fraction of his or her former independence. Dramatic changes in body image, coupled with others' reactions to the veteran's altered physical appearance, further complicate the recovery process. One young soldier, a quadriplegic, stated, "I want to commit suicide, but I can't move my arms or legs. No one will help me do it. My mother keeps telling me things will get better if I just have patience. I'm 21 years old... how can things ever get better? I was an athlete. I planned to become a physical therapist. I wanted to get married and start a family someday. Who would want me now? I am completely helpless until someone cleans me up and sits me in my motorized chair. All my dreams are gone. What's the point?"*

Sustained exposure to potentially life-threatening experiences escalates the risk for psychological problems. This is especially true in a war zone where death and serious injury are not only feared but also expected. In a study targeting the effects of combat on the mental health of soldiers in Afghanistan and Iraq,[5] researchers discovered a strong correlation between combat experiences (being shot at, handling dead bodies, witnessing the death of a peer, killing enemy combatants) and the prevalence of posttraumatic stress disorder (PTSD). The presence of PTSD increased proportionately with the number of battles in which soldiers engaged during their deployment. Mental illnesses most commonly identified among study participants include acute stress disorder, posttraumatic stress disorder, generalized anxiety disorder, major depression, traumatic brain injury (TBI), and substance abuse. An even more recent study conducted by the U.S. Army Surgeon General's Office[6] indicated that 15 to 20 percent of all soldiers fighting in Iraq and Afghanistan experienced PTSD, and that rate increased to 30 percent for those serving their third tour of duty. In addition, the number of Army suicides hit a record in 2007, and two in ten soldiers reported that their marriages were in trouble.

Despite the high incidence of mental distress among combat troops, few soldiers express interest in pursuing mental health treatment. This holds true even when the soldiers are presented with opportunities to visit "wellness tents" in the field, participate in debriefings post-deployment, or meet with mental health professionals in more formal settings. Researchers in one study[7] determined that only 38 to 45 percent of soldiers who met criteria for a mental disorder were interested in receiving help. Even more startling, only 23 to 40 percent of those expressing a desire for assistance actually sought help post-discharge. The stigma of mental illness (i.e., "I am weak, crazy, not normal") and the fear that seeking mental health care will adversely affect future career opportunities were primary factors in their decision-making process. Thus

---

*All stories told by soldiers and veterans throughout this chapter were reported to social workers in veterans' centers and hospitals.

mental health conditions often become interpreted as "adjustment issues" so that seeking help does not become a negative experience for the soldier.

Social Work with the Families of Soldiers and Veterans

Combat survivors struggle to escape traumatic memories that assault them through intrusive thoughts and nightmares. At the same time, their loved ones struggle to understand what happened to the individual they sent to war. The person who returns is altered in ways that cannot always be seen or explained. One soldier's mother poignantly stated, "I sent my son to war. The person they sent back is not my son... it is a shell that looks like my son. He is angry and distant. My heart is breaking because nothing I say or do can recapture what he, and we, have lost."

When soldiers receive orders for deployment into a combat zone, a kaleidoscope of emotional reactions emerge from both the soldier and from his or her family members: denial, "this isn't really happening... is it?"; fear, "what if he or she is seriously injured, crippled, or killed in combat?"; anger, "I never really thought he or she would be sent to war"; confusion, "what will become of our family before, during, and after my loved one's deployment into a war zone?" The emotional impact of impending deployment is magnified by the reality that war inevitably results in death and sacrifice.

The free-floating sea of emotional reactions within and between family members can wreak havoc on a family's ability to prepare for, endure, and recover from the deployment experience. Individuals process and cope with emotional distress in ways uniquely their own. Age, gender, and past experiences influence each family member's willingness and ability to openly challenge and move through their collective emotional experience. During this critical time in the family's life cycle, forging a united front is crucial to the healthy adjustment of all involved. Without adequate guidance and support, many of these "at-risk" families will become "collateral casualties" of war.

Social Programs for Soldiers and Veterans

In the event of the death of a soldier, family members not only must deal with the death of a loved one, but most families will also be poorer. Initially, government programs help to offset expenses and the wages of the soldier who died, but these resources are designed to decline over time, thus challenging social workers to help the families develop alternate sources of income. Further, many families require emotional assistance as they cope with grief and loss. Social workers in hospice agencies and mental health centers regularly provide valuable counseling to parents, siblings, spouses, and children of soldiers killed while performing military duty.

Social workers also encounter soldiers returning from a war zone who experience problems meeting basic social needs. If the individual is a professional soldier who has not yet fulfilled his or her commitment to military service, reassignment to a new duty station often occurs. This forestalls any immediate concerns about housing and income. If, however, the individual has fulfilled his or her military obligation, an additional challenge of separation from service and transition to civilian life ensues. The presence or absence of extended family support during this time of transition is a primary variable in determining post-discharge outcomes. If family support is not present, homelessness may become an issue. The National Alliance to End Homelessness, for example, reports that, although veterans make-up 11 percent of the population, one-fourth of all homeless people in the United States are veterans.[8]

The financial issue is more complex for reservists and National Guard personnel mobilized to an active duty status. Although job security is guaranteed, many of these individuals incur significant financial reversals while on active duty. The military cannot, and does not, match the salaries these individuals receive from their civilian employers. This disparity in income often generates far-reaching consequences for these individuals and the family members they leave behind. In one instance, a young mother of three stated, "What does the military expect us to do? My husband made over $100,000 a year as a computer analyst. I am a housewife. How am I supposed to pay the mortgage and keep our household running on what the Army is paying him? We will probably have to file bankruptcy. So much for supporting those willing to serve their country!"

Social Work Practice during Reintegration Efforts

Outreach and Resource Mobilization

Although several disciplines work with active duty military personnel and veterans, social workers are best qualified to address their subsequent emotional and social needs. Historically what sets the social work profession apart from other disciplines is the willingness to meet individuals "where they are," emotionally and geographically. Social workers display great flexibility in their willingness to engage in outreach efforts designed to identify and engage elusive populations. This willingness to aggressively pursue populations most at risk "where they work, live, and play" allows social workers to intervene early on, before the problems escalate.

Social workers assigned to active duty military positions, and those working civilian contracts for the Department of Defense or other divisions of the federal government, play a critical role in outreach efforts. Their presence at military bases, in the field, and at veterans' outreach centers and hospitals across the country provide opportunities to identify the needs of soldiers and veterans at each stage of the deployment process. The following case study highlights the role social work plays in promoting a healthy transition for soldiers and their family members.

Mr. X. is a 22-year-old, married Marine sergeant recently discharged from the military after a tour of duty in Iraq. He was discharged approximately two months before the social worker's initial contact with him at a local veterans' outreach center. The social worker assigned to his case identified a number of problem areas. The veteran had limited income and needed temporary financial assistance. He was interested in securing employment and returning to school but had no idea how to access vocational services. He and his spouse were experiencing a variety of marital problems they had not been able to resolve on their own. Both partners had little understanding of the emotional problems this soldier was experiencing.

The social worker immediately set forth to identify and mobilize available resources. The veteran and his wife received referrals to community-based agencies for financial services. A referral to the vocational counseling department at the local veterans' hospital was initiated to assess his readiness for training and job placement services. The social worker also initiated a referral to the hospital's PTSD program so the veteran and his spouse could receive assistance coping with the veteran's psychiatric problems. The couple also received a list of Internet referrals where they could download information pertinent to issues encountered by veterans of Middle Eastern wars.[9]

The social worker met with this couple weekly at the outreach center for several months. She provided emotional support and monitored their progress accessing identified resources. When the couple expressed frustration due to snags in the referral process to several agencies, the social worker assumed an advocacy role. Several months later when the veteran returned for follow-up services at the veterans' hospital, he was asked what had been most helpful during the initial months following his military discharge. The veteran replied, "The Vet Center social worker. We felt lost, alone, and confused. Our social worker was very kind. She guided us through a maze of resources we would never have figured out on our own. She seemed to really care about what happened to us and gave us hope that, in time, things would get better. I don't know where we would be if this caring professional had not stepped up to bat for us."

Education and Skill Building

The transition from soldier to civilian, especially after serving in a war zone, is challenging. If physical and/or mental disabilities factor into the equation, the adjustment process becomes even more complicated. Through individual, group, and family sessions, social work professionals provide knowledge about specific conditions, identifying existing treatment options and introducing coping skills so those affected can more readily navigate the challenges at hand. The simple act of "naming the problem" brings relief and provides direction. As one veteran so aptly stated, "Now that I know what the problem is, I can begin identifying ways to attack it."

Skill building is another critical piece of the recovery process. The majority of combat veterans are young, and they possess a limited range of coping skills. Exposure to a variety of problem-solving techniques, offered through educational classes and skill-building sessions, provides them with a "toolbox for recovery." These tools, once acquired and reinforced, empower individuals to assume the lead in creating their own solutions. The social worker's role during this process is to impart knowledge and guide individuals through role-play sessions designed to enhance their effectiveness in skills application. The case of a young female amputee clearly illustrates this point.

Ms. P. is a 23-year-old female soldier severely wounded during a terrorist attack in Iraq. She was standing guard when a jeep carrying explosives crashed into a building near her position. She lost both legs below the knees. Emotionally devastated by her loss, this young veteran had no idea how to cope with the drastic life changes brought about by her amputations. Her family was equally at a loss. The social worker assigned to her case provided information about typical reactions experienced by amputees and their family members. He invited them to attend a support group with other amputees and their families. This provided opportunities for mutual support and the exchange of ideas and information. He also invited the family to attend a series of classes that focused on independent living skills. During these classes, the veteran developed strategies to assertively communicate her needs. Role-plays where family members assumed the role of amputee helped sensitize them to the challenges faced by their loved one on a daily basis. The veteran and her family also received instruction on the variety of prosthetic devices she would need to normalize her life. Stress management and play therapy classes introduced healthy alternatives for coping with distress inherent after traumatic losses.

When asked to describe this educational experience Ms. P. replied, "My first reaction... this is a big waste of time. I didn't see how going to classes would help me or my family deal with the fact I have no legs. I attended grudgingly at first to humor the social worker. Then, as the weeks went by, I realized things were getting better. We were learning new ways to get things done that really worked. I learned to communicate with my family more productively, and they stopped being afraid to tell me how they really felt. We have even learned to laugh together when the going gets tough. Meeting with other amputees and their family members was also helpful. We learned a lot from each other and made some new friends, too. I never realized how important these classes would be to my recovery. I hope all the other veterans coming back with injuries like mine have a chance to participate in this kind of program. The classes made me realize I still have a life to live, but it is up to me to get out there and live it."

Supportive Interventions

Taking a human life or witnessing the traumatic death of another human being produces far-reaching consequences for even the most psychologically sound individual. Although loss is a normal part of the life cycle, most humans never encounter the type of traumatic losses identified above. During the heat of battle, most soldiers report feeling numb. One young soldier described his experience by saying, "I was on auto-pilot. I saw people dying all around me, and all I could focus on was staying alive. I had to kill several enemy soldiers and didn't think much of it at the time."

The psychological impact of one's actions in combat may take days, weeks, even months to surface. Another young veteran reported the following experience: "I was a helicopter door gunner in Iraq. My job was to kill enemy soldiers on the ground. One day we came across a band of rebels, and they started shooting at our helicopter. I returned fire, knowing I would kill at least some of them. After the battle, we landed to do a body count. Among the dead were a young woman and her baby. As we flew back to base camp, it felt like I was dying inside, one piece at a time. Things have never been the same since that day."

Survivors of combat trauma face three significant challenges as they strive to recover from traumatic losses incurred on the battlefield. First, taking human life, even in the name of self-preservation, transforms them into "old souls." An *old soul* is a young person who has seen the darkest side of him- or herself. Although all humans have the capacity to kill when confronted with life-and-death situations, few of us ever cross this line. Thinking you can kill someone, and knowing you have, are very different experiences.

Second, the taking of a human life generates tremendous conflict between one's beliefs and values, and actions taken during the heat of battle. One young soldier participating in a PTSD program expressed the following thoughts. "I grew up in the church. I learned that harming others was a mortal sin. I remember one day, when my unit was preparing for battle, a preacher stopped by our tent to pray with us. He asked God to protect us and keep us safe. Then he told us to go out there and kill those bastards. His comment really confused me. He sanctioned behavior that is in direct conflict with what I spent the first 18 years of my life believing. It really messed me up. Now I question if God even exists. I also worry about my soul... if there is a God, am I doomed to hell because of what I did in Iraq?"

Finally, returning combat soldiers often experience profound guilt. This guilt stems not only from taking human lives but also for surviving when others do not. One young man, traveling in a convoy, described the following experience. "My buddies and I were driving supplies between two base camps. My truck was scheduled to take the lead, but the other driver begged me to let him go first. He was new in the country and wanted to prove himself. I said yes against my own better judgment. We were on a narrow road with a steep ravine on one side. The truck in front of me hit a mine. All I could do is watch in horror as the truck plunged over the cliff. Bodies flew everywhere. I stopped my truck and we scrambled down the cliff to rescue survivors. There weren't any.... We ended up collecting dead bodies instead. If I had refused to let the new guy lead the way, this wouldn't have happened. It's a hell of a burden to carry around each day."

Social workers provide the bulk of mental health services to individuals seeking assistance from veterans' outreach centers, hospitals, and mental health trauma programs. The focus of treatment is empowering veterans to identify, process, and move beyond their traumatic experiences. Social workers conducting individual and group therapy sessions encourage trauma survivors to "remember and let go" of traumatic memories, since forgetting is not a realistic option. Multifamily group therapy adds yet another dimension to the recovery process. Allowing veterans and family members to share their common experiences provides hope and encouragement that life can, and will, go on. A final case study illustrates the social worker's role as change agent when addressing veterans' mental health concerns.

Mr. M. is a 25-year-old, married combat veteran who served two tours of duty in Iraq. During the second tour, his unit encountered a group of insurgents, which resulted in intense hand-to-hand combat. Several of his buddies were killed during the attack. Mr. M. sustained only minor injuries. Unfortunately, his traumatic experience continued to haunt him after discharge. He reported a great deal of inner conflict about having killed several enemy soldiers during the battle. He also felt guilty for surviving when many of his peers did not. During his first session with a social worker in an outpatient trauma program, he shared the following information: "I have been a wreck since I got back from Iraq. I have nightmares about killing and being killed. I think about the war all the time and have to avoid watching the news or I get all stressed out. I am irritable a lot of the time and don't want to be around anyone. Life just doesn't seem worth living anymore."

The social worker's first intervention involved consultation with the clinic psychiatrist. The psychiatrist prescribed medication to help alleviate Mr. M.'s symptoms. Next, Mr. M. was enrolled in both individual and group therapy. The goal of individual therapy was to provide a milieu where the veteran could discuss the most painful aspects of his combat experience. The social worker identified a number of techniques to aid him in redirecting painful thoughts when they occurred. Mr. M. was also assisted in challenging self-defeating thoughts about his survival and reframing his feelings about killing enemy soldiers in the line of duty.

During group therapy sessions, the focus was helping Mr. M. realize he is not alone in his struggle. Opportunities to process thoughts and feelings with other veterans experiencing similar reactions helped him develop a new appreciation of his own situation. It also provided exposure to others' coping strategies, some of which he adopted with great success. During one session, he remarked that things at home were not going very well between him and his spouse. This resulted in a referral to a multifamily group. In this context, Mr. M. and his wife learned how to join forces so they could combat symptoms of the veteran's PTSD instead of fighting with one another.

After three months of treatment, the veteran and his wife met with the treatment team to discuss his progress and identify ongoing issues for work. Both expressed great relief that things were beginning to improve. Mr. M. was less irritable and anxious. His nightmares were less frequent and intense. He noted a return of optimism about the future. His wife reported that participating in the multifamily group was the best possible thing that could have happened. She felt supported and validated both by the social work leader and other members of the group. She stated, "Attending family group made me realize we are not in this alone. I heard our story coming out of the mouths of other veterans and their wives. Some of them have been in treatment longer than we have. Their testimonies gave us hope that things can and will get better if we just hang in there. I don't know what might have happened if we hadn't come in for help. We still have a long way to go, but at least we are moving in the right direction!"

Special Considerations Regarding Today's Victims of War

It is clear that social workers have an important role to play in assisting individuals who are survivors of war and their families. There is, however, special knowledge and unique insights required of social workers as they serve these individuals.

Quality of Care for Veterans

For a period of time in 2007, the news was filled with stories reporting substandard treatment provided to Afghanistan and Iraq war veterans at the nation's premiere medical facility, Walter Reed Army Hospital in Washington, D.C. This firestorm was partially initiated by the resignation of a social worker on the Walter Reed Army Medical Center staff, Joe Wilson, who was frustrated with the failure of the hospital's administrators to address the deplorable conditions experienced by wounded soldiers at Walter Reed. The situation was pushed into the public spotlight by an article published in the *Washington Post* on February 18, 2007, that eventually resulted in the replacement of the hospital commander, the Army Surgeon General, and the Secretary of the Army and the creation of a presidential-level task force headed by former senator Bob Dole and former Health and Human Services Secretary Donna Shalala. Another social worker, Kristin Day, then–acting national director of Social Work Service at the Department of Veterans Affairs (VA), actively supported the Commission's recommendations, calling for better coordination between the Department of Defense and the VA, creation of a comprehensive recovery plan to provide the right care at the right time for hospitalized soldiers and veterans, a restructuring of the disability determination and compensation systems, additional efforts to prevent and treat PTSD and TBI, and a stronger role in treating families.[10]

If these changes are eventually accomplished, they will be too late for many veterans. A 2008 investigation of the Army's care of returning soldiers by *Time* magazine focused on the subsequent death of Sergeant Gerald Cassidy, who had suffered a traumatic head injury in Iraq. The report summarizes:

> Soldiers fall through the cracks in every war. But the death of Sergeant Gerald (GJ) Cassidy, a cheerful 31-year-old husband and father of two, highlights the tragic and persistent shortcomings of Army medicine. The same Army that spends $160 billion on tomorrow's fighting machines is shortchanging the shell-shocked troops coming home from war in need of healing. Cassidy was promised world-class health care. But he didn't get the simple help—quick treatment, pain-management classes, knowledge of his whereabouts or even a roommate—that could have saved his life.[11]

Serving an All-Volunteer Force

Previous generations of soldiers resulted from a combination of draftees and enlistees. Present-day soldiers are members of an all-volunteer force who have elected to spend at least part of their careers in the military. This difference affects the characteristics of who is in the military and how they respond when they face physical or mental injuries, presenting special challenges for the social workers who serve them. For example, more than 50 percent of soldiers serving in Afghanistan and Iraq are between the ages of 20 and 29. Although early intervention and outreach efforts are much improved since the Vietnam War, youth often deters returning soldiers from accepting available support. Young veterans tend to minimize symptoms and avoid seeking professional help. When problems are psychiatric in nature, these problems are even more difficult to identify, and young soldiers are more reluctant to engage in treatment.

Further, more than 50 percent of service members are married, and about 11 percent of marriages are to other service members. This generates serious concerns when married couples are simultaneously deployed to high-risk areas, especially when minor children are involved. Complex issues facing couples in this situation include the constant worry that one's partner will be injured or killed, child care during the parents' deployment, the impact of separation from parental figures on offspring at critical points during the developmental process, and reestablishing family ties once members reunite. Of even greater concern are the consequences for children when one or both parents die in combat.

Finally, the ability to choose whether or not one engages in military service affects post-discharge adjustment, especially for individuals deployed to a war zone. When an individual is free to choose whether or not to join the military, it creates a sense of self-determination (i.e., "This is something I elected to do, and going to war may or may not be part of the package"). When one is conscripted, it generates a sense of powerlessness and anger, especially when bad things happen (i.e., "I had no choice... the government ruined my life").

Women in the Military and Associated Gender Issues

During previous wars, female soldiers were forbidden to participate in direct combat. Present-day women can and do select military occupation specializations (MOS) that place them on frontlines of the battlefield. As a result, female combat veterans face the same physical and mental health risks as their male counterparts. This role transition creates far-reaching consequences in regard to treatment. Patients currently treated by veterans' hospitals are predominately male. When females do seek treatment, the primary focus, until now, has been military sexual trauma and health-related issues. The influx of females joining the military is changing the face of post-military intervention. As female veterans become a larger percentage of those seeking care, clinicians must create and implement programming designed to meet the unique needs of this population.

The Need for Cultural Competence When Serving Returning Troops

America has made great strides in addressing racial discrimination since the 1960s, when African American soldiers who had been drafted into the military often felt they were fighting to free the South Vietnamese people from oppression but continued to experience oppression themselves at home. Today, ethnic minorities make up a portion of military personnel that is very close to the minority distribution in the United States. As of September 30, 2004, combined deployment lists from the Afghanistan and Iraq wars report the following racial analysis of troops: 70 percent white, 15 percent African American, 9.5 percent Hispanic, and 5 percent other or unknown. These figures do not include soldiers deployed within the United States.[12]

Despite these gains in addressing racial discrimination, prejudice is still very much present in certain segments of U.S. society. Professionals working with returning veterans of color must be careful to avoid assumptions based on race or ethnicity. It is imperative to remember that strategies applied to the dominant culture with great success might fail miserably with minority groups. Cultural and racial sensitivity affords clinicians the opportunity to learn from their patients what is most and least helpful during the reintegration process.

The Affects of Guerrilla Warfare and Acts of Terrorism

As opposed to the more traditional forms of battlefield warfare, in Iraq and Afghanistan the greatest sources of danger are guerrilla warfare and terrorist acts, not direct combat.[13] In an urban war, threats are ambiguous. Anyone, anywhere, might be the enemy. This lack of an "identified enemy" places soldiers in a constant state of alert. During the Iraq War, the ratio of seriously wounded to those killed in action was the highest in U.S. history.[14] Ninety-four percent of soldiers in Iraq reported exposure to hostile small arms fire, 86 percent reported knowing someone who was seriously injured or killed, and 68 percent reported seeing dead or seriously injured Americans. The majority of these losses were the result of random acts of violence. One young Iraq veteran relayed his feelings by saying, "I never felt safe over there. I was a truck driver, not a combat soldier, but every time I got in my vehicle, I worried about being ambushed or hitting a mine. I saw too many of my friends die that way. ...I always worried I might be next."

Social Work and the Prevention of War

Social workers directly serve the survivors of war and, drawing upon the person-in-environment perspective, further contend it is important to address the broader issues that are the causes and consequences of war. Identifying the cause of war is a complex issue. Surely one factor is the grossly unequal distribution of wealth and resources throughout the world when a few rich and developed countries (and especially the United States) possess a significant part of the world's wealth and use a substantial proportion of the earth's natural resources (e.g., oil, timber, minerals), allowing their people to enjoy a substantially higher quality of life than exists elsewhere. It is not surprising that others who experience the social consequences of such poverty (i.e., poor housing, inadequate diet, poor health, limited transportation, etc.) are willing to go to war to correct this inequality. Another factor contributing to wars is growing religious fanaticism, both in the United States and throughout the world, in which one extremist religion attempts to force its religious beliefs onto others. This condition polarizes people and leaves little room for compromise, often preempting efforts to address other human concerns. Finally, excessive emphasis on "nationalism" and "patriotism," although laudable in spirit, too often leads to a false sense of superiority and unwillingness to compromise national desires for the greater good of the world's people.

The cost of war in terms of both human and economic resources is enormous. The loss of life and the maiming of human beings not only have a substantial emotional impact on those affected but also have a significant economic drain on the nation. Resources that might have been devoted to resolving the social, health, and economic issues discussed elsewhere in this book are diverted to maintaining a military presence throughout the world, protecting homeland security, and absorbing the direct costs of active battle. For example, the change in U.S. expenditures reflects the diversion of resources from 2000 (before the Afghanistan and Iraq wars) to the estimated fiscal year (FY) 2009 budget (see Table 13.1).[15]

Clearly, the cost of war has shifted resources away from meeting the needs of vulnerable U.S. citizens. The spiraling national debt resulting from this action must be paid off by future generations—with financial interest. In their book, *The Three Trillion Dollar War: The True Cost of the Iraq Conflict*, noted economists Joseph Stiglitz and Linda Bilmes project that only a fraction of the cost is represented in the federal budget. Most of the costs are funded offline through increasing the public debt and that many costs related to lifetime health care, maintaining a military presence in Afghanistan and Iraq, combat pay, death benefits, Social Security, disability and medical care, and other hidden costs were not made public by the George W. Bush Administration.[16]

In its policy statement on "Peace and Social Justice,"[17] the National Association of Social Workers takes a stand on three issues related to war:

▶ Although we have recently gone through a new military buildup and actions against terrorist groups and the countries that harbor them, the United States needs to emphasize economic support rather than Western dominance. ...Whenever possible, the United States must foster cooperation in its foreign policy rather than unilateral military action. A long-range goal should be the reduction of military spending and diversion of the subsequent savings to social needs.

▶ Even in the face of overt terrorist attacks on the United States, it is still vital that we work in creative ways with other nations and international organizations to reduce violence against innocent civilians.

▶ The United States needs to continue using qualified professional social workers to serve the armed forces and military dependents to ensure that a high priority is given to human values and social welfare needs in those settings.

Table 13.1

Change in Actual U.S. Expenditures for National Defense (2000 to 2007) Compared with Expenditures for Domestic Social Programs

	2000	2007	Increase
National defense	$294.4 billion	$549.2 billion	86.6%
Training/employment/social services	15.3 billion	20.0 billion	30.7%
Income security	41.4 billion	56.4 billion	36.2%

Note: The Bush Administration budget for 2009 further increased defense spending to $670.7B, reduced training/employment/social services to $19.7B, and increased income security to $58.4B.

Concluding Comment

War has far-reaching consequences for combat soldiers, their family members, and society as a whole. Without timely and effective intervention, soldiers returning from Afghanistan and Iraq are at risk for a lifetime of maladjustment and misery. Social work professionals—acting as teachers, guides, and advocates—can significantly reduce this risk. Strategic placement of social workers during all stages of the recovery process will enhance soldiers' potential to move beyond their combat experiences. Although social workers cannot stop wars, prevent deaths during combat, or undo physical and/or psychiatric injuries incurred during war, they can empower survivors to live happier, more productive lives. Further, they can use their advocacy skills to help prevent wars and improve the quality of life for all people throughout the world.

KEY WORDS AND CONCEPTS

Role of social work during reintegration efforts

Collateral casualties

Social implications of war for returning veterans

Consequences of deployment for families

Old souls

Women in the military

Cultural competence in social work practice with soldiers

SUGGESTED INFORMATION SOURCES

Farber-Silk, Lisa H. *Giving My Heart: Love in a Military Family.* Ann Arbor, MI: Modern History Press, 2008.

Riverbend. *Baghdad Burning: Girl Blog from Iraq.* New York: Feminist Press at the City University of New York, 2005.

Roberts, Cheryl A. *Coping with Post-Traumatic Stress Disorder: A Guide for Families.* Jefferson, NC: McFarland, 2003.

Sheeler, Jim. *Final Salute: A Story of Unfinished Lives.* New York: Penguin Press, 2008.

Tripp, Elise Forbes. *Surviving Iraq: Soldiers' Stories.* Northampton, MA: Olive Branch Press, 2008.

ENDNOTES

1. Ross Doutkat, Abigail Cutler, and Terrence Henry, "Casualties of War," *Atlantic* 29 (March 2004): 50.
2. "Iraq Coalition Casualty Count," icasualties.org. Retrieved January 6, 2008, from http://icasualties.org/oif.
3. Walter I. Trattner, *From Poor Law to Welfare State: A History of Social Welfare in America,* 6th ed. (New York: Free Press, 1999), p. 77.
4. Nancy Gibbs, "The Lucky Ones," *Time Magazine* 165 (March 21, 2005): 36.
5. C. Hoge, C. Castro, S. Messer, D. McGurk, D. Cotting, and R. Koffman, "Combat Duty in Iraq and Afghanistan, Mental Health Problems, and Barriers to Care," *New England Journal of Medicine* 351 (2004): 13–22.

6. Gregg Zoroya, "A Fifth of Soldiers at PTSD Risk: Rate Rises with Tours, Army Says," *USA Today* (March 7, 2008): 11A.
7. Hoge, et al., op. cit.
8. Kimberly Hefling, "Veterans Make Up Quarter of Homeless," *The Coloradoan* (November 8, 2007): A11.
9. The National Center for Posttraumatic Stress Disorder, www.ncptsd.org, identifies multiple links to Internet sites offering education materials, support networks, and benefits and resource information. For detailed information, refer to the following: National Center for PTSD and Walter Reed Army Medical Center, *Iraq War Clinician Guide,* 2nd ed. (Washington, DC: Department of Veterans Affairs, June 2004) and *VHA Office of Public Health and Environmental Hazards Analysis of VA Health Care Utilization among Southwest Asian War Veterans Combined: Operation Iraqi Freedom/Operation Enduring Freedom* (Washington, DC: Department of Veteran's Affairs, March 2005).
10. Paul R. Pace, "Reforming Care for Afflicted Soldiers," *NASW News* (October 2007): 4.
11. Mark Thompson, "Death at the Army's Hands," *Time* (February 25, 2008), 40–42.
12. Han Kang, Director of Epidemiology Services, Department of Veterans Affairs, e-mail communiqué on May 9, 2005.
13. "The Unique Circumstances and Mental Health Impact of the Wars in Afghanistan and Iraq: A National Center for PTSD Fact Sheet." Retrieved May 3, 2005, from http://www.ncptsd.va.gov.
14. T. Ricks, "Where Does Iraq Stand Among U.S. Wars? Total Casualties Compare to Spanish-American, Mexican, and 1812 Conflicts," *The Washington Post* (May 31, 2004): A16.
15. *The U.S. Budget for Fiscal Year 2009: Historical Tables,* "Table 8.7—Outlays for Discretionary Programs: 1962–2009." (Washington, DC: Office of Management and Budget, 2008): 154–155.
16. Joseph Stiglitz and Linda Bilmes, *The Three Trillion Dollar War: The True Cost of the Iraq Conflict* (New York: W. W. Norton, 2008).
17. National Association of Social Workers, *Social Work Speaks: National Association of Social Workers Policy Statements, 2003–2006,* 6th ed. (Washington, DC: NASW Press, 2003): 267–269.

Social Work Becoming a Global Profession

Prefatory Comment

People everywhere need assistance in addressing social issues that affect their lives, as well as help in resolving or reducing specific social problems that individuals from time to time confront. Thus, the need for social work, as the profession dedicated to both serving people and improving social conditions, is global.

Other sections of this book focus on the ways in which social work evolved in the United States. Lest the reader assume that the functioning of social workers in the United States is the only model for this profession, this chapter is concerned with similarities and differences in the expressions of social work throughout the world. In addition, it reflects the growing globalization of social work and the evolving efforts to address international social issues.

With increasing speed, people throughout the world are becoming interdependent. Concerning the environment, for example, global warming (thought to be caused largely by industrial and auto emissions in developed countries) alters the rainfall and growing seasons for crops worldwide and threatens to melt the icebergs and flood coastal cities. In relation to the economy, the extreme poverty experienced by persons in underdeveloped countries often forces them to work for relatively little pay and accept deplorable working conditions, thus reducing the cost of products in developed countries but also contributing to outsourcing of manufacturing and services and the loss of employment in the developed countries. Or the failure to curb an epidemic (e.g., HIV/AIDS, bird flu) in one area of the world causes that health problem to spread throughout the world. Indeed, people are more interdependent than at any other time in history.

Directly affecting the work of social workers are such international issues as refugees and immigration, international adoptions, engagement in wars (e.g., Afghanistan, Iraq), epidemics of diseases, terrorist threats, natural disasters, and so on. International tension increases when some segments of the population conclude that others experience a substantially better quality of life. Although quality of life is influenced by many factors, wealth (or lack of wealth) is often considered a broad indicator of human well-being and a signal for the need of human services. Information accumulated by the World Bank indicates that the gap in wealth between the richest one-fifth of the world's population and the poorest one-fifth is increasing at the rate of approximately 3 percent each year.[1] More specifically, the bottom 20 percent of the population has an average per capita income with a buying power of approximately $326 per year. For the lowest 44 percent of the world's population, the buying power increases to $786 per year. Contrast that with the average income in the thirty-three highest income nations (plus Hong Kong), where the average per capita income is $26,000 per year. The stark difference in income between the lowest almost one-half of the population and the highest one-fifth suggests a substantial difference in many quality-of-life factors. Of the 6.7 billion people worldwide, it is estimated that the following numbers of people experience the identified poverty-related conditions.[2]

▶ 790 million people lack adequate nutrition
▶ 880 million people lack access to basic medical care
▶ 1 billion people lack safe drinking water
▶ 1 billion people lack adequate shelter
▶ 1 billion people are illiterate
▶ 2 billion people lack access to electricity
▶ 2.4 billion people lack adequate sanitation

Clearly, many people are suffering in a world that currently has the resources to improve the well-being of millions of people. For social workers with a global perspective, addressing these conditions multiplies their concerns regarding the prevalence of social injustices in the United States.

Most social workers would accept that some of the wealth in the United States should be reallocated to reduce poverty throughout the world. Some would argue that these funds could come through more efficient use of tax funds by the various levels of government; others believe that corporate taxes or taxes on the wealthy could be increased; and still others contend that even the cost of current wars, if redistributed to the poor of the world, could improve the lives of millions of people and reduce the likelihood of wars and terrorist activities. To use the cost of wars as an example, consider the following data.[3]

6,700,000,000	Estimated world population
$60,000,000,000	Initial Bush administration estimate of the cost of Iraq War, 2003
$600,000,000,000	Pentagon estimate of the cost of first five years of Iraq War, 2008
$2,000,000,000,000	Congressional Budget Office estimate of long-term total expenditures on Iraq War, 2008

The reallocation of the Iraq War funds would provide nearly $9 to every person in the world, reallocation of the Pentagon five-year estimate of actual expenditures would add $90 to each person's income, and the long-term estimate by the Congressional Budget Office would yield $290 per person. Compared to the $786 average income of the lowest 44 percent of the world's population, the funds devoted by the Unites States to the Iraq War could make a substantial difference in the quality life for many people throughout the world.

World Population Changes: Creating a Global Demand for Social Work in the Future

The projections for future population changes suggest additional issues social workers should be particularly prepared to address. It is estimated that, as of 2008, the world's population was more than 6.7 billion people, which is double the population as recently as 1965.[4] It had taken all of human history until 1804 to reach 1 billion people, and the earth easily supported this population. Now, even with vastly increased agricultural productivity, it is recognized that the world's food supply cannot indefinitely support a growing population. Nor can the air support increasing pollution, or the oceans produce a sufficient supply of fish, or the rivers provide the needed drinking water for the people and animals, and so on. As Figure 15.1 indicates, this growth and the ensuing demands on the earth and its people will continue through at least the next fifty years.

There is encouraging news in the fact that, worldwide, the fertility rates are decreasing. Where in 1970 the annual rate of population growth was 2 percent, that figure has now dropped to about 1.25 percent, and by 2050 it is expected to be down to less than 0.5 percent. Although the growth trend looks favorable, the sheer number of people being added places great demand on the earth and its people to accommodate

Figure 15.1

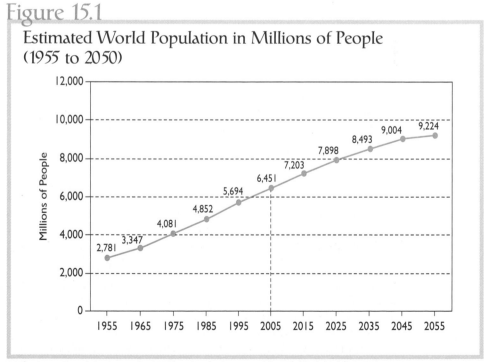

Estimated World Population in Millions of People (1955 to 2050)

Source: U.S. Census Bureau, "Total Midyear Population for the World: 1950–2050." http://www.census.gov/ipc/www/worldpopinfo.html.

the increased population. To place this growth in perspective, consider the following: the Census Bureau estimates that in one month in 2005 there were 10.8 million births, 4.7 million deaths, and an overall population increase of 6.2 million people (approximately the number of people living in the state of Massachusetts.[5] Population experts predict that the earth's carrying capacity for people is in the 7.7 billion to 12 billion range.[6] Within a relatively few years (i.e., by 2023), we will reach the lower limit of this estimate, and the projection for 2050 is above 9.4 billion people, well toward the middle of the estimated capacity of the earth to support its population. Virtually every country in the world will be challenged to find the means to purify the air, manage the forests, secure an adequate supply of water, protect the land to sustain necessary food production, provide required energy resources (e.g., for heat, light, and transportation), and—of special interest to social workers—develop social structures to allow the people to achieve quality lives and live peacefully in an overcrowded world.

The problems associated with this growth are more than sheer increases in the number of people. The demographics, too, are shifting, which will require changes in many of our social institutions. Projections by the United Nations indicate that, in the next one-half century, the percentage of children will decline by 9.5 percent, and the percentage of people age 60 and over will increase by 10.6 percent. Those in the "breadwinner" age group will remain about the same (around 60 percent of the population), supporting both the children and older people. What are the implications for these population changes? This aging of the population will have many social implications. For example, today only 10 percent of the older population is made up of those people who draw most heavily on health and human services, that is, individuals ages 80 and older. That percentage is expected to double by the year 2050 and will include approximately 400 million people worldwide. Also, as the population ages, a greater percentage of the survivors are female, who have a life expectancy much longer than that of males. At age 60, 55 percent of the population is female; at age 80, that portion increases to 65 percent; and by age 100, females make up 83 percent of the population.[7] Unique financial, social, and health issues will confront this growing number of older women.

The United Nations highlights three areas in which the changes in age structure will have an impact.[8]

> Population ageing is profound, having major consequences and implications for human life. In the economic area, population ageing will have an impact on economic growth, savings, investment and consumption, labour markets, pensions, taxation and intergenerational transfers. In the social sphere population ageing affects health and health care, family composition and living arrangements, housing and migration. In the political arena, population ageing can influence voting patterns and representation. (p. xxviii)

Similar patterns of change will occur related to increased urbanization and the issues associated with living in overcrowded conditions, the spread of communicable diseases, the protection of women and children from abuses, opportunities for employment and economic supports for those who cannot be employed, care for mentally disabled persons, and so on.

Such global population stresses call for world communication, collaboration, and planning to address impending problems. Social work has an important role to perform in helping the world address these and related issues, but action is sometimes hampered by the difficulty of speaking with a single professional voice. Hokenstad indicates that, with increasing globalization, "social workers need to think about the equitable sharing of both its benefits and burdens so that the marginal sectors of society are not overlooked" and by advocating "on such matters as development, refugees, health care, human rights, discrimination, children's rights, and peacekeeping."[9]

Social Welfare Programs: A Varied Response to Human Need

Each country, according to its own culture, resources, and the extent of its human needs, has developed a unique mix of social welfare programs. The structures of those programs affect what services can be provided and, for social workers, the roles they will perform. No two countries have evolved identical human services, although they have borrowed ideas from each other.*

Social Welfare in Preindustrial Nations

Several social welfare philosophies characterize the different approaches to human services throughout the world. For example, in preindustrial or agriculture-based societies, social needs are met primarily by families, churches, the few wealthy persons in the society, and various guilds (e.g., agricultural trade groups and civic organizations). This type of society is typically found among developing countries in Africa, Latin America, Asia, and elsewhere. In these societies, direct human services are most likely to be provided on a natural helping or volunteer basis, and social work practice tends to evolve as a macro social change profession. Thus, in many of these societies, social workers' efforts have been orientated toward *social development,* that is, social, economic, and political change to improve basic human conditions.

The country of Rwanda, located in east-central Africa, provides an example of an underdeveloped country and the manner in which very serious human needs are being addressed. As the most densely populated country in Africa, the people of Rwanda find community and extended family networks of kin and fictive-kin relationships the primary resource for meeting basic human needs. The absence of any substantial governmentally administered social welfare services and programs places this responsibility to provide the basic needs such as clean drinking water, basic health care, education, and the provision of adequate nutrition solidly in the hands of the people. Perhaps, what is more remarkable concerning many of the lay people of Rwanda is the high degree of

---

*A particularly informative source when examining social work in several different countries is M. C. Hokenstad, S. K. Khinduka, and James Midgley, eds., *Profiles in International Social Work* (Washington, D.C.: NASW Press, 1992). Included in this book are descriptions of social work in Chile, Great Britain, Hungary, India, Japan, Hong Kong, Singapore, South Korea, Taiwan, South Africa, Sweden, Uganda, and the United States. A second useful source is Pete Alcock and Gary Craig, eds., *International Social Policy: Welfare Regimes in the Developed World* (New York: Palgrave, 2001).

vigilance in their commitment to unity, self-determination, creativity, and collective work and responsibility for rebuilding their country in the aftermath of the genocide of 1994. In spite of this horrific and tragic past and the slow progress toward any comprehensive social service infrastructure, ordinary citizens (e.g., those with little formal education or training) share the little they have with those with even fewer resources (i.e., the elderly, widows, and orphans specifically). This is testament to the strength and resilience of the people and of their humanity, civic responsibility, and duty. The absence of such humane efforts by everyday people would assuredly result in the needless deaths of thousands. Professionally credentialed social work practitioners are virtually nonexistent in Rwanda, particularly among Rwandan natives, and professional training or education does not exist in any formalized manner. In this and similar social welfare systems, professional social work practitioners generally are working through international nongovernmental organizations (NGOs) or other faith- or community-based nonprofit international groups and organizations that require highly specialized and trained personnel to direct, organize, and coordinate their international aid efforts to provide services in these preindustrial countries.

Social Welfare in Postindustrial Nations

Another philosophy tends to emerge when industrialization begins to occur in a country. When this happens, individual and family mobility is required, urbanization increases, and people are viewed as commodities whose time and talent can be bought and sold. There is reliance on the market system to provide people with needed resources because the extended family may not be present or have the capacity to meet its members' social needs. Thus a set of social programs and persons to deliver these programs evolves. It is in these postindustrial societies that professional levels of social work are most likely to develop.

Epsing-Anderson has developed a typology of three distinct social welfare systems that have emerged in postindustrial societies. Epsing-Anderson's typology is based on the analysis of the degree to which the social welfare system (1) treats people as having a right to services, and not just as commodities used in the production of goods and services; (2) redistributes money and other resources to achieve greater equality and reduce poverty; and (3) maintains a balance between the government and private sectors having responsibility for the well-being of people.[10] Examination of how countries differ on these three points (i.e., comparative social welfare) yields the following distinct variations in postindustrial welfare approaches—or social welfare states.

First, the *corporatist welfare state* is designed to maintain existing social class differences and the distribution of resources by the system. Services are distributed primarily by private or corporate entities, and people are not viewed as having the right to services. This approach to social welfare is at the most conservative side of the continuum of approaches and attempts to maintain the status quo. Examples of countries where this approach is dominant include France, Italy, Spain, and Austria. In these countries, social workers' activities are primarily related to delivering social provisions and resolving marriage and family issues. Social work practice under this system is highly specialized, and most recognized social workers are required to hold a social work credential, usually with training at the vocational level.[11]

Second, the *liberal welfare state* is best represented by the United States, Canada, Great Britain, Australia, India, and Japan—although these countries differ in the degree to which each of Epsing-Anderson's criteria for comparing welfare systems is embraced. These programs typically focus on redistributing income to the low-income population; are designed to reinforce the work ethic and view peoples' labor primarily as an economic commodity; maintain minimum standards of well-being through government programs, yet also subsidize the private for-profit and nonprofit welfare programs; tend to stigmatize people receiving services, thus maintaining social stratification; and only minimally treat people as having a right to services. In these countries, social workers provide a range of services, from direct practice interventions to efforts to facilitate at least incremental change in social structures. Professional social workers in these countries hold a social work credential at the undergraduate or graduate level.[12]

Last, the *social democratic welfare state* provides universal services and contends that the peoples' work should not simply be treated as another commodity. Social programs in countries that have adopted this model (e.g., Norway, Sweden, and the Netherlands) attempt to achieve maximum standards of human well-being through universal health insurance systems and are designed to socialize the costs of family living through governmental transfers such as children's allowances, sharing costs of caring for the aged and handicapped, and guaranteeing full employment to all who can work. In this type of welfare system, relatively few of the service providers hold a social work credential. Those who have credentials are prepared at the vocational or secondary levels, except when offering therapeutic services typically related to child behavior issues and parenting problems.

Of special note are Russia, the Czech Republic, Romania, Bulgaria, and other countries formerly associated with the United Soviet Socialist Republics (USSR). During the existence of the USSR, social work and its democratic orientation to helping people individually or collectively address social injustices was banned, and social work, at least as we know it today, disappeared in these countries. Although these are postindustrial countries, social welfare programs, social work, and social work education have just recently begun to re-emerge.

The Emergence of Social Work Training and Education

It is difficult to mark the beginning of a profession. In the United States, for example, the National Association of Social Workers designated 1998 as the centennial year for the profession, presumably because in 1898 the New York Charity Organization created a six-week training program known as the New York School of Philanthropy. If one holds social work up to all the criteria for professions proposed by Abraham Flexner and other experts on the sociology of professions (see Chapter 4), it is more likely that social work in the United States met the criteria to become a recognized profession somewhere around the late 1920s. Nevertheless, the initiation of education and training programs is usually documented and thus is used here to signal the advent of professions. It is informative, therefore, to note a few of the dates when significant training or education in social work was introduced. The following is a partial list of the approximate starting dates for social work education in countries throughout the world.

1898	United States	1924	South Africa
1899	The Netherlands	1931	Ireland
1903	England	1932	Spain
1908	Germany	1936	India and Egypt
1920	Belgium	1963	Uganda
1921	Sweden	1989	Hungry
1922	Chile	1992	Italy

Social work also varies in different countries in the educational levels recognized as preparation for practice. In some countries, it is *training,* with no particular academic preparation (not even a high school diploma required). In others, high school or specific community college vocational training is the requisite preparation, while in many countries college-level *professional education* is the requirement to enter social work. In a few countries, including the United States, a professional master's degree is the terminal practice degree. Nowhere is a doctoral degree the expected preparation for social work practice.

Barretta-Herman's analysis of social work education throughout the world suggests that the educational programs are relatively consistent in the content they offer.[13] More than two-thirds of the respondents to her survey from 35 different countries indicated that the schools required coursework in the following areas: personal communication, research, social and public policy, community intervention, ethnic or culturally focused content, organizational theory, and biopsychosocial theory. In the social work practice areas, there was again considerable consensus in requiring content regarding work with groups, case work, work with communities, marital and family counseling, and work with social agencies. These data indicate there is relatively high consistency throughout the world regarding the fundamental content required for social work practice.

A Global Approach to Social Work

As recently as the late 1900s, a worldwide perspective on social work was accurately termed *international social work* and was concerned with comparing social work as it existed in the different countries and how the different social welfare conceptions shaped social work practice. As social work has matured, it has become possible to address social work from a *global perspective,* that is, as one profession practicing in different countries. However, in some countries, social work is almost entirely offered through government agencies; in others, it is mostly in the private sector; and in yet others it is balanced between the two. Sometimes it is highly clinical and oriented toward change in the person, and in other countries it is mostly focused on changing the structure of the society and the human services delivery system.

When social work education is required, there is a common set of knowledge, values, and competencies that unite social work activities into a single worldwide profession. In 2005, Weiss[14] published the results of a study in which she surveyed 781 BSW-level student social workers from ten countries reflecting all three social welfare conceptions defined by Epsing-Anderson (discussed previously) and located in North and South America, Europe, Africa, Australia, and the Middle East. The results of this study pinpoint (statistically significant at the < 0.001 level) three fundamental perspectives that serve as the theoretical and value center of social work:

> The major finding of this study is the substantial similarity in the students' perceptions of the source of poverty, the way to deal with poverty, and the goals of the profession....The similarities in students' views are indicative of a common understanding of poverty as rooted in social or structural, rather than individual, causes and as requiring state intervention for its alleviation. The similarities also reflect the dual commitment of the profession to social justice, understood as the need for the redistribution of resources for the benefit of those who have been deprived, and to (enhancing) individual well-being. (p. 108)

In a world in which people and countries are highly interdependent, the existence of a global social work profession is a step toward addressing the major issues that shape the quality of life for the peoples of the world. To facilitate the development of and advocacy for positions to address these global issues, to encourage sharing of relevant knowledge and skills for social work practice, and to educate social workers who can strengthen the human services throughout the world, several important steps have been taken.

International Professional Organizations

Two international organizations provide the basic leadership for the globalization of social work. One, the International Federation of Social Workers (IFSW), is structured to work through various national professional membership organizations such as the National Association of Social Workers and the professional trade unions of social workers that exist in some countries. Begun in 1928 following the International Conference on Social Work held in Paris, today organizations from approximately eighty-four countries, representing 470,000 social workers, participate in the IFSW. The activities of IFSW include publication of a newsletter, maintaining a commission that advocates for the protection of human rights throughout the world, the development of a statement of ethical guidelines for social workers, and maintenance of updated policy positions on global social welfare issues.[15]

The second important international social work organization is the International Association of Schools of Social Work (IASSW), which was also formed in 1928. This organization now includes 410 member social work education associations (e.g., Council on Social Work Education) and individual schools from 90 countries. The IASSW is concerned with facilitating the inclusion of international content into social work education programs, providing consultation to the United Nations and the United Nations Children's Fund, and facilitating the transfer of academic credit among schools from different countries. With the IFSW, it publishes the journal *International Social Work*.[16]

Defining Social Work Globally

Arriving at a generally accepted definition to describe social work in the United States proved difficult (see Chapter 3). Finding a definition that embraced the common features of social work throughout the world was even more challenging. However, in 2000 the IFSW adopted a definition of social work that encompassed the many expressions of this profession throughout the world. This definition was a major accomplishment that makes it possible for social work to act as a single profession in addressing global issues, to allow workers to gain employment in other countries, and to create educational programs that transfer from country to country. The strong social justice and humanitarian emphasis of social work is evident in the IFSW definition:[17]

> The social work profession promotes social change, problem solving in human relationships and the empowerment and liberation of people to enhance well-being. Utilising theories of human behaviour and social systems, social work intervenes at the points where people interact with their environments. Principles of human rights and social justice are fundamental to social work.

Although this definition is similar to the NASW definition that characterizes social work in the United States, the strong orientation toward changing the social structures that affect people, as opposed to the U.S. emphasis on individual change, is evident.

Values and Ethics Held by Social Workers Globally

The underlying beliefs about the inherent value of people and the responsibility of societies to create conditions in which people can thrive are perhaps the glue that binds social workers together. These basic principles transcend the particular cultures and social welfare systems in various parts of the world and are the most universal expressions of the common beliefs that characterize social work globally.

The International Federation of Social Workers has devoted considerable effort to developing an international code of ethics. Underpinning the statement of ethical principles is recognition that "Ethical awareness is a necessary part of the professional practice of social workers. Their ability and commitment to act ethically is an essential aspect of the quality of the services offered to those who use social work services."[18] This code addresses three sets of basic principles that characterize social work practice throughout the world:

▶ *Human Rights and Human Dignity.* Social work is based on respect for the inherent worth and dignity of all people and the rights that follow from this. Social workers should uphold and defend each person's physical, psychological, emotional, and spiritual integrity and well-being, including respecting the right to self-determination, promoting the right to participation, treating each person as a whole, and identifying and developing client strengths.

▶ *Social Justice.* Social workers have a responsibility to promote social justice, in relation to society generally and in relation to the people with whom they work, e.g., challenging negative discrimination, recognizing diversity, distributing resources equitably, challenging unjust policies and practices, and working in solidarity with others to break down barriers to an inclusive society.

▶ *Professional Conduct.* Social workers should act in accordance with the ethical code or guidelines current in their countries that will provide more nationally relevant guidance to ethical practice. However, several universal guides to conduct are suggested, including, for example, maintaining practice competence, acting with integrity and maintaining appropriate boundaries, giving priority to the interests of clients over personal interests, maintain confidentiality, and so on.

Global Views of Social Issues

One direct result of the similar values held by social workers is that agreement has been reached regarding understanding and developing approaches to resolving social problems that are experienced throughout the world. For example, workers and organizations of social workers are concerned with such worldwide issues as achieving and preserving peace, distributing human and economic resources more equitably, protecting the rights and preventing the exploitation of children and youth, enhancing women's status and safety, facilitating international adoptions, and so on. Evidence of these concerns is found in the issues addressed in the IFSW policy statements that have been adopted to date.*

▶ Health
▶ Human Rights
▶ Older Persons
▶ Refugees
▶ Women
▶ Peace and Social Justice
▶ Globalization and the Environment

▶ HIV-AIDS
▶ Migration
▶ The Protection of Personal Information
▶ Conditions in Rural Communities
▶ Youth
▶ Displaced Persons
▶ Indigenous People

The value of these position papers is not only to identify topics for which social workers are in general agreement but also to provide a more influential voice to international organizations such as the United Nations (UN). In that venue, social workers have been actively involved with a number of UN-related agencies, including the United Nations Children's Fund (UNICEF), the UN Development Program, the Department of Policy Coordination and Sustainable Development, the Office of the UN High Commissioner for Refugees, and the World Health Organization.

---

*All position papers are available from the International Federation of Social Workers Secretariat, PO Box 6875, Schwarztorstrasse 22, CH-3001 Berne, Switzerland, in English, French, and Spanish. They are also available at the IFSW web site: http://www.ifsw.org/en/p38000079.html.

Employment in International Social Work

Many of the basic principles imbedded in social work are also important contributors to successful international work. Social workers with considerable international experience identify the following as critical in international work: skills in interdisciplinary collaboration, sensitivity to other cultures, attention to the person in environment, searching to address the whole picture, emphasis on self-sufficiency, comfort in serving as a generalist, and maximizing self-determination.[19]

Four forms of international practice are possible for a social worker. One form is to secure a position in an international organization that advances human services on a worldwide basis. The UN serves as the primary agency to coordinate the efforts of the various countries to overcome oppression, facilitate the delivery of health and welfare services that cross international boundaries, and promote social justice. Social work with UN-related agencies such as UNICEF, the Economic and Social Council, the World Health Organization, and the UN High Commissioner on Refugees are examples of such positions.

Second, the U.S. government, too, has positions concerned with international social welfare issues. The Department of Health and Human Services maintains an international affairs staff to give attention to worldwide human services issues, and its Office of Refugee Resettlement is actively involved in promoting the safety, welfare, and rights of refugees. The International Development Cooperation Agency (USAID) administers foreign aid programs in approximately one hundred countries throughout the world, and the Peace Corps has provided developing countries with the human and technical resources to improve their physical infrastructure (e.g., water, sanitation, roads), health care, and human services.

Third, perhaps the most common form of international employment for social workers is to find a social work job in a government or voluntary agency in another country. These roles typically include service provision, consultation, and teaching or training activities. Particularly for countries that are in the process of developing services to individuals and families, the skills possessed by most U.S. social workers are highly valued. The reverse is true, too, for social workers from developing countries, who often have a strong social development background and bring a helpful expertise not typically found among U.S.-educated social workers.

Last, some international social work positions exist in multinational corporations or the U.S. military, which locate personnel in foreign countries. When families are relocated (or left behind), there are inevitable social adjustments to be made. As in other social work practice in business and industry, social workers provide direct services to help individuals and families to deal with their social problems, assist the company in sharpening its cultural sensitivity, and represent the company as a participant in the local community, making contributions to and interfacing with the human services delivery system.

How does one become prepared for international social work? Certainly, the demands on workers differ depending on the nature of a country's social welfare system and the type of position that the social worker holds. Specific preparation, then, cannot be identified that is essential for all positions. However, a few fundamental areas of preparation are somewhat universal.

First, become informed and stay current regarding international affairs, particularly issues of social and economic justice, human rights, and peace. Careful reading of both the social work literature on international issues and the general news sources is essential.

Second, develop competence in the use of one or more foreign languages. Although English is used for general communication in most parts of the world, it is respectful to others to attempt to speak to clients in their language (however faltering) and, particularly if providing direct services, much subtle meaning in communication is lost if one does not know the language.

Third, it is also essential to develop knowledge of the host county's culture. This is prerequisite to helping to avoid the tendency toward *ethnocentrism* (i.e., to believe that one's own culture is superior) and, therefore, to force his or her way of doing things into the other culture. The concept of "the ugly American" reflects the reputation persons from the United States have developed by reflecting such cultural insensitivity. The study of the others' culture and experience is a first step in increasing awareness and avoiding inadvertent acts of insensitivity, such as not recognizing cultural patterns related to age and gender when addressing family members or becoming frustrated by differing commitments to timeliness and punctuality.

Finally, the unique contribution that a professional social worker brings is his or her professional knowledge and skill. Experience in practicing social work after completing one's professional education is prerequisite for most international social work positions.

Although all the above competencies are necessary for successful international social work practice, one research project identified the basic social work principles of "individualizing the client," "maximizing client empowerment," "maximizing client participation," and "maximizing client self-determination"[20] as the factors most associated with successful Peace Corps and USAID projects. Ghavam's study of 74 projects throughout the world found that "the greater the villagers' role and participation in start-up, assessment, and design phases of the projects resulted in more overall success of the development projects." This study also found that the project director's technical preparation for the position, experience in international work, and adequacy in the culture and language of the area were also associated with the overall success of the projects.[21] In short, good social work practice, plus orientation to the language and culture of the specific country, corresponds with successful international practice. The competent social worker already has a foundation for international practice.

Concluding Comment

As technology advances, the world shrinks. The presence of a worldwide economy makes countries increasingly interdependent. The ability of the media to immediately transmit information around the globe creates an unprecedented awareness of events as they occur in even remote areas of the world. And the availability of the World Wide Web and e-mail allows human services agencies and human services providers to exchange information through a virtually cost-free and instantaneous process. Although some parts of the world have not yet fully experienced the Technological Revolution, in many ways international boundaries have become less significant.

Parallel to the diminishing isolation of individual countries, social work, too, is beginning to blur national distinctions and think of itself as a global profession. Writing for the *NASW News,* Sheryl Fred suggests that global social work might accurately be considered an emerging field of practice:

> Counseling victims of the tsunami disaster. Helping immigrants and refugees in the United States receive the services they need. Empowering tribal communities in India to fight for their land rights. All of these are direct practice examples of the international field of practice in social work, a career path that has long been in practice, but is only recently gaining attention from the social work profession as a whole.[22]

A challenge for the next generation of social workers will be to evolve a concept of social work that will bridge the differing philosophies of society's role in meeting human needs and yet maintain the social worker's unique mission as the profession that addresses individual and family needs and, simultaneously, is concerned with changing the society to reduce or eliminate factors that contribute to people's problems in social functioning.

KEY WORDS AND CONCEPTS

Global social work
International social work definition
International Declaration of Ethical
    Principles for Social Work
Corporatist welfare state
Liberal welfare state

Social democratic welfare state
International Federation of Social
    Workers
International Association of Schools of
    Social Work

SUGGESTED INFORMATION RESOURCES

Brinkerhoff, Derick W., and Jennifer M. Brinkerhoff. *Working for Change: Making a Career in International Public Service.* Bloomfield, CT: Kumarian Press, 2005.

Gray, Mel, John Coates, and Michael Yellow Bird. *Indigenous Social Work Around the World: Towards Culturally Relevant Education and Practice.* Williston, VT: Ashgate, 2008.

International Federation of Social Workers. http://www.ifsw.org.

Robb, Matthew. "International Social Work: Go Global!" *Social Work Today* (January/February) 2005, pp. 15–18.

Ramanathanm, Chathapuram S., and Rosemary J. Link. *Principles and Resources for Social Work Practice in a Global Era.* Belmont, CA: Brooks/Cole-Wadsworth, 1999.

ENDNOTES

1. "Global Poverty: The Gap Between the World's Rich and Poor Is Growing, and the Dying Continues," *Public Affairs Report,* 2001 (Berkeley, CA: Institute of Governmental Studies 42(2)).
2. Ibid.
3. David M. Herszenhorn, "Estimates of Iraq War Cost Were Not Close to Ballpark," *New York Times.* Found at http://www.nytimes.com/2008/03/19/washington/19cost.html?_r=1&oref=slogin.
4. U.S. Census Bureau, "U.S. and World Population Clocks—POPClocks." Found at http://www.census.gov/.
5. U.S. Census Bureau, "World Vital Events Per Time Unit 2008." www.census.gov/ipc/www/idb/worldpopinfo.html.
6. Geoffrey Gilbert, *World Population: A Handbook* (Santa Barbara, CA: ABC-CLIO Press, 2001), pp. 16–17.
7. United Nations, *World Population Aging 1950–2050* (New York: United Nations Population Division, 2001).
8. Ibid.
9. M. C. Hokenstad, cited in Peter Slavin, "Profession Has a Global Role," *NASW News* 47 (March 2002): 1–2.
10. Gøsta Epsing-Anderson, *The Three Worlds of Welfare Capitalism* (Princeton, NJ: Princeton University Press, 1990), pp. 21–29.
11. Matthew Colton, Ferran Casas, Mark Drakeford, Susan Roberts, Evert Scholte, and Margaret Williams, *Stigma and Social Welfare: An International Comparative Study* (Brookfield, VT: Ashgate, 1997), pp. 138–140.
12. Judith Norman and Heather Hintze, "A Sampling of International Practice Knowledge," *International Social Work* 48(5) 2005: 553–567.
13. Angeline Barretta-Herman, *A Re-Analysis of the IASSW World Census 2000;* unpublished manuscript (St. Paul, MN: University of St. Thomas, 2002), pp. 16 and 18.
14. Idit Weiss, "Is There a Global Common Core to Social Work?" *Social Work* 50 (April 2005): 101–110.
15. International Federation of Social Workers, "General Information," http://www.ifsw.org.
16. International Association of Schools of Social Work, "Welcome," http://www.iassw-aiets.org.
17. International Federation of Social Workers, "Ethics in Social Work, Statement of Principles," http://www.ifsw.org/en/p38000324.html.
18. Ibid.
19. Sheryl Fred, "Building an International Field of Practice," *NASW News* 50 (April 2005), p. 4.
20. Bradford W. Sheafor and Charles R. Horejsi, *Techniques and Guidelines for Social Work Practice,* 8th ed. (Boston: Allyn & Bacon, 2008), pp. 66–79.
21. Hamid Reza Ghavam, "Characteristics of External Activators in Third World Village Development." Unpublished Doctoral Dissertation, Colorado State University, Fort Collins, CO, pp. 148–149.
22. Fred, op. cit.

part five

Social Work Practice with Vulnerable Populations

The term "vulnerable populations" is used throughout this book. In this context, vulnerable populations are groups of people who are especially susceptible to experiencing problems in some aspect of social functioning. They are populations at risk because of factors in the environment, imbedded in the social structures and stereotypes about these groups, which increase the probability they will experience social problems. The populations addressed in the following chapters have the same universal needs as all humans, but in addition a higher percentage experience the need for special attention by social workers. These are population groups who are characterized by uniqueness based on race, ethnic origin, gender, age, sexual orientation, a handicapping condition, or other characteristics that make them more vulnerable to problematic social conditions and second-class status in the society.

It is important to recognize that the term *vulnerable populations* is applied to groups of people with a common characteristic, where an increased incidence of social issues is associated with people sharing that characteristic. When applied to individuals, vulnerability is often countered by *resilience*. Many individuals overcome their vulnerability, and, although the conditions making them vulnerable persist, they are not affected by them to the extent that they experience the social issues typically associated with vulnerable populations.

In addition to helping people individually address the issues they confront, the social worker also addresses the forces in American society that keep these groups vulnerable. For example, poverty, poor physical and mental health, premature death, chronic substance abuse, and education deficits are all factors that are symptomatic of vulnerability. Some people would argue that these special population groups are vulnerable because they are biologically or emotionally inferior to the majority—leading to a view labeled "isms," i.e., racism, sexism, classism, ageism, and so on. Social workers reject the "isms" and conclude that, when a group consistently experiences a social condition more severely than others, there is systematic bias built into the society's structure that can, and should, be changed.

In the following chapters, important practice considerations for several special population groups are identified as a means of sensitizing the new social worker to the unique characteristics and experiences of each group. Each of the eleven chapters in Part Five addresses a different special population. Chapters 16 through 20 are concerned with groups that are disadvantaged because of physical characteristics such as gender, age, sexual orientation, and physical disability. Chapters 21 through 26 address populations who experience discrimination and oppression due to race, ethnicity, and culture—including the experiences of the Muslim American community (especially since 9/11), Asian Americans, American Indians and Alaska Natives, Mexican Americans, African Americans, and Puerto Ricans. For populations in which the authors did not have sufficient expertise, nationally recognized experts in working with that population were commissioned to write those chapters. To bring continuity to the chapters, each author was provided with guidelines that suggested including demographic information about that population, analyzing the group's experience in U.S. society through a five-level ecosystems model (see Box P5.1), discussing issues in social work practice when working with this population, and providing case material that would help readers recognize the application of these materials to social work practice.

In working with special population groups, once a sound knowledge base is established through the use of a conceptual tool such as the ecosystems model, the social worker is pointed toward intervening at both micro- and macro-intervention levels—attending to both the person and the environment. Usually a variety of assessment tools to identify biological, psychological, sociological, cultural, and historical factors influencing the client's situation are used to know what is needed and, more important, what should be done. Fitting that information into this ecosystems model

helps organize these varying factors affecting the clients, thus assuring there is consideration of both individual characteristics and factors that contribute to one's vulnerability.

One useful tool for social work assessment is the ecosystems model derived from ecological theory[1] and general systems theory.[2] This model provides a structured way to examine system interactions that should be considered regarding a client situation. Figure P5.1 provides a synopsis of this model.

First, at the *individual level,* the focus is on the biopsychological endowment each person possesses, including personality strengths, level of psychosocial development, cognition, perception, problem-solving skills, emotional temperament, habit formation, and communication and language skills. Additionally, it is important to be knowledgeable about the person's attitudes, values, cultural beliefs, lifestyle, skills, and abilities; their view of the world; and how they respond to and cope with physical and psychological stress and problems. This listing represents some of the key factors at the individual level; the list is by no means exhaustive.

Second, at the *family level,* the focus is on the nature of family lifestyle, culture, organization, family division of labor, sex role structure, and interactional dynamics. Within a cultural context, each family is unique. It is therefore

Box P5.1

An Ecosystems Model for Assessing Special Populations

Professions require the disciplined used of values, knowledge, and skills when serving clients. One expression of this discipline is in how one organizes information to make an assessment of the client situation. For social workers, that means drawing together considerable information about the client's past and present and the factors in the world around the client that may affect the situation. The next step is to plan interventions to facilitate change in the client and his or her environment. The intervention phase of the change process will usually require the investment of time and energy from the client and resources from the community. Thus an accurate and thorough assessment, as the essential first step in the process of change, is prerequisite to a successful outcome.

Figure P5.1

Ecosystems Model for Analysis of Psychosocial Factors Affecting Special Populations

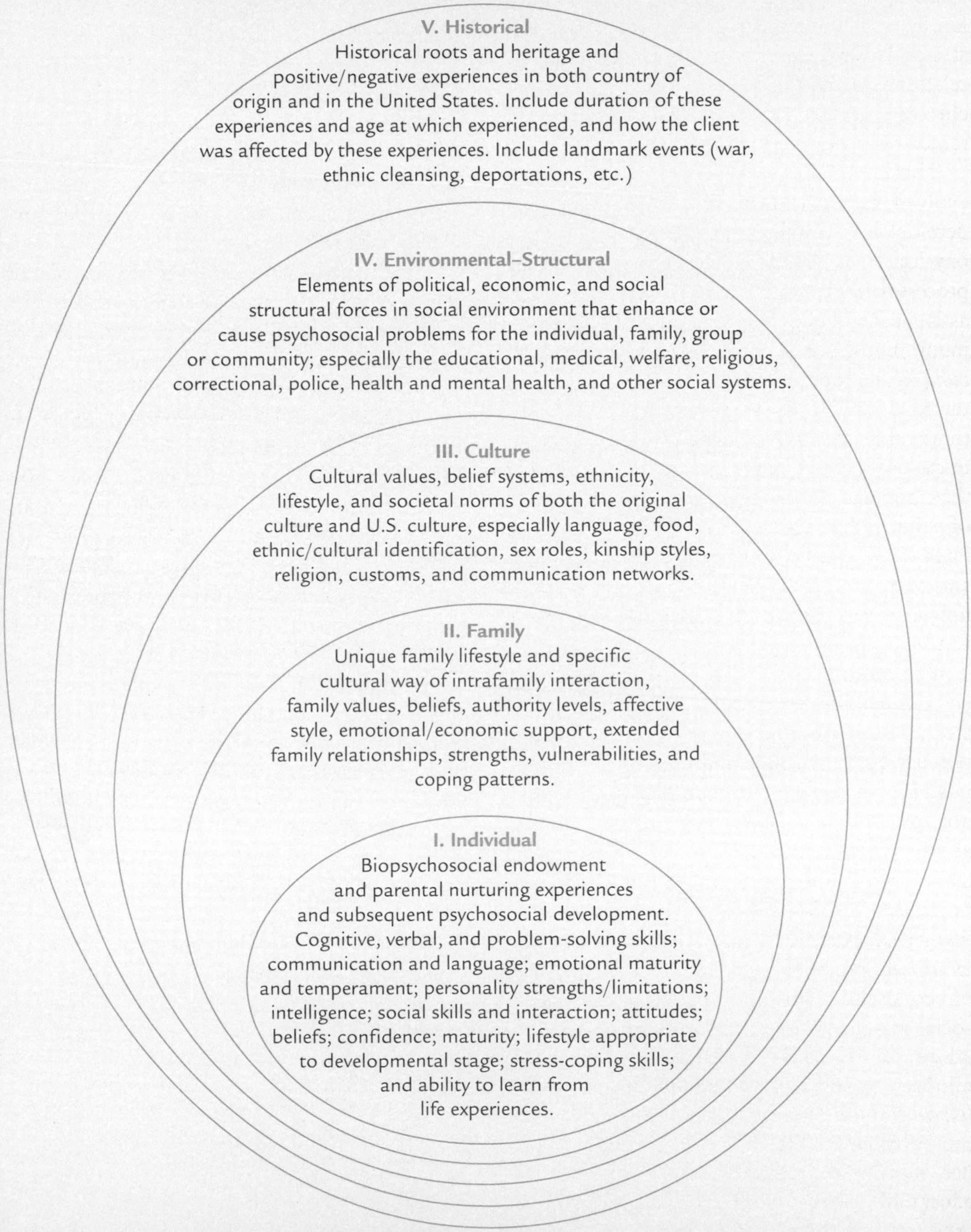

V. Historical
Historical roots and heritage and positive/negative experiences in both country of origin and in the United States. Include duration of these experiences and age at which experienced, and how the client was affected by these experiences. Include landmark events (war, ethnic cleansing, deportations, etc.)

IV. Environmental–Structural
Elements of political, economic, and social structural forces in social environment that enhance or cause psychosocial problems for the individual, family, group or community; especially the educational, medical, welfare, religious, correctional, police, health and mental health, and other social systems.

III. Culture
Cultural values, belief systems, ethnicity, lifestyle, and societal norms of both the original culture and U.S. culture, especially language, food, ethnic/cultural identification, sex roles, kinship styles, religion, customs, and communication networks.

II. Family
Unique family lifestyle and specific cultural way of intrafamily interaction, family values, beliefs, authority levels, affective style, emotional/economic support, extended family relationships, strengths, vulnerabilities, and coping patterns.

I. Individual
Biopsychosocial endowment and parental nurturing experiences and subsequent psychosocial development. Cognitive, verbal, and problem-solving skills; communication and language; emotional maturity and temperament; personality strengths/limitations; intelligence; social skills and interaction; attitudes; beliefs; confidence; maturity; lifestyle appropriate to developmental stage; stress-coping skills; and ability to learn from life experiences.

A special thanks to Professor Lois Miranda and social work faculty and students at the University of Wisconsin, Oshkosh, for assisting in the further refinement of the ecosystems model.

important to know its values, beliefs, emotional support capacity, affective style, tradition, rituals, overall strengths and vulnerabilities of the family, and how it manages internal or external stress. The nature and quality of the spousal relationship and the depth of connectedness to children and extended family are other areas requiring examination.

Third, in all civilizations, cultures have evolved for survival purposes. Each culture develops behavioral responses influenced by the physical environment, and historical and social processes incorporating specific structures such as language, food, kinship styles, religion, communications, norms, beliefs, and values. At the *cultural level* of the ecosystems model, therefore, the focus should be on understanding the cultural values, belief systems, and societal norms of the host culture and, in the case of minorities, their original culture. There may exist a conflict of cultures that may result in mental–emotional impairment due to culture shock. The enhancing and nurturing aspects of the culture(s) should be noted, as well as noxious elements such as sexism, ageism, and racism.

The fourth level of analysis involves *environmental–structural* factors and the positive or negative impact they have on special populations. Environmental–structural theories postulate that many of the problems of vulnerable populations are caused by the economic and social structure of U.S. society. Women, for example, are not poorer as a group than men because of biological or cultural inferiority. Rather, sexism is a U.S. cultural value that is expressed and reinforced through the structure of economic, political, educational, and other social institutions. Ryan states that when U.S. white society looks at the poorly educated minority group of children in the ghetto or *barrio* school, blame is placed on the parents (no books in the home), the child (impulse-ridden, nonverbal), minority culture (no value on education), or their socioeconomic status (i.e., they are socially and economically deprived and don't adequately provide for their children). In pursuing this logic, Ryan adds, no one remembers to ask questions about the collapsing buildings; old, torn textbooks; insensitive teachers; relentless segregation; or callous administrators—in short, the environmental structure imposed upon the person with its accompanying negative consequences.[3] These are important considerations for social workers to introduce into the assessment.

The fifth and final level of the ecosystems model concerns positive and problematic factors in the *historical experience* of the special population members. The historical roots and experiences of female subordination by males, for example, will affect the nature and quality of women's interaction with human services agencies and their representatives. The male social worker may not be aware of his unconscious sexist behavior—the result of decades of conditioning—as he attempts to "help" female clients with their problems. Years of minority group oppression and exploitation, at times including genocide, lynching, and police executions without trial, have left deep scars on minority group members and will affect the way they relate to human services agency representatives. Some elderly whites may recall very positive historical experiences remembering how supportive and encouraging U.S. social institutions have been, only to become depressed and discouraged when abandoned by the government when old. One more example of knowing about the U.S. historical experience is to appreciate the historical experience of immigrants and the countries from which they came.

ENDNOTES

1. Urie Bronfenbrenner, "Toward Experimental Ecology of Human Development," *American Psychologist* 32 (1977): 513–551.
2. Lars Skyttner, *General Systems Theory: Ideas and Applications* (River Edge, NJ: World Scientific, 2001).
3. William Ryan, *Blaming the Victim* (New York: Pantheon Books, 1971), p. 4.

Social Work Practice with Muslims in the United States*

Prefatory Comment

The attack on Pearl Harbor on December 7, 1941, shocked and angered the United States and thrust Americans into a more than three-year war with Japan. Domestically, *all* Japanese immigrants and U.S.-born Japanese Americans were perceived as dangerous enemies and were placed in relocation centers for the duration of the war. They lost their land, property, and possessions. Sixty years later, nineteen Muslim al-Qaeda terrorists crashed three civilian airliners into the Pentagon and New York World Trade Center towers, killing approximately 3,200 American citizens. This launched the United States into a war in Afghanistan in search of Osama bin Laden, who was believed to have masterminded the attacks on the United States, and into a more prolonged war in Iraq. Foreign-born Muslims were spared the extreme public backlash visited upon Japanese, but, nevertheless, American Muslims were and still are being subjected to prejudice, discrimination, and stereotyping.

In adhering to the proactive spirit of this text in guiding students and practitioners into uncharted waters requiring the profession's attention, this chapter is concerned with the treatment of Muslims in the United States during the years following the 9/11 attacks. To be effective in serving Muslim clients and effecting unwarranted negative attitudes about the estimated four million to six million Muslims in the United States, social workers must be accurately informed about the Muslim religion and Muslim people. This chapter introduces this basic information.

Muslims have existed in American society since the founding of the United States.[1] In the past few decades, the size of the Muslim population has grown dramatically.[2] At least three factors underlie this growth: high levels of immigration, comparatively high birth rates among Muslim women, and Americans converting to Islam. Ascertaining the exact size and composition of the Muslim population in the United States is problematic, however, as U.S. law prohibits the Census Bureau from

---

*This chapter was prepared by Dr. David Hodge, assistant professor, Arizona State University, West.

inquiring about respondents' religion. Although estimates vary, a number of observers believe that Muslims may now be the second largest spiritual tradition in the nation.[3]

As the Islamic community continues to grow, social workers will increasingly be called upon to provide services to this discrete cultural group. Islam, however, represents a distinct worldview that differs substantially from the dominant secular worldview that informs American society. Consequently, widespread concern exists among Muslims that helping professionals trained in secular educational settings will have little knowledge or understanding of Islamic values.[4] Indeed, although this textbook represents a step in the right direction, research indicates that most social work students receive no educational content on religious diversity during their education.[5]

It is important to note that social workers are ethically mandated to develop and exhibit spiritual competency.[6] *Spiritual competency* can be understood as a more specific, faith-based form of cultural competency.[7] Accordingly, spiritual competency can be thought of as the process of developing (1) an empathic understanding of the client's spiritual worldview; (2) intervention strategies that are appropriate, relevant, and sensitive to the client's worldview; and (3) knowledge of one's own biases that might affect the proper implementation of steps one and two.[8] It is helpful to think of spiritual competency as a lifelong endeavor in which no one ever achieves complete competency. All of us are in process.

The ecosystems model cited in the introduction to Part Five of this text is particularly useful in developing spiritual competency with Muslims. This method represents a holistic approach in which four external systems to the individual—family, culture, environmental–structural factors, and history—are viewed as salient aspects in the client's life. Flowing from the European Enlightenment's emphasis upon the rational, autonomous person, the secular culture tends to accent the role of the individual *apart from* environmental systems. Conversely, Islamic culture tends to view the individual as a person who is *part of* environmental systems.[9] In other words, the ecosystems model offers the advantage of understanding reality in a manner that is congruent with how Muslims tend to view the world. As the following section implies, Islam is not as much an individualistic belief system as it is a way of life that unifies the metaphysical and material systems.[10]

 ## A Preliminary Understanding of Islam

Islam is commonly understood to mean submission, specifically submission to Allah, the supreme and only God. Individuals who practice this submission are called *Muslims*. Both terms, Islam and Muslim, appear repeatedly in the Quran, making Islam the only world religion to have a built-in name from its inauguration.[11] The Quran was revealed to the honored founder of Islam, the Prophet Muhammad

(570/580AD–632), the "Messenger of God." The Quran is held to be God's revelation to humankind. While the Quran states that Allah communicated with other prophets, recognized by Jews and Christians, the Quran is God's final, immutable revelation.

Out of gratitude for Allah's goodness and compassion, Muslims seek to follow the straight path of God's precepts, the *shari'a.* The common Western demarcation between the personal, which may incorporate the spiritual, and the public, which is secular, is foreign to Islam. The shari'a governs all aspects of one's life. In other words, Islam offers adherents a holistic way of life in which the personal and the public are integrated. The primary basis for the shari'a is the Quran. The shari'a is also informed by the *hadith,* the recorded collections of the sayings of the Prophet.[12]

Significantly, Muslims date their history from the creation of the Islamic community, or *ummah,* rather than from their founder's birth or death or the inception of the Quran.[13] Two significant expressions of Islam characterize the worldwide Islamic community. Approximately 90 percent of Muslims are *Sunnis.* The remaining 10 percent are *Shiites,* who form the overwhelming majority in Iran.[14] Renard suggests a helpful comparison can be made between Protestantism and Sunni Islam, and Roman Catholicism and Shiite Islam.[15] In Sunni Islam and traditional Protestantism, there is an emphasis upon a direct relationship between the believer and God, unmediated by external authority structures. Similar to Roman Catholicism, Shiites have a hierarchical authority structure of legal scholars, based upon the consensus of the Shiite community, who hold an added responsibility for interpreting the Word of God for the faithful.

Since the time of the Prophet Muhammad, the Islamic community has grown to approximately a billion people.[16] Islam is frequently associated with the predominantly Islamic Arab nations of the Middle East where the faith originated. Yet, among the global Islamic community, Arab Muslims are a minority.[17] The largest populations of Muslims are found in South and Southeast Asia.[18] Indeed, the Islamic community encompasses the globe.

Local culture, political concerns, issues of interpretation, and other factors all function to shape the expression of Islam among self-identified Muslims. While there is extensive agreement that the shari'a should govern all facets of one's conduct, the practices that exemplify a "true Muslim" are contested throughout the Islamic world.[19] In reality, the Islamic community comprises many smaller Muslim communities, each with its own distinct characteristics.

Consequently, readers should bear in mind that no particular set of beliefs and values are representative of all Muslims. Many individuals who self-identify as Muslims are likely to disavow a number of the perspectives presented in this chapter. Rather than offering the final word on Islam, this chapter is better viewed as providing readers with an initial, tentative understanding of Islam. Although much diversity exists within Islamic discourse, it is important to acknowledge that a number of commonalities also exist that serve to demarcate Muslims from other populations. Perhaps the most significant of these distinguishing commonalities are the "five pillars" upon which the Islamic faith rests.[20]

The Five Pillars of Islam

The five pillars of faith are widely affirmed by Muslims as central facets of Islam. These practices can be thought of as the heart of a wider set of beliefs and practices.[21] While the wider framework of beliefs and practices is often influenced by local cultural factors, the five pillars are viewed by Muslims around the world as providing a basic outline for the expression of Islamic spirituality.[22]

The first and most fundamental tenet of the Islamic faith is the Declaration of Faith.[23] The declaration is the method by which individuals enter into the worldwide Islamic community. Individuals simply profess, "There is no god but God, and Muhammad is His Messenger." The declaration testifies to the absolute, singular theism of Islam and the primary role of Muhammad as his last prophet.[24] Thus, it serves to remind Muslims that they are part of a worldwide community of believers under the care of a compassionate, merciful God, who is personally involved with his creation.

The second pillar of faith is the performance of ritual prayers. Prayer is preceded by symbolic physical cleansing and is understood to be a holistic practice that encompasses body, mind, and emotions. Different positions are adopted, including standing straight, bending over at the waist, and kneeling with the head to the floor. The prayers are performed five times throughout the day, with the individual facing Mecca, the holy city of Islam, in Saudi Arabia, where God first entered into a covenant with the Islamic people. The offerings of prayers at dawn, midday, midafternoon, sunset, and an hour after sunset reinforce the concept that daily life and faith are continuously intertwined.[25] Similarly, for many Muslims, the uniformity of practice embodied in the ritual observance symbolizes the equality of humankind before God.[26]

The third pillar is charity, or alms giving. Each year a percentage, typically 2.5 percent of accumulated wealth, is given to address economic inequalities and promote the general welfare of the Islamic community.[27] Individuals who are poor are exempt from giving. The act of giving helps to ameliorate materialistic desires and reminds the giver that the source of all wealth is God rather than oneself.[28] Put differently, giving fosters a sense of thanksgiving to God for his goodness and a sense of community identity and responsibility.[29]

The fourth pillar is the yearly fast held during the month of Ramadan. Because Ramadan is based on the lunar calendar instead of on the solar calendar, Ramadan occurs roughly ten days earlier each year. Able-bodied adults abstain from eating, drinking, smoking, and sexual activity from sunrise to sunset to foster spiritual renewal.[30] In addition to facilitating a closer relationship to God, the Ramadan fast also encourages Muslims to empathize with those less fortunate than themselves.[31]

The final pillar of faith is the pilgrimage to Mecca. At least once during their lifetime, individuals are expected to make the pilgrimage unless financial or physical impediments exist.[32] During the pilgrimage, individuals often experience a oneness with God and recognize the equality of all people before God, as Malcolm X's experience illustrates.[33] The pilgrimage was instrumental in changing Malcolm X's hatred of whites into an affirmation of the equality of all races.[34]

In many cases, the degree to which individual Muslims practice the five pillars may be a good indication of the salience of faith in their lives. Conversely, it is also important to note that Muslims may say extra prayers later in the day or trust in God's benevolent understanding when faced with circumstances that make compliance difficult (e.g., an employer refusing to allow time for prayer during work hours, restrictive school policies, child care responsibilities, etc.).[35] For Muslims in the United States, this may be a particularly important consideration, as the cultural context in the United States often differs radically from that experienced in one's culture of origin.

The Demographics of Muslims in the United States

Obtaining data that accurately reflect the status of Muslims in the United States is difficult due to the methodological limitations associated with surveying relatively small, faith-based communities that may not be evenly dispersed across the nation. For instance, perhaps the most representative survey to date, the American Muslim Poll based upon a national sample of 1,781 self-identified Muslims in 2001, may have underweighted the views of African Americans, nominal Muslims, and perhaps Anglo converts. With these limitations in mind, the American Muslim Poll indicates that close to two-thirds (64 percent) of Muslims in the United States were born outside of the country.[36]

In 1965, the United States immigration policy was changed so that the needs of the labor market replaced racial/ethnic criteria.[37] The implementation of a more equitable immigration policy allowed highly skilled Muslims from around the world to join previous generations of European immigrants in seeking a better life for themselves and their families in America. This has led to the development of a richly diverse community. Currently, the Islamic community in the United States is composed of individuals from at least eighty nations.[38] In many ways, American Muslims are a microcosm of the global Islamic community, with significant numbers arriving in recent decades. Among those born outside the United States, 36 percent arrived between 1980 and 1989, and 24 percent arrived between 1990 and 2001.[39]

Estimates of the number of Muslims in the United States range from one million[40] to eleven million,[41] with most authorities suggesting a population of four million to six million.[42] Approximately 80 percent of American Muslims are Sunnis.[43] Although most major cities have Muslim populations, large concentrations are located in Boston, Chicago, the Detroit–Toledo corridor, Houston, Los Angeles, and New York City.[44] Shiites, who constitute the remaining 20 percent, form significant communities in Chicago, Detroit, Los Angeles, New York City, and Washington, D.C.[45] While almost every state has a Muslim population of some size, particularly heavy concentrations exist in California and New York.[46]

Reflecting global demographics, the American Islamic community is composed of significant populations from Asia and the Middle East and North Africa, as well as African Americans.[47] Data on ethnicity from the American Muslim Poll are reported in Table 21.1. As stated above, this survey may underestimate the number of African American Muslims since the survey methodology specified that 20 percent of the

Table 21.1

Demographics of Muslims in the United States (*N* = 1,781)

Ethnicity		Age Group	
South Asian	32%	18–29 years	23%
Pakistani	17%	30–49 years	51%
Indian	7%	50–64 years	20%
Bangladesh	4%	65 + years	7%
Afghan	4%	Education	
Arab	26%	< High school	6%
African American	20%	High school graduate	12%
African	7%	Some college	24%
Other	14%	College graduate	58%
Unsure	1%	Income*	
Gender		<$15,000	10%
Male	59%	$15,000–$24,999	10%
Female	41%	$25,000–$34,999	13%
Marital Status		$35,000–$49,999	17%
Married	69%	$50,000–$74,999	22%
Single, never divorced	19%	$75,000 or more	28%
Divorced, separated, widowed	11%		

*17 percent of respondents declined to report their income.

Source: American Muslim Poll (Washington, D.C.: Project MAPS, 2001).

respondents were African Americans. Estimates of the number of African Americans in the Islamic community tend to be higher, typically in the 30 to 40 percent range.[48]

The vast majority of African American Muslims, who are largely converts to Islam, are Sunnis.[49] Although the Nation of Islam, headed by the charismatic Louis Farrakhan, is often portrayed in the media as representative of African American Muslims, it speaks for only a small portion of African American Muslims. The Nation of Islam, which has an estimated membership of 10,000[50] to 50,000,[51] is widely considered by other Muslims to be outside the bounds of mainstream Islam.

As the demographic data in Table 21.1 suggest, Muslims in the United States tend to be highly educated and financially secure.[52] More than 40 percent work in managerial, medical, or professional/technical occupations, and half earn more than $50, 000 annually.[53] Foreign-born Muslims, in particular, tend to be members of the middle to upper-middle class.[54]

Concurrently, it is important to recall that many Muslims are disadvantaged. There tends to be a significant cultural, occupational, and economic gap between foreign-born and African American Muslims. In addition, some immigrants are quite poor, such as those individuals who were forced to immigrate because of political unrest in their country of origin. Roughly a quarter of regular mosque participants live in households with incomes below $20,000, less than half the median household income.[55]

As one might expect, given the diversity that exists among American Muslims, some degree of tension exists within the Islamic community.[56] These tensions are frequently mitigated, however, by the community's need to face the dominant secular culture with a united front. As they struggle to preserve their faith, Muslims often focus on points of shared interest that are particularly important to the Islamic community at large, such as the family.

Muslim Families

Family plays a central role in Islamic culture. The word *family* can be used in a more expansive sense than is typical in Western secular culture. Within secular culture, the image that the term family tends to bring to mind is that of the "nuclear family," two adults and possibly one or more children. Within Islamic culture, the term family is often associated with what the secular culture would refer to as the extended family or kin network. In its broadest usage, family can even refer to the local, national, or global Islamic community.[57]

Marriage is perceived, not just as the joining of two individuals, but also as a union of two extended kin networks. The concept of lifelong singleness is foreign to Islam, and divorce, while permitted, is strongly discouraged. Marriage is viewed as a means of spiritual and personal fulfillment that fosters the social good.[58] In contrast with the secular culture's emphasis on appearance, qualities such as education, spirituality, and quality of character are emphasized in mate selection in Islamic culture. As is the case with many other important decisions in life, many Muslims seek the wisdom of the wider kin networks for advice on appropriate marriage partners.[59] In some cases, this trust may be exemplified by marriages that are arranged by the kin networks. The family also bears responsibility for ensuring that the marriage succeeds and that all parties are content.

The American *egalitarian marriage model* held up as an ideal in secular culture generally holds little appeal to Muslims, who value mutual respect rather than secular notions of equality.[60] Husbands and wives are traditionally held to be of equal worth but also to have complementary roles.[61] Men are responsible for the material provision and leadership of the family, while women have the primary responsibility for maintaining the home and raising the children. Men generally oversee and have the final word on decisions in the public sphere, while women make the decisions about child-rearing and household concerns.

Affirmation of a *complementary marriage model* does not necessarily mean that women are precluded from working outside the home or that men do not participate in housework.[62] In actuality, women commonly work outside the home, and men frequently assist with housework. As a mark of mutual respect, spouses often consult with each other when faced with important decisions.[63]

Women's employment outside the home is typically held in tension with providing a nurturing environment for the family, particularly young children. Children

are considered a blessing from God, and large families are generally encouraged. A secure mother–child attachment is held to be critical to children's well-being and, by extension, the future health of the Islamic community. Mothers generally prefer to spend as much time as possible with their children, which also allows them the opportunity to enculturate Islamic values and preserve their heritage.[64]

Parents often play a role in the lives of their children that is analogous to the role played by peer groups in the lives of children in the secular culture.[65] Girls participate with their mothers in various activities, and boys often accompany their fathers. Children typically bond closely with their parents, siblings, and other family members. Youth are considered to be men and women upon reaching puberty, at which point they often begin practicing the five pillars of faith. Furthermore, little concern is expressed that post-puberty youth differentiate from the family unit, as interconnectedness among family members is valued.[66] Youth are encouraged to care for other family members, and it is common for parents to role model this value by having elders stay with the family rather than placing them in an institutional setting.[67] Elders are respected for their wisdom and experience and often function as mediators for other members of the kin network when family problems arise.

Families are typically marked by a strong sense of cohesion and interdependency. Group counseling may be seen as a violation of family privacy and consequently is not widely accepted among Muslims.[68] Family and individual counseling is usually advised. Utilizing spiritual ecomaps,[69] which highlight an existential relationship with environmental resources, and spiritual genograms,[70] which focus on family relationships over time, can be useful in identifying personal and environmental assets.

For social workers socialized to view secular norms as "universal," Muslim families can seem to be enmeshed in a maladjusted, unhealthy manner.[71] As an expression of spiritual competency, it is important for social workers to work within the family's value system to find solutions to problems. Practitioners must refrain from imposing, either explicitly or implicitly, secular values that popular culture may affirm as "normal" and "universal." Social workers must ensure that they respect complementary marriages, cohesive family units, and other Islamic values that Muslims may hold.

Common Cultural Values in Islamic Discourse

Muslims commonly affirm a number of values, including community, God's sovereignty, modesty, virtue, and nutrition. Rather than understanding these values as a series of separate entities, they should be viewed as interrelated constructs reflecting the unified, holistic Islamic cosmology.

Community

Community is a significant Islamic value.[72] Flowing from the belief that all people are equal under God, Muslims tend to see themselves a part of an extended, faith-based family—the Islamic community. As occurs with a family, members care for and are responsible to the community, and the community is responsible for and cares for its members in a reciprocal relationship.

Because Muslims see themselves as part of a larger community, individual aspirations are held in tension with the preferences of others. Muslims tend to emphasize benevolence, care for others, cooperation between individuals, empathy, equality and justice between people, the importance of social support, and positive human relatedness.[73] As part of being in a community, individual preference is often circumscribed so as not to harm other members of the community. Consequently, in contrast to the explicit, overt communication valued in the secular culture, Muslims often prefer implicit forms of communication that are highly sensitive to others' needs and concerns.[74] Similarly, secular individualistic values such as personal success, self-actualization, self-reliance, and personal autonomy hold somewhat less attraction for Muslims, who tend to find meaning in group success, community development, interdependence, and consensus.[75]

Much like the extended family, the community protects and empowers the individual.[76] For instance, African American women report finding a safe social space from the inequalities they experience in the larger culture, and this empowers them to redefine themselves in a positive manner.[77] Similarly, immigrant Muslim women report that the Islamic community provides a haven of safety that is instrumental in helping them cope with the stresses of adapting to a new societal context.[78]

Because individual identity is intertwined with the community's identity, every individual has a responsibility to protect the community.[79] In school settings, for instance, Muslim students may feel responsible to defend siblings, family, and faith when these dimensions of community are attacked.[80] Similarly, as an expression of their desire to protect the well-being of the community, elders often mentor other community members.

God's Sovereignty

Muslims believe that God brought the Islamic community into being. God is understood to be omnipotent and personal—at the center of the Muslim's existence.[81] Nothing happens to the Muslim apart from God's will. While this belief is sometimes thought to engender fatalism, more properly it prepares Muslims to face hardship and fosters perseverance during trials. Further, because life is a transitory journey on the road to eternal life, Muslims can face the future with optimism. The eternal perspective can foster a sense of existential meaning that facilitates coping during difficult situations.[82]

In keeping with the centrality of God in the Muslim's life, cognitive interventions based upon the shari'a may be particularly effective. While traditional psychotherapy and group counseling may not be widely accepted among Muslims,[83] cognitive therapy, in which unproductive beliefs are identified and replaced with God's precepts, has been demonstrated to be at least as effective as traditional forms of therapy with anxiety disorders,[84] bereavement,[85] and depression,[86] while concurrently ameliorating problems at a faster rate.

In addition to God, the Muslim cosmology includes belief in Satan, angels, and supernatural beings referred to as *jins*. Possession by a jin is a legitimate possibility in the Muslim cosmology and, accordingly, should not automatically be taken as an indication of psychosis.[87] As noted in the DSM, it is important to take cultural norms and values into account when conducting an assessment.[88]

Modesty

Another cultural value that is widely affirmed is modesty, particularly around members of the opposite sex.[89] While there is wide agreement in the Islamic community that modesty is an important value, much debate has occurred regarding how this value should be operationalized in American society. For men, the issue is not as keenly felt since Islamic standards regarding what is considered modest clothing for men overlap with secular views. The issue is more significant for women. Views on what constitutes modest apparel for women range from what secular culture deems modest to clothing that covers everything except the hands and face. Thus, many Muslim women wear a headcovering of some type, such as a scarf, a practice referred to as veiling or *hijab*. Because the practice of veiling has no mainstream cultural counterpart, women who choose to veil often face ridicule and discrimination.[90]

Related to modesty are Islamic views on social relationships between the sexes. Many Muslims feel that men and women should not mix socially with members of the opposite gender.[91] Some Muslims feel that, outside of interactions that occur within the family, the sexes should be separated after kindergarten.[92] Others believe that interaction between the sexes is permissible in a group context. When working with youth, in particular, social workers should be careful to respect Islamic norms about mixing with members of the opposite gender. In cases where it is necessary to meet with someone of the opposite gender, holding the meeting in an open, public forum may be acceptable.[93]

Secular dating patterns are widely seen as problematic, especially for youth. Dating can be a contentious issue in Muslim households, particularly when parents and youth hold different views of what constitutes proper Islamic behavior.[94] While social workers may be tempted to side with a youth's desire for greater freedom, it is advisable to explore solutions that are congruent with the family's value system.

Virtue

Modesty can be seen as one dimension of virtue. In classic Islamic thought, virtue provides the foundation for human happiness.[95] Islam affirms a set of moral and ethical norms that have much in common with other theistic faiths. Behavior that is injurious to others—whether mentally, physically, or morally—is forbidden. The equality of all individuals before God is upheld, along with the need to treat others with respect and honesty.[96]

Muslims also affirm the sanctity of human life, generally from conception to natural death. Thus, euthanasia, suicide, and abortion, except in instances when the mother's life is at stake, are not permitted.[97] Homosexuality, which is understood to be socially constructed, is not sanctioned.[98] Sexual activity is reserved for marriage and is viewed as a gift from God.[99]

Nutrition

As part of a holistic cosmology, Muslims generally follow a dietary code to promote physical and spiritual well-being. Many Muslims only eat meat that is considered *halal*, a term used to describe beef, poultry, and sheep that have been lawfully slaughtered according to Islamic specifications.[100] Some Muslims adopt a vegetarian diet to avoid meat that is not halal.[101] Others may accept kosher-prepared meals, which, although not the same as halal food, may be similar enough to be acceptable to some Muslims.[102] Still others will eat items from a standard Western menu as long as the food does not contain pork. The dietary code also prohibits mind-altering substances, such as alcohol.

As an aid to developing spiritual competency with Muslims, Table 21.2 delineates a number of values that are commonly affirmed in Islamic discourse and secular discourse. As emphasized above, social workers should not assume that Muslims

Table 21.2

Value Differences in Secular and Islamic Discourses*

Secular Discourse	Islamic Discourse
Individualism	Community
Separateness	Connectedness
Self-determination	Consensus
Independence	Interdependence
Self-actualization	Community actualization
Personal achievement and success	Group achievement and success
Self-reliance	Community reliance
Respect for individual rights	Respect for community rights
Self-expression	Self-control
Sensitivity to individual oppression	Sensitivity to group oppression
Identity rooted in sexuality and work	Identity rooted in culture and God
Egalitarian gender roles	Complementary gender roles
Pro-choice	Pro-life
Sexuality expressed based on individual choice	Sexuality expressed in marriage
Explicit communication that clearly expresses individual opinion	Implicit communication that safeguards others' opinions
Spirituality and morality individually constructed	Spirituality and morality derived from the *shari'a*
Material orientation	Spiritual/eternal orientation

*Table adapted from D. R. Hodge, "Social Work and the House of Islam: Orienting Practitioners to the Beliefs and Values of Muslims in the United States," *Social Work* 50 (2005): 162–173.

or secularists will affirm all the delineated values. Many secularists, for example, hold pro-life views, and many self-identified Muslims exhibit explicit communication styles that clearly express their opinions. In addition, many of the values listed in Table 21.2 are held in tension with one another. Muslims retain a sense of individualism, for example, while conceiving of themselves as a community. In short, Table 21.2 should not be viewed as a rigid typology but rather should be seen as a visual means of creating awareness regarding possible value differences that may exist between adherents of an Islamic worldview and a secular worldview.

Structural Factors in the Social Environment

Social work theory on oppression states that a difference in worldviews in conjunction with a power differential between the worldviews tends to foster bias toward the worldview without access to power.[103] In other words, the dominant culture tends to oppress the subordinate culture in areas where a conflict in worldviews or value systems occurs. As Gilligan's[104] work illustrates, females and males affirm different value systems; consequently, females tend to encounter discrimination in settings where males have more power.

Diaphobia and Religious Stereotypes

Just as the term sexism was developed to describe gender-based bias, the term *diaphobia* has been used to describe animosity that is directed toward a divine worldview in which a transcendent God serves as the ultimate point of reference.[105] As adherents of a subordinate, theistically based culture in the dominant secular culture, Muslims often encounter bias. Diaphobia is manifested in the formation of spiritual prejudices and religious stereotypes among secularists. The beliefs, values, and practices of Islamic culture are not evaluated on their own terms. Rather they are evaluated according to the criteria established by the secular culture. Secular culture functions as the final arbitrator of right and wrong. Values falling outside of the secular value system are implicitly characterized as morally deficient. In short, diaphobic tendencies manifest themselves most prominently in areas where Islamic values differ from those affirmed by the secular culture.[106]

Muslims consider prejudice and stereotyping to be one of the most important issues facing the Islamic community in the United States.[107] Spiritual prejudices and religious stereotypes are disseminated throughout American society via the media, educational sector, and other culture-shaping institutions. Research has documented that secular actors, such as the *New York Times*, exhibit bias toward Muslims.[108] Observers have delineated how the rich diversity of Islamic culture is frequently transformed in media depictions of Muslims into denigrating images connoting ignorance, oppression, fanaticism, and violence.[109] Muslims are acutely aware of how they are characterized. More than two-thirds (68 percent) think that the media is unfair in its portrayal of Muslims and Islam, and almost eight in ten (77 percent) think that Hollywood portrays Muslims and Islam unfairly.[110]

Similar tendencies have been documented in the social work literature. Research has explored how people of faith, including Muslims, are portrayed in social work textbooks.[111] The small amount of material devoted to faith groups tends to reflect the worldview of the dominant secular culture rather than the perspective of Muslims and other people of faith. In other words, Muslims are not depicted as they would tend to characterize themselves, a practice that leaves social workers unequipped to work in a spiritually sensitive manner. Rather, texts tend to depict Muslims as they are seen through the lens of the dominant secular culture, a practice that sets social workers up to reinforce the diaphobic stereotypes and prejudices that exist in the larger secular culture.

For instance, one social work textbook reports that the Muslim world abounds with "horror tales of crimes against humanity," and that the "moral agenda" of Middle Eastern countries "is the complete enslavement of women."[112] Such portrayals do not represent the self-descriptions of most Muslims. The Muslim world, of course, is not completely devoid of human atrocities, but then neither is the secular world free of "crimes against humanity." As Gellner[113] has observed, the secular worldview flowing from the European Enlightenment directly fostered the French Revolution, communism, and, indirectly, National Socialism. These movements have resulted in the deaths of tens of millions of human beings and inflicted untold suffering upon millions of others. It is noteworthy that human atrocities of this magnitude are essentially without parallel in the Muslim world.

Research that has examined the relationship between Islam and human rights has found that governments rooted in Islam do not foster the abuse of human rights.[114] An examination of 23 predominantly Muslim countries with a control group of non-Muslim nations found that both upheld the same level of human rights. Highlighting examples of human depravity in Muslim nations while simultaneously downplaying or even ignoring instances of human depravity flowing from a secular worldview does little to foster understanding between people.

As implied above, similar dynamics occur when discussing women. The issue of veiling in particular is a flashpoint in secular discourse. In some Western nations, secularists have even worked to abrogate Muslims' rights by attempting to ban girls from wearing the hijab in public schools.[115] For many in the secular culture, hijab has come to symbolize the oppression of women that is believed to occur in Islamic culture.[116]

Muslim women, however, frequently view the situation quite differently. From the perspective of many Muslim women, it is secular culture that oppresses women.[117] Secular culture is viewed as fostering lack of respect for women by, for example, reducing women to sexual objects; engendering high levels of debilitating eating disorders; promoting a hedonistic, narcissistic climate in which men walk away from their commitments to their wives and children; producing popular music that glamorizes the humiliation of women; and creating a milieu in which rape, sexual assault, and physical violence against women are everyday occurrences. Such degradation of women is comparatively rare in Islamic communities, where, it is held, women are treated with respect.[118]

Counter to secular assumptions, many women view the practice of hijab as liberating.[119] Veiling is seen as emancipation from a secular culture that celebrates immodesty. Donning hijab communicates that the woman is to be elevated above the level of a sexual object and that she is to be treated with respect based upon her abilities. It is also important to note that veiling occurs for many other mutually compatible reasons. For example, as an expression of their spirituality, many women veil to express their obedience to God. Many Muslims veil for the sense of safety and peace that the practice engenders. The practice may also symbolize pride in Islam.

Social workers must guard against reducing complex, multifaceted issues to simplistic caricatures. Portraying secular values as liberating and Islamic values as oppressive does little to foster understanding. To work effectively with Muslims, it is important to be able to see the world through an Islamic lens. Spiritually competent practice occurs at the point where social workers have developed an empathetic understanding of how Muslims view the world.

The biased characterizations in the secular culture have fostered a sense of mistrust and dislocation among Muslims in the United States. These portrayals also help create an atmosphere in which discrimination against Muslims is legitimated in schools, workplaces, and other public forums.[120] Employers, for instance, may fire Muslims for praying during lunch hour. Public school teachers may attempt to abrogate Muslims' constitutional rights by banning students from wearing the hijab or discriminating against papers that deal with Islamic topics.

Due to fear that they will be misunderstood or discriminated against, Muslims may be reluctant to seek assistance from social workers and other human services professionals.[121] Social workers can address this concern by showing interest in Islam[122] and becoming familiar with Islamic values.[123] Emphasizing traditional empathetic qualities, such as care, genuineness, respect, support, and warmth, can also help overcome initial concerns.[124] Similarly, meeting practical needs, such as advocating on behalf of oppressed Muslims, can also help build bridges.[125]

Civil Rights

To advocate for Muslim concerns, social workers must be aware of the environmental resources that exist. Social workers should take the time to familiarize themselves with relevant statutes, organizations, and institutions so that the appropriate resources can be brought to bear in a given context. The free exercise clause of the U.S. Constitution protects individuals' right to freely express their faith in public settings. The web sites of the U.S. Equal Employment Opportunity Commission (EEOC) and the Department of Education contain information on, respectively, employees' and students' free exercise rights. Particularly useful is the updated version[126] of former President Clinton's[127] memorandum on the free exercise rights of students in public schools.

School social workers, in particular, should also be aware of the Equal Access Act (P.L. 98-377) and Protection of Pupil Rights Amendment (PPRA) (20 U.S.C. §1232h). The Equal Access Act ensures that students of faith have the same right to school facilities as secular students. Schools cannot, for example, allow an environmental club to meet in an empty classroom and refuse to provide a classroom for Muslim students to perform daily prayers.[128] The PPRA provides federal protection for parents' and students' rights whenever federal funding is involved. Under PPRA, parents have the right to inspect instructional material that addresses a number of controversial areas, including content on sexuality, to ensure that it conforms to their values. To prevent the imposition of secular values, schools must make parents aware that such material is being presented and obtain written consent from parents before exposing children to any of the material.

Muslim Organizations

Social workers should also be aware of the institutions that Muslims have developed to cope with living in a secular culture. Perhaps the most prominent is the *masjid*, or *mosque*. More than 1,200 mosques exist in the United States, and almost 90 percent were founded since 1970.[129] The services offered by mosques in the United States have evolved substantially to meet the unique needs of the Islamic community. In traditional Muslim countries, mosques tend to be places where Muslims have the option of gathering for prayer, particularly Friday midday prayers. In North America, to provide a greater degree of social support to the Islamic community, mosques have tended to expand the range of services they offer. In addition to traditional prayer services, mosques often function as centers for an increasingly diverse array of services, including education for children and adults, counseling services, prison programs, daycare, and youth activities.[130]

The Muslim Student Association (MSA) is the largest student organization serving the Islamic community in the United States. According to Altaf Husain (personal communication), president of the MSA, there are currently more than 500 chapters in the United States. They offer a number of religious and cultural services, including, perhaps most importantly, social support to the hundreds of thousands of Muslims enrolled in American college campuses.[131]

As an outgrowth of the MSA, former students founded the Islamic Society of North America (ISNA), perhaps the most prominent Muslim organization in the United States.[132] The ISNA attempts to foster a degree of commitment and community among American Muslims, both through its own actions and by facilitating a large number of locally based organizations throughout the country.[133] ISNA activities are diverse and address most dimensions of Muslim life in America. Services include the provision of instructional materials, journals, workshops, library facilities, housing assistance, a charity fund, women's services, and a marriage bureau that operates a computerized database for matching single individuals with potential partners. Although ISNA attempts to serve all segments of the Muslim population, it tends to be perceived as an organization tailored primarily to meet the needs of immigrants.[134] The Muslim American Society performs many of the same functions for African American Muslims, and numerous additional Muslim organizations have been founded in recent years, with varying degrees of support among the general Muslim population.

Recently emigrated Muslims may be unaware of the range of programs available, since many of the services that have evolved are unique to the American Islamic community. Social workers who are familiar with the array of services in a given area can often function as brokers, linking Muslims to extant programs. The resources and social support such programs provide are often crucial in helping Muslims deal with the stress associated with religious stereotypes, racism, gender inequality, and immigration.[135]

Similarly, many Muslims may be unaware of the legislative statutes that protect their religious liberties in the United States. The history of their own people in their nation of origin may incline Muslims to believe that the justice system in this nation is also partial and prejudiced. While the court system in the United States is far from perfect, perpetrators of violence and discrimination against Muslims are regularly convicted.

Historical Factors

While historical influences are critical to any population, they may be especially salient with Muslims who have recently immigrated to the United States. As noted previously, Muslims in the United States originate from at least 80 different nations.[136] Traumatic events, such as war, famine, and persecution in individuals' culture of origin, can shape how individuals interact with governments, the extent to which they trust "the system," and even their willingness to trust social workers. Similarly, African American Muslims are shaped by a history of racism that often affects their ability to trust European American institutions.

Social workers who regularly work with Muslims from a particular ethnic or national background should consider learning more about that cultural group and the historical influences that shape its interpretation of Islam. For instance, social workers who regularly work with African American Muslims might review Solomon's article on African Americans.[137] Even though the article does not specifically address Muslims, readers are likely to find many of the historical and cultural insights useful in work with African American Muslims. The ramifications of events from previous eras echo down through time, influencing present attitudes and practices.

In tandem with culturally specific influences, it is also important to develop an awareness of historical developments that have shaped the collective Islamic identity. In attempting to work out the implications of an Islamic worldview, Muslims have provided numerous scientific, literary, and artistic contributions to the world. Social workers are unlikely to be familiar with many of these developments since the dominant secular culture tends to highlight advancements that flow from the European Enlightenment. Consequently, social workers might consider familiarizing themselves with some of the major Islamic innovations in these fields.

September 11th

Another historical influence that all Muslims in the United States share is the legacy of the terrorist attacks on American facilities, the most prominent being the September 11, 2001, attacks on the Pentagon and the World Trade Center towers. The effects on the Islamic community and the general population have been complex. The fact that the terrorists were Arab and self-identified as Muslims played into lingering stereotypes and prejudices with the result that innocent law-abiding Muslims were often victimized in the immediate aftermath of the attacks.[138] In a series of high-profile appearances, President Bush stressed that Islam is a religion of peace, emphasized that Muslims should be treated with respect, and defended the right of Muslim women to wear the hijab in public settings without fear.[139]

Subsequently, public perceptions of Muslims became significantly more favorable. In fact, the general public's view of Muslims was more favorable six months after September 11 than it was before the terrorists' attack.[140]

These developments seem generally congruent with the experience of Muslims in the United States in the months after the attack. When asked to give their opinion on Americans' attitudes toward Muslims since September 11, approximately three-quarters (74 percent) stated that, in their personal experience, Americans had been respectful and tolerant of Muslims.[141]

Concurrently, it is important to note that September 11 fostered an increase in anti-Muslim discrimination. Incidents of alleged discrimination filed by Muslims with the Equal Employment Opportunity Commission (EEOC) from September 11, 2001, to May 7, 2002, more than doubled compared with the number filed one year previously (497 vs. 193).[142] Muslim organizations that track reports of bias reported a threefold increase, including incidents of murder, with reports of discrimination being particularly prominent at airports and ports of entry.[143] Just over half of Muslims (52 percent) know of at least one incident of anti-Muslim discrimination in their community since September 11.[144]

While incidents of discrimination may have declined in the months following September 11,[145] a more long-term concern may be The Uniting and Strengthening America by Proudly Appropriating Tools Required to Intercept and Obstruct Terrorism Act of 2001 (H.R. 3162), better known by its acronym, the USA Patriot Act. The USA Patriot Act was passed by Congress in the aftermath of September 11 with little debate. Criticized by members of both the political right and left, the legislation expands government powers, critics argue, at the expense of civil liberties, while the erosion of civil liberties diminishes everyone's freedom, and many Muslims are concerned that they will be unduly targeted.

Implications for Micro and Macro Practice

The ecosystems approach helps social workers look beyond the level of the individual to complex environmental realities that shape Muslims' existence in the United States. More specifically, it is important to remember the following: the Muslim client is part of an extended family that is informed by Islamic values, which exists in a social environment animated by both detrimental and beneficial structural factors, which in turn is influenced by culturally specific historical events such as September 11. As noted previously, Figure 21.1 encapsulates some of the issues that should be examined at each level of the ecosystems model when working with Muslims.

In assessing problems and designing solutions, social workers should consider each of the concentric spheres of the ecosystems approach. Interventions can be aimed at any single level or combination of levels. Clients, however, are much more likely to own and apply suggested interventions if social workers have considered the multiple facets of existence that are represented by the ecosystems model. As the following example illustrates, developing intervention strategies that are appropriate, relevant, and sensitive to the client's worldview typically requires consideration of each level of the ecosystem model.

Figure 21.1

Example of Ecosystems Model for Muslims in the United States

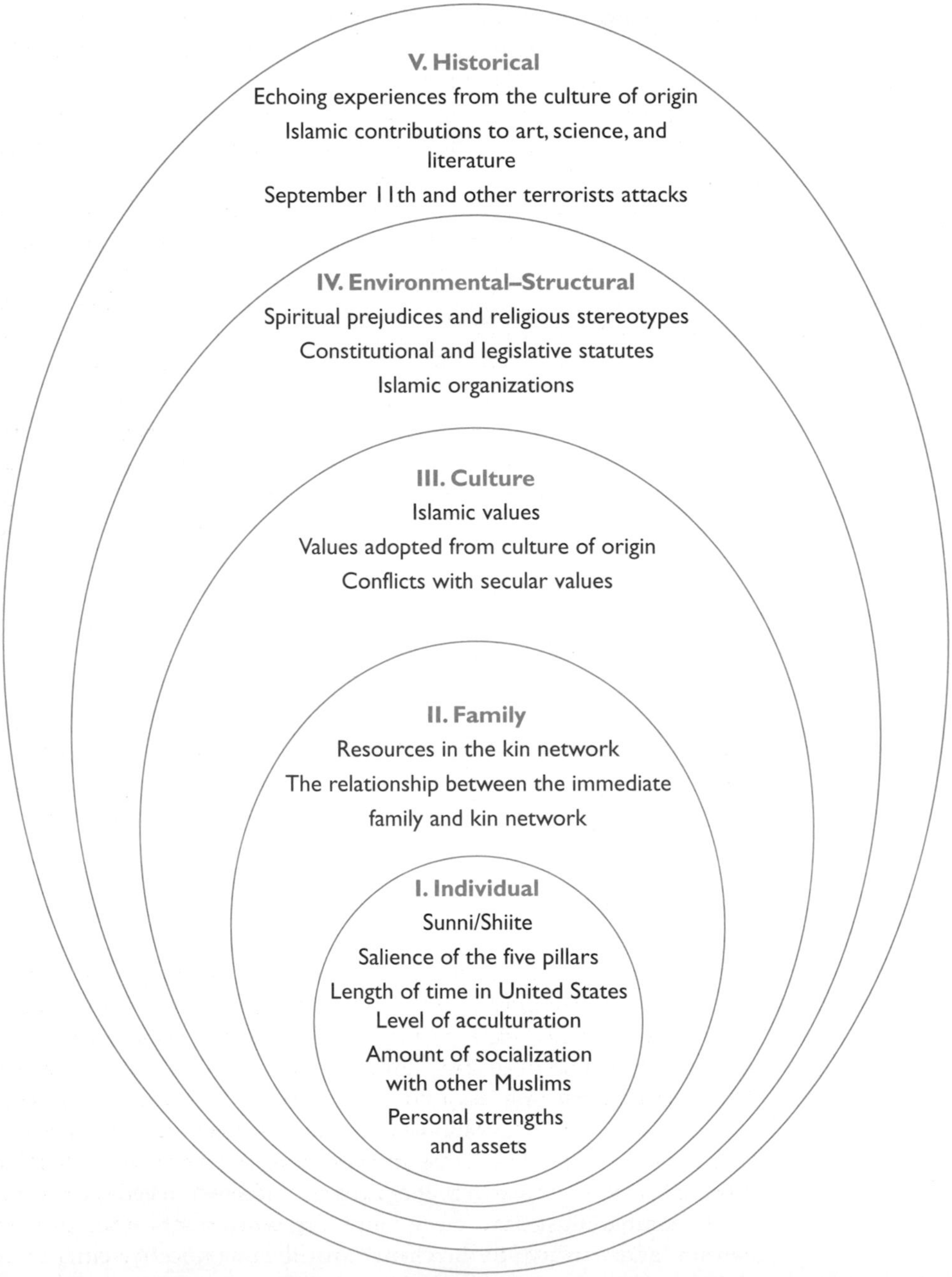

V. Historical

Echoing experiences from the culture of origin

Islamic contributions to art, science, and literature

September 11th and other terrorists attacks

IV. Environmental–Structural

Spiritual prejudices and religious stereotypes

Constitutional and legislative statutes

Islamic organizations

III. Culture

Islamic values

Values adopted from culture of origin

Conflicts with secular values

II. Family

Resources in the kin network

The relationship between the immediate family and kin network

I. Individual

Sunni/Shiite

Salience of the five pillars

Length of time in United States

Level of acculturation

Amount of socialization with other Muslims

Personal strengths and assets

THE INDIVIDUAL

Mustafa, a 12-year-old boy, was in danger of being expelled from public school for fighting. A Sunni Muslim, Mustafa was born in Detroit, to where his parents had emigrated from Turkey. In previous years, Mustafa had attended a private Islamic school. When Mustafa's father was transferred to California, the family decided to enroll Mustafa in a public school since there were no Islamic schools in the local vicinity. Bright and articulate, and in previous years an excellent student, Mustafa's grades had dropped considerably since he started attending public school a few months ago.

Although Kerry, the school social worker, initially found Mustafa to be somewhat uncommunicative, Mustafa became increasingly open as Kerry wondered about the difficulty Mustafa must have encountered switching from an Islamic school to a public school. Mustafa slowly began sharing some of the problems he was facing as a student of faith in a secular environment. He often found himself going hungry on days the cafeteria served food that contained pork. On Earth Day, one of his teachers had led the class in a meditation session in which students were to visualize themselves as part of Mother Nature, a practice that made Mustafa extremely uncomfortable due to its spiritual overtones. Another teacher had given a writing assignment in which students could write about any subject and then rejected Mustafa's paper, which argued for the sanctity of life from an Islamic perspective, on the grounds that it was "too religious." Although he got along with most students, some ridiculed his faith, called him a "terrorist," and disparaged his mother, who wears a veil, when she came to pick him up at school. Mustafa felt that he had to defend his faith and family, with his fists if necessary.

THE FAMILY

Kerry arranged a meeting between Mustafa and his main system of social support, his immediate family. His family was surprised at the situation. Mustafa had not shared the problems he encountered at school because he felt that he had to stand up for the Islamic community on his own. His parents resolved to support Mustafa and communicated to him that they would handle the situations together, as a team. His mother and sisters volunteered to come to school and give a classroom presentation on hijab, explaining the reasons why Muslim women choose to veil. His father offered to share some of his experiences at his place of employment along with strategies he had developed to address the religious stereotypes and prejudices he encountered at work.

CULTURAL ISSUES

Upon meeting Mustafa's family, Kerry built trust by addressing the husband first and then, later in the conversation, asking his permission to speak to his wife and daughters. Kerry also wore modest attire and used more indirect forms of communication (e.g., "In my professional judgment..." rather than "I feel..."). Adopting a slightly more directive approach, Kerry explored a number of concrete options that might meet the family's goals. Sensitivity was shown to nonverbal forms of communication, as Kerry worked toward coming to a consensus regarding how to tackle the situation. Trust was enhanced by Kerry's demonstrated willingness to advocate with school officials on the family's behalf in a number of areas.

To address the dietary issues concerning pork, Kerry contacted the food services personnel. They arranged for school menus to be sent to Mustafa's mother a week in advance. With prior notice, she was able to prepare a lunch for Mustafa to take to school when the menu consisted of food that was not halal.

ENVIRONMENTAL–STRUCTURAL ISSUES

After contacting the U.S. Department of Education and obtaining constitutional guidelines on the free exercise of religion, Kerry set up a meeting with school officials. In the ensuing discussion, Kerry emphasized two points that directly addressed Mustafa's situation. First, the establishment clause of the U.S. Constitution stipulates that schools must maintain neutrality between competing spiritual belief systems. The classroom implementation of New Age forms of visualization and meditation are prohibited. Second, Kerry noted that the free exercise clause protects students' right to express their religious beliefs. Teachers cannot discriminate against a student's paper just because it presents a religious perspective.

Kerry also phoned a number of mosques in the wider vicinity to ascertain if any offered youth programs or knew of any Islamic organizations that sponsored youth programs. After locating a couple of programs, Kerry sent a letter to Mustafa's father, drawing his attention to the options.

HISTORICAL ISSUES

The historical, media-propagated associations between Islam and terrorism represented a difficult issue to address. Kerry decided to use the school's interest in environmentalism in an attempt to weaken the link between Islam and terrorism. Kerry worked with school officials to highlight that Ted Kaczynski, the Unabomber, self-identified as an environmentalist and was in a significant following in the environmental movement. Yet, because environmentalists generally affirm a value system that resonates with the dominant secular worldview, the media carefully distinguished between the majority of self-identified environmentalists, who advocate for the environment peacefully, and those self-described environmentalists who use terrorist tactics in the name of environmentalism. Consequently, few people associate environmentalism with terrorism.

Kerry pointed out that the media adopt a different agenda with Muslims since their spiritual value system fails to resonate with the secular values held by most members of the media. Even though the overwhelming majority of Muslims condemn the use of violence in the name of Islam, the media often fail to distinguish between peaceful Muslims and those who commit acts of violence. Yet, just as it is inappropriate to judge all environmentalists by those who commit violence, so too it is inappropriate to judge all Muslims by those who commit violence. We must deconstruct the ethnocentric discourse propagated by the dominant culture, Kerry argued, and welcome the enriching perspectives Muslims bring to our school, society, and nation.

From one perspective, Kerry's interventions met with mixed results. Having access to the school menus resolved the dietary issues. The presentation by Mustafa's mother and sisters on veiling, in conjunction with Kerry's coupling of Islam and environmentalism, helped foster a more tolerant environment at the school. Conversely, while the school eventually implemented a policy to end the imposition of New Age religious practices on the student population, some teachers still exhibited reluctance to accept spiritually themed papers, and Mustafa often felt that he received lower grades when his work presented an Islamic perspective. Although this discrimination was grounds for a lawsuit, Mustafa's parents declined to press the issue in court.

From the perspective of Mustafa's parents, however, Kerry's combination of micro- and macro-level interventions was a success. Mustafa's grades had improved to their former level. While Mustafa's peers at school still didn't always accept or agree with his Islamic views, they were more respectful, and, consequently, fights were a thing of the past. As is the case in other situations, consideration of each level of the ecosystems model is vital for effective, spiritually competent work with Muslims.

Concluding Comment

Muslims in the United States face an uncertain future. International events over which individual Muslims have little control, such as the U.S. military attack and occupation of Iraq, have the potential to dramatically affect the well-being of innocent, law-abiding Muslims. In addition to living with this unpredictability, Muslims must continually deal with the oppression that people of faith encounter in the dominant secular culture.

As a minority population in a hostile cultural environment, Muslims are often in need of advocacy on their behalf. Individual initiatives, legislative efforts, and international actions are needed to ensure that the rights of Muslims and other people of faith are protected. Social workers, due to their unique skill sets, are often ideally situated to provide this advocacy.

Unfortunately, in at least some instances, the social work profession itself has adopted the stance of dominant culture, propagating diaphobic stereotypes that foster misunderstanding and bias toward Muslims. Social workers, however, are called to deconstruct the assumptions of the dominant culture that affect their ability to provide services. Personal biases must be identified and addressed.

As an ethically based profession, the NASW Code of Ethics provides clear guidelines regarding the stance that social workers must adopt toward Muslims and other people of faith. More specifically, social workers should educate themselves about the oppression religious people encounter, avoid derogatory religious language, and refrain from facilitating any form of religious discrimination while actively working to prevent and eliminate religious discrimination. As the NASW Code of Ethics states, social workers are to foster respect for cultural and social diversity within the United States and globally, seeking to ensure justice for *all* people.

KEY WORDS AND CONCEPTS

Muslim
Islam
Hijab
Mosque

Diaphobia
The Five Pillars
Spiritual competency

SUGGESTED INFORMATION SOURCES

Aswad, B. C., and B. Bilge, eds. *Family and Gender Among American Muslims*. Philadelphia: Temple University Press, 1996.
Carolan, M. T., G. Bagherinia, R. Juhari, J. Himelright, and M. Mouton-Sanders. "Contemporary Muslim Families: Research and Practice," *Contemporary Family Therapy* 22, no. 1 (2000).

Crabtree, S. A., F. Husain, and B. Spalek. *Islam and Social Work: Debating Values, Transforming Practice*. London: British Association of Social Workers, 2008.

Esposito, J. L., ed. *The Oxford Encyclopedia of the Modern Islamic World*. New York: Oxford University Press, 1995.

Hodge, D. R. "Social Work and the House of Islam: Orienting Practitioners to the Beliefs and Values of Muslims in the United States," *Social Work* 50 (2005): 162–173.

Mahmoud, V. "African American Muslim Families," in M. McGoldrick, J. Giordano, and J. K. Pearce, eds., *Ethnicity and Family Therapy*, 2nd ed. New York: Guilford Press, 1996, pp. 122–128.

Smith, J. I. *Islam in America*. New York: Columbia University Press, 1999.

ENDNOTES

1. Yvonne Yazbeck Haddad and Jane I. Smith, "United States of America," in John L. Esposito, ed., *The Oxford Encyclopedia of the Modern Islamic World*, vol. 4 (New York: Oxford University Press, 1995), pp. 277–284.

2. J. Gordon Melton, *The Encyclopedia of American Religions*, 6th ed. (London: Gale Research, 1999).

3. Yvonne Yazbeck Haddad, "Make Room for the Muslims?" in Walter H. Conser Jr. and Summer B. Twiss, eds., *Religious Diversity and American Religious History* (Athens: The University of Georgia Press, 1997), pp. 218–261; P. Scott Richards and Allen E. Bergin, *A Spiritual Strategy* (Washington, D.C.: American Psychological Association, 1997).

4. Belkeis Y. Altareb, "Islamic Spirituality in America: A Middle Path to Unity," *Counseling and Values* 41, no. 1 (1996): 29–38; Manijeh Daneshpour, "Muslim Families and Family Therapy," *Journal of Marital and Family Therapy* 24, no. 3 (1998): 355–390; Anahid Kulwicki, "Health Issues Among Arab Muslim Families," in Barbara C. Aswad and Barbara Bilge, eds., *Family and Gender Among American Muslims* (Philadelphia: Temple University Press, 1996), pp. 187–207; Eugene W. Kelly, Amany Aridi, and Laleh Bakhtiar, "Muslims in the United States: An Exploratory Study of Universal and Mental Health Values," *Counseling and Values* 40, no. 3 (1996): 206–218; Vanessa Mahmoud, "African American Muslim Families," in Monica McGoldrick, Joe Giordano, and John K. Pearce, eds., *Ethnicity and Family Therapy*, 2nd ed. (New York: Guilford Press, 1996), pp. 122–128.

5. Edward R. Canda and Leola Dyrud Furman, *Spiritual Diversity in Social Work Practice* (New York: The Free Press, 1999).

6. NASW Code of Ethics, 1999, http://www.socialworkers.org/pubs/code/default.asp (accessed November 24, 2008).

7. David P. Boyle and Alyson Springer, "Toward a Cultural Competence Measure for Social Work with Specific Populations," *Journal of Ethic and Cultural Diversity in Social Work* 9, no. 3/4 (2001): 53–71.

8. Derald Wing Sue, Patricia Arredondo, and Roderick J. McDavis, "Multicultural Counseling Competencies and Standards: A Call to the Profession," *Journal of Counseling and Development* 70, no. 4 (1992): 477–486.

9. Daneshpour, op. cit.

10. Marsha T. Carolan, et al., "Contemporary Muslim Families: Research and Practice," *Contemporary Family Therapy* 22, no. 1 (2000): 67–79.

11. Dale F. Eickelman, *The Middle East and Central Asia*, 3rd ed. (Upper Saddle River, NJ: Prentice Hall, 1998).

12. David Waines, *An Introduction to Islam* (Cambridge: Cambridge University Press, 1995).

13. John L. Esposito, *Islam* (New York: Oxford University Press, 1988).

14. Eickelman, op. cit.

15. John Renard, *Responses to 101 Questions on Islam* (Mahwah, NJ: Paulist Press, 1998).

16. Waines, op. cit.; Syed Arshad Husain, "Religion and Mental Health from the Muslim Perspective," in Harold G. Koenig, ed., *Handbook of Religion and Mental Health* (New York: Academic Press, 1998), pp. 279–291.

17. Paul Lawrence and Cathy Rozmus, "Culturally Sensitive Care of the Muslim Patient," *Journal of Transcultural Nursing* 12, no. 3 (2001): pp. 228–233.

18. Eickelman, op. cit.

19. Ibid.

20. Mahmoud M. Ayoub, "United States of America," in John L. Esposito, ed., *The Oxford Encyclopedia of the Modern Islamic World*, vol. 3 (New York: Oxford University Press, 1995), pp. 333–334.

21. Esposito, *Islam*, op. cit.

22. Ayoub, op. cit.

23. Gamal Abou El Azayem and Zari Hedayat-Diba, "The Psychological Aspects of Islam: Basic Principles of Islam and Their Psychological Corollary," *The International Journal for the Psychology of Religion* 4, no. 1 (1994): 41–50.

24. Esposito, *Islam*, op. cit.

25. Gamal Abou El Azayem, op. cit.

26. Eickelman, op. cit.

27. Husain, op. cit.

28. Renard, op. cit.

29. Esposito, *Islam*, op. cit.

30. Eickelman, op. cit.

31. Altareb, op. cit.

32. Esposito, *Islam*, op. cit.

33. Altareb, op. cit.

34. Akbar S. Ahmed, "Popular Religion in Europe and the Americas," in John L. Esposito, ed., *The Oxford Encyclopedia of the Modern Islamic World*, vol. 3 (New York: Oxford University Press, 1995), pp. 354–358.

35. Elise Goldwasser, "Economic Security and Muslim Identity: A Study of the Immigrant Community in Durham, North Carolina," in Yvonne Haddad and John L. Esposito, eds., *Muslims on the Americanization Path?* (Atlanta: Scholars Press, 1998), pp. 379–397; Jane I. Smith, *Islam in America* (New York: Columbia University Press, 1999).

36. American Muslim Poll (Washington, D.C.: Project MAPS: Muslims in the American Public Square, 2001).

37. Haddad and Smith, "United States of America," op. cit.

38. American Muslim Poll, op. cit.

39. Ibid., op. cit.

40. Barry A. Kosmin and Seymour P. Lachman, *One Nation Under God* (New York: Harmony Books, 1993).

41. Haddad, "Make Room for the Muslims?", op. cit.

42. Richards and Bergin, op. cit.; Eickelman, op. cit.; Akbar S. Ahmed, op. cit.; Smith, op. cit.; Frederick Mathewson Denny, "Islam in the Americas," in John L. Esposito, ed., *The Oxford Encyclopedia of the Modern Islamic World*, vol. 2 (New York: Oxford University Press, 1995), pp. 296–300.

43. Smith, op. cit.
44. Haddad and Smith, "United States of America," op. cit.; Smith, op. cit.; Denny, op. cit.; Carol L. Stone, "Estimate of Muslims Living in America," in Yvonne Yazbeck Haddad, ed., *The Muslims of America* (New York: Oxford University Press, 1991), pp. 25–36.
45. Haddad and Smith, "United States of America," op. cit.; Raymond Brady Williams, "South Asian Religions in the United States," in John R. Hinnells, ed., *A New Handbook of Living Religions* (New York: Penguin Books, 1997), pp. 796–818.
46. Kosmin and Lachman, op. cit.
47. American Muslim Poll, op. cit.; Denny, op. cit.
48. Haddad and Smith, "United States of America," op. cit.; Richards and Bergin, op. cit.; Smith, op. cit.; Kosmin and Lachman, op. cit.
49. Melton, op. cit.; Smith, op. cit.
50. Melton, op. cit.
51. Jonah Blank, "The Muslim Mainstream," *U.S. News and World Report* 20, 7 (1998): 22–25.
52. American Muslim Poll, op. cit.; Kosmin and Seymour P. Lachman, op. cit.; Denny, op. cit.
53. American Muslim Poll, op. cit.
54. Denny, op. cit.
55. Ihsan Bagby, Paul M. Perl, and Bryan T. Froehle, *The Mosque in America: A National Portrait* (Washington, D.C.: Council on American–Islamic Relations, 2001).
56. Haddad and Smith, "United States of America," op. cit.; Denny, op. cit.
57. Elizabeth Warnock Fernea, "Family," in John L. Esposito, ed., *The Oxford Encyclopedia of the Modern Islamic World,* vol. 1 (New York: Oxford University Press, 1995), pp. 458–461.
58. Dena Saadat Hassouuneh-Phillips, "'Marriage is Half of Faith and the Rest is Fear of Allah,'" *Violence Against Women* 7, no. 8 (August 2001): 927–946.
59. Smith, op. cit.
60. Carolan, et al., op. cit.
61. Altareb, op. cit.
62. Carolan, et al., op. cit.
63. Kulwicki, op. cit.
64. Smith, op. cit.
65. Yvonne Y. Haddad and Jane I. Smith, "Islamic Values Among American Muslims," in Barbara C. Aswad and Barbara Bilge, eds., *Family and Gender Among American Muslims* (Philadelphia: Temple University Press, 1996), pp. 19–40.
66. Daneshpour, op. cit.
67. Kulwicki, op. cit.
68. Munir A. Shaikh, *Teaching About Islam and Muslims in the Public School Classroom,* 3rd ed. (Fountain Valley, CA: Council on Islamic Education, 1995).
69. David R. Hodge, "Spiritual Ecomaps: A New Diagrammatic Tool for Assessing Marital and Family Spirituality," *Journal of Marital and Family Therapy* 26, no. 1 (2000): 229–240.
70. David R. Hodge, "Spiritual Genograms: A Generational Approach to Assessing Spirituality," *Families in Society* 82, no. 1 (2001): 35–48.
71. Daneshpour, op. cit.
72. Alphonso W. Haynes, et al., "Islamic Social Transformation: Considerations for the Social Worker," *International Social Work* 40 (1997): 265–275.
73. Kelly, op. cit.
74. Daneshpour, op. cit.

75. Kelly, op. cit.
76. Mumtaz F. Jafari, "Counseling Values and Objectives: A Comparison of Western and Islamic Perspectives," *The American Journal of Islamic Social Sciences* 10, no. 3 (1993): 326–339.
77. Michelle D. Byng, "Mediating Discrimination: Resisting Oppression Among African American Muslim Women," *Social Problems* 45, no. 4 (1998): 473–487.
78. Fariyal Ross-Sheriff, "Immigrant Muslim Women in the United States: Adaptation to American Society," *Journal of Social Work Research* 2, no. 2 (2001): 283–294.
79. Haynes, et al., op. cit.
80. Mahmoud, op. cit.
81. Altareb, op. cit.
82. Rafic Banawi and Rex Stockton, "Islamic Values Relevant to Group Work, with Practical Applications for the Group Leader," *The Journal for Specialists in Group Work* 18, no. 3 (1993): 151–160.
83. Ibid.
84. M. Z. Azhar, S. L. Varma, and A. S. Dharap, "Religious Psychotherapy in Anxiety Disorder Patients," *Acta Psychiatrica Scandinavica* 90 (1994): 1–2.
85. M. Z. Azhar and S. L. Varma, "Religious Psychotherapy as Management of Bereavement," *Acta Psychiatrica Scandinavica* 91 (1995): 233–235.
86. M. Z. Azhar and S. L. Varma, "Religious Psychotherapy in Depressive Patients," *Psychotherapy and Psychosomatics* 63 (1995): 165–168.
87. Husain, op. cit.
88. *Diagnostic and Statistical Manual of Mental Disorders*, 4th ed. (Washington, D.C.: American Psychiatric Association, 1994).
89. Haddad and Smith, "Islamic Values Among American Muslims," op. cit.
90. Carolan, et al., op. cit.
91. Mahmoud, op. cit.
92. Cyril Simmons, Christine Simmons, and Mohammed Habib Allah, "English, Israeli-Arab and Saudi Arabian Adolescent Values," *Educational Studies* 20, no. 1 (1994): 69–86.
93. Richard B. Carter and Amelia E. El Hindi, "Counseling Muslim Children in School Settings," *Professional School Counseling* 2, no. 3 (1999): 183–188.
94. Ibid.
95. Majed A. Ashy, "Health and Illness from an Islamic Perspective," *Journal of Religion and Health* 38, no. 3 (1999): 241–257.
96. Haddad and Smith, "Islamic Values Among American Muslims," op. cit.; Julia Mitchell Corbett, *Religion in America*, 2nd ed. (Englewood Cliffs, NJ: Prentice Hall, 1994).
97. Haddad and Smith, "Islamic Values Among American Muslims," op. cit.
98. J. Mark Halstead and Katarzyna Lewicka, "Should Homosexuality Be Taught as an Acceptable Alternative Lifestyle? A Muslim Perspective," *Cambridge Journal of Education* 28, no. 1 (1998): 49–64.
99. Husain, op. cit.
100. Smith, op. cit.
101. Charles Kemp, "Islamic Cultures: Health-Care Beliefs and Practices," *American Journal of Health Behavior* 20, no. 3 (1996): 83–89.
102. Kulwicki, op. cit.
103. Tim Hamilton and Satish Sharma, "The Violence and Oppression of Power Relations," *Peace Review* 9, no. 4 (1997): 555–561; Kathryn G. Wambach and Dorothy Van Soest, "Oppression," in Richard L. Edwards, ed., *1997 Supplement*, 19th ed. (Washington, D.C.: NASW Press, 1997), pp. 243–252.

104. Carol Gilligan, *In a Different Voice: Psychological Theory and Women's Development* (Cambridge, MA: Harvard University Press, 1993).

105. David R. Hodge, "Conceptualizing Spirituality in Social Work: How the Metaphysical Beliefs of Social Workers May Foster Bias Towards Theistic Consumers," *Social Thought* 21, no. 1 (2002): 39–61.

106. Bobby S. Sayyid, *A Fundamental Fear* (New York: St. Martin's Press, 1997).

107. American Muslim Poll, op. cit.

108. Amal Omar Madani, "Depiction of Arabs and Muslims in the United States News Media," Dissertation, California School of Professional Psychology—Los Angeles, 2000, p. 9-B; Nadege Soubiale and Nicolas Roussiau, "Social Representation of Islam and Changes in the Stereotypes of Muslims," *Psicologia, Teoria e Pesquisa: Brasilia* 14, no. 3 (September–December 1998): 191–202.

109. Greg Noakes, "Muslims and the American Press," in Yvonne Haddad and John L. Esposito, eds., *Muslims on the Americanization Path?* (Atlanta: Scholars Press, 1998), pp. 361–378; Ronald Stockton, "Ethnic Archetypes and the Arab Image," in Ernest McCarus, ed., *The Development of Arab-American Identity* (Ann Arbor: The University of Michigan Press, 1994), pp. 119–153.

110. American Muslim Poll, op. cit.

111. David R. Hodge, Lisa M. Baughman, and Julie A. Cummings, "Moving Toward Spiritual Competency: Deconstructing Religious Stereotypes and Spiritual Prejudices in Social Work Literature," Paper presented at the [Forty-Eighth Annual Program Meeting] Council on Social Work Education, February 24–27, Nashville, TN, 2002.

112. Katherine Van Wormer, *Social Welfare* (Chicago: Nelson-Hall Publishers, 1997).

113. Ernest Gellner, *Postmodernism, Reason and Religion* (New York: Routledge, 1992).

114. Daniel Price, "Islam and Human Rights: A Case of Deceptive First Appearances," *Journal for the Scientific Study of Religion* 41, no. 2 (2002): 213–225.

115. Sayyid, op. cit.; Esmail Shakeri, "Muslim Women in Canada: Their Role and Status as Revealed in the Hijab Controversy," in Yvonne Haddad and John L. Esposito, eds., *Muslims on the Americanization Path?* (Atlanta: Scholars Press, 1998), pp. 159–178.

116. Shakeri, op. cit.

117. Carolan, et al., op. cit.; Debra Reece, "Covering and Communication: The Symbolism of Dress Among Muslim Women," *The Howard Journal of Communication* 7, no. 35 (1996): 35–52.

118. Renard, op. cit.; Louise Cainkar, "Immigrant Palestinian Women Evaluate Their Lives," in Barbara C. Aswad and Barbara Bilge, eds., *Family and Gender Among American Muslims* (Philadelphia: Temple University Press, 1996), pp. 41–58.

119. Carolan, et al., op. cit.; Reece, op. cit.

120. Council on American-Islamic Relations Research Center, *The Status of Muslim Civil Rights in the United States 2002: Stereotypes and Civil Liberties* (Washington, D.C.: Council on American-Islamic Relations, 2002).

121. Altareb, op. cit.; Daneshpour, op. cit.; Kelly, op. cit.; Mahmoud, op. cit.; Zari Hedayat-Diba, "Psychotherapy with Muslims," in P. Scott Richards and Allen E. Bergin, eds., *Handbook of Psychotherapy and Religious Diversity* (Washington, D.C.: American Psychological Association, 2000), pp. 289–314.

122. Vanessa Mahmoud, "African American Muslim Families," in Monica McGoldrick, Joe Giordano, and John K. Pearce, eds., *Ethnicity and Family Therapy*, 2nd Edition (New York: Guilford Press, 1996) pp. 122–128.

123. Kelly, op. cit.

124. Sarah Shafi, "A Study of Muslim Asian Women's Experiences of Counseling and the Necessity for a Racially Similar Counselor," *Counseling Psychology Quarterly* 11, no. 3 (1998): 301–314.

125. Alean Al-Krenawi, "Group Work with Bedouin Widows of the Negev in a Medical Clinic," *Affilia* 11, no. 3 (1996): 303–318.

126. Richard W. Riley, "Religious Expression in Public Schools," 1998. http://www.ed.gov/Speeches/08–1995/religion.html (accessed July 11, 2001).

127. William J. Clinton, "Memorandum for the U.S. Secretary of Education and the U.S. Attorney General," 1995, http://w3.trib.com/FACT/1st.pres.rel.html (accessed December 11, 1999).

128. Riley, op. cit.

129. Bagby, Perl, and Froehle, op. cit.

130. Smith, op. cit.; Bagby, Perl, and Froehle, op. cit.; Corbett, op. cit.

131. Haddad and Smith, op. cit.

132. Denny, op. cit.; Bagby, Perl, and Froehle, op. cit.

133. Smith, op. cit.; Gutbi Mahdi Ahmed, "Muslim Organizations in the United States," in Yvonne Yazbeck Haddad, ed., *The Muslims of America* (New York: Oxford University Press, 1991), pp. 11–24.

134. Smith, op. cit.

135. Byng, op. cit.; Ross-Sheriff, op. cit.

136. American Muslim Poll, op. cit.

137. Barbara Bryant Solomon, "Social Work Practice with African Americans," in Armando T. Morales and Bradford W. Sheafor, *Social Work: A Profession of Many Faces*, 9th ed. (Needham, MA: Allyn & Bacon, 2001), pp. 519–539.

138. RNS News Service, "Report: Anti-Muslim Violence May Be Declining," Religion News Service, October 26, 2001, http://pewforum.org/news/index.php3?NewsID-827, accessed May 23, 2002).

139. Shelvia Dancy, "Bush Visits Mosque, Warns Against Anti-Muslim Violence," Religion News Service, September 17, 2001, http://pewforum.org/news/index.php3?NewsID=730 (accessed May 23, 2002).

140. Luis Lugo, "Muslim-Americans Gaining Respect," *The Atlanta Journal-Constitution*, March 25, 2002, http://accessatlanta.com/ajc/opinion/0303/0325muslims.html (accessed May 23, 2002).

141. American Muslim Poll, op. cit.

142. U.S. Equal Employment Opportunity Commission, "EEOC Provides Answers About Workplace Rights of Muslims, Arabs, South Asians and Sikhs," U.S. Equal Employment Opportunity Commission, May 15, 2002, http://www.eeoc.gov/press/5-15-02.html (accessed July 23, 2002).

143. Council on American-Islamic Relations Research Center, op. cit.

144. American Muslim Poll, op. cit.

145. RNS News Service, op. cit.

Social Work Practice with Indigenous Peoples and Tribal Communities*

Prefatory Comment

The concept of *cultural competency* is central to social work but often difficult for new students to fully comprehend. Perhaps this difficulty is not surprising because, for a long period of time, the United States embraced a "melting pot" philosophy, assuming that, as generations passed, people would throw off their old cultures and meld into a similar set of beliefs and cultural practices. Of course, the descendants of each immigrant group thought the resulting culture would be much like theirs and chafed at the vestiges of other cultures, particularly those racially and ethnically different, that persisted in their difference.

Perhaps more than any other group, the Indigenous population (variously called Native Peoples, American Indians, Alaska Natives, First Nation Peoples, and Native Americans) resisted assimilation. After all, they did not experience a voluntary or involuntary transition to a new land—others invaded their land. Although there were hundreds of tribes, each with some unique elements of culture, their preservation of cultural uniqueness was substantial enough that the new social worker must carefully consider practice modifications that are specifically responsive to the needs of America's 4.5 million Indigenous people. Indeed, social workers can expect to work with members of the Indigenous population group, as it is the most vulnerable to social problems of all racial or ethnic groups addressed in this section of *Social Work: A Profession of Many Faces*.

In this chapter, some specific adaptations are identified through the lens of the Ecosystems Model and illustrative case examples. The chapter does not intend to be inclusive of all of the variations in Native culture or to address all of the social issues they experience. Rather, it is anticipated that readers will increase their *cultural competency* to this part of the U.S. population, avoid initial assumptions

---

*This chapter was prepared by Roe Bubar, associate professor of social work, ethnic studies, and women's studies, Colorado State University, and Dana Klar, assistant professor of social work, Lindenwood University, St. Charles, Missouri.

that might harm relationships with Native clients, and provide a base for continued learning.

Indigenous peoples today are located in rural areas (i.e., homelands, reservations, pueblos, Rancherias, villages, colonies), urban and suburban communities, and in geographically isolated areas throughout the United States. The movement of Indigenous peoples among these locations is common, and sense of place, as well as connection to tribal homelands, remains important in the twenty-first century. *Indigenous peoples* define themselves tribally, and tribalism affects the social, cultural, and political aspects of daily life. Therefore many Native peoples define themselves in terms of their tribal affiliation first and then as Native or Native American. There continues to be reclamation of all things Indigenous, and recognition of enculturation is emerging in the social science literature as one potential protective factor for Native youth. Given the high out-of-marriage rates in the Indigenous population, many Native people today identify as "mixed bloods" and claim descendency, which presents individual complications for enrollment and thus identity challenges. Some tribes have responded to the needs of their members and descendents by adjusting enrollment criteria.

In some tribal communities, economic development has enabled tribes to reduce unemployment and improve conditions in their homeland areas, whereas other tribes less strategically located or less resource rich continue to struggle with some of the highest levels of poverty and unemployment in the country. Indian nations, tribal communities, and Indigenous peoples remain the most diverse group within the United States today.

The power to name and label oneself is both cultural and political. Even though Indigenous peoples refer to themselves as "Indian," the term "Indian" is not a preferred label for non-Natives to use. However the term "Indian" remains embedded in many legal and political terms defined within policies and legislation and thus provides a particular legal meaning and status. Use of the term *Indigenous* is the most inclusive yet may not be preferred by many tribal communities and peoples since it is not tribally specific, although it is more inclusive globally. The term Native American will not be used in this chapter since it is not as inclusive and does not specifically include Alaska Natives or Native Hawaiians and First Nations, a term most often used in reference to the Indigenous peoples in Canada. The terms Native and Indigenous are used interchangeably in this chapter to refer to this population group.

Native people today are located in communities often set apart from the American mainstream. In addition, Native issues and concerns are highly invisible in the U.S. mainstream, whether we consider the news, Internet, or other media sources. Many have come to refer to Indigenous peoples as the "invisible" minority, partially because 65 percent of the population lives off reservation and remains somewhat "hidden" in urban or rural areas. Most Americans study about Native peoples as though they were the people of the past with little emphasis on contemporary issues or contemporary tribal communities. This tendency, coupled with the fact that Natives make up just over 1.5 percent of the U.S. population, also contributes to the "invisibility" of Native peoples and Indigenous issues.

Current Demographics

In 2007 the U.S. Census indicated that Indigenous peoples comprise 4.5 million people. The Native population is younger than the population as a whole, with a median age of 31, compared with 36.4 years for the U.S. total,[1] and Indigenous peoples have one of the highest out-of-marriage rates. More people are identified as Cherokee than any other tribal affiliation, yet the Navajo Nation, the second largest tribe, maintains the largest land base of any Indian nation. Their reservation extends into three states: New Mexico, Arizona, and Utah.[2]

Currently there are 562 federally recognized tribes, 230 of which are located within the state of Alaska. There are 322 federally recognized Indian reservations, and most are located in the West.[3] Federally recognized tribes are eligible for services that are provided by the Bureau of Indian Affairs (BIA). In addition, there are a number of state-recognized tribes, which means they are recognized and have a certain status within the state in which they reside but are not necessarily recognized by the federal government. Federal recognition is a process in which tribes either apply to meet set criteria within the BIA's administrative process or lobby Congress for recognition via legislation. Today there are many tribes that remain unrecognized by either state or federal governments.

Key Social Issues

Sovereignty

Tribal communities represent sovereign Indian nations, and their sovereign status predates both the U.S. Constitution and the arrival of colonist or settler populations in this country. *Sovereignty* includes the concept of self-governance and thus internal control over land, resources, and membership. Therefore, there are federal, state, and also tribal governmental structures within the United States. The U.S. Constitution is the organic authority for federal and state existence but not for tribes. As a result, Native people are not considered minorities but instead are viewed as Indigenous. Because of their nationhood status, tribes have a unique relationship with the U.S. government. Many people believe that Indigenous peoples receive money or entitlements from the government for being "Indian," which is not accurate. Instead, the federal government's relationship with Indian nations is described as a *trust relationship:* one in which the federal government is obligated or has a duty to uphold treaty promises. Indigenous nations were compelled to grant to the United States large tracts of aboriginally held lands and reserved unto themselves smaller pieces of land in exchange for promises that the United States is obligated to fulfill as a party to treaty agreements. The United States is thus obligated via laws, treaties, and pledges to protect the sovereign status of tribes in this country, to protect tribal resources, and to provide education and health care to federally recognized tribes and tribal members. Native peoples place a high value and emphasis on the sovereign status of Native nations, and sovereignty is considered a critical concept for social workers to understand and respect when interacting with tribal communities and Indigenous peoples, whether working with urban or reservation-based communities.

Socioeconomic and Persistent Poverty Issues

On virtually every social indicator, the U.S. Native population falls substantially behind the dominant population—the white, non-Hispanic segment of the population. Consider the comparison of the two population groups in Table 23.1, compiled from data released by the U.S. Census Bureau in 2007. It is apparent that the Indigenous people in the United States are exceptionally vulnerable to social problems.

Poverty is apparent in most reservation communities, as well as the experience of many urban Native people. Housing is a serious challenge in reservation communities with 40 percent of available housing considered inadequate, and one in five homes is found without plumbing.[4] In urban areas, the average household income reported for

Table 23.1

Social Indicator Comparison of U. S. White, not Hispanic Population with American Indian Alaska Native (AIAN) Population in 2004

Social Indicator	White, not Hispanic	AIAN, not Hispanic
Median age	40.1 years	32.7 years
Married (age 15 and older)	57.3 %	42.2 %
Birth to unmarried woman in past year	20.5 %	50.2 %
Household headed by female, no husband present	8.9 %	20.9 %
Education level		
Less than high school	11.4 %	21.6 %
High school graduate	88.6 %	78.4 %
College graduate	29.7 %	15.1 %
Median household income	$48,784	$30,815
Poverty rate		
All ages	8.8 %	25.1 %
Under age 18	11.0 %	31.6 %
65 and older	7.2 %	19.7 %
Owner of own home	73.9 %	56.8 %
Median value of home	$153,396	$92,753

Source: U.S. Census Bureau, *The American Community—American Indians and Alaska Natives: 2004* (Washington, D.C.: U.S. Department of Commerce, 2007).

the 2000 Census was $15,312, compared with the average urban non-Native house-hold income of $22,736.[5] Creating economic solutions to poverty and unemployment is key to addressing social challenges within Indigenous homeland and urban areas.

Over the past 25 years, there has been a push for Indigenous economic development. One common method to encourage such development is nation-owned business enterprises. These enterprises are extremely diverse and include the use of tribally owned natural resources seen in timber enterprises or in tribally created recreational offerings, best known for gaming operations. Casinos, in particular, are often thought of as "the solution" for Indigenous poverty given the economic development challenges in most tribal areas. However, while gaming has been successful for strategically located tribes, many tribes have yet to experience much profit. For the small number of tribes where gaming operations have been successful, profits have been used to subsidize schools, recreation, health care, and provide more social services for tribal members.

Gaming as an economic enterprise is limited in its capacity to enrich many tribal communities. Most reservations were established on "undesirable" land, in rural and extremely isolated locations. The successful casinos are located on or near major interstates, thus able to draw from large metropolitan areas, or have access to the traveling public. There are only a dozen or so large, successful tribally owned and operated gaming operations. It is important to consider that tribal members remain divided over economic development opportunities such as casinos, tourism, and development of natural resources. While some Native people see such development as positive sources of income, others view it as devastating compromises to cultural and spiritual integrity.[6]

Sovereignty and nation-building are critical components of Indigenous economic development. It is important to understand that for economic development in Indian country to be successful it must take account of sovereign nation status, historical realities, and tribally specific and culturally appropriate methodology. Cornell and Kalt recognize that economic success is tied to a *nation-building approach,* one that puts genuine decision-making power in Indigenous hands, backs up that power with capable institutions of self-governance, matches those institutions to Indigenous political culture, has a strategic orientation toward long-term outcomes, and is guided by public-spirited leadership.[7]

Unfortunately, Indigenous economic development is subjected to continued threat of discrimination and oppression as witnessed with the fraud perpetuated on six separate gaming Native nations, and the general public, by Jack Abramoff and Michael Scanlon, former political lobbyists. These six nations together contributed more than $82 million for lobbying efforts to occur on their behalf. Unbeknownst to the tribes, Abramoff and Scanlon devised a scheme together where they pocketed $40 million of that money, in effect providing to the nations much less than the original bargain. These six nations were not found to be participants in the actual fraud, yet they experienced national embarrassment in their association with Abramoff.[8] This crime amplified the reality that Native nations remain a target of negative stereotypes that can lead to attempts to take advantage of the less sophisticated consumer. Until more tribal members complete higher education and gain experience in mainstream politics and the global economy, the potential for such crime perpetuation exists.

Education

The history of Indian education in the United States is often contextualized in a *historical trauma* framework. Forced removal of children to distant boarding schools created serious harm for individual children, families, and tribal communities and is often considered one of the most genocidal policies ever passed in the history of the country. Starting in the late 1800s and continuing into the early 1970s, forced Indian education removed Native children as young as 4 to live in boarding school settings located far away, as well as more local institutions. Boarding schools were often run and administered by a myriad of Christian missionaries, and children were typically kept in boarding school settings until the age of majority, when many returned to their tribal communities. Separated from family and tribal communities, children were forced to assimilate into white mainstream Christian culture—where use of Native language, spirituality, clothing, or culture was forbidden—was enforced, and compliance was obtained with physical punishment and, in extreme cases, torture.[9] There are some Natives who consider their boarding school experiences to be more positive and were thankful that, in times of great economic struggle, boarding school offered both food and shelter. However, the majority of Indigenous peoples in the United States, Canada, and Australia consider the policy to be a genocidal example of Indigenous historical trauma and liken their experiences to those who lived through the holocaust. The Canadian government has made a formal apology and reached a settlement to compensate First Nations peoples for the trauma that was caused from their country's boarding school policies. In Australia, aboriginal children taken from their homeland areas and placed in institutionalized school settings are referred to as the "stolen generation."*

In the United States today, Indian boarding schools still exist but are voluntary in attendance. The 1975 Indian Self-Determination and Education Assistance Act, the Tribally Controlled Schools Act of 1988, and the 1978 Educational Amendments Act have each affected Indian education issues, thus providing for more local control, as well as restructuring BIA and tribally operated schools to obtain direct funding.[10] Indian education continues to face serious challenges in tribal communities, and students are not afforded the same access to educational resources available to other American students. Today the National Indian School Board Association is responsible for addressing local school board training, and the trend has been to empower Native communities around education. Public schools are also eligible to obtain funding for Native student special needs under the Johnson-O'Malley Act of 1934. Bilingual and Native language immersion programs have started up in more recent years. For example, in the Kamehameha schools, a new online program allows Native Hawaiian adults to study alongside other family members in an effort to reclaim their culture and language. Other new trends include making classrooms more culturally relevant by including elders and tribal members in the classroom, providing more Native-appropriate curriculum, and incorporating Native language in the curriculum.

---

*The movie *Rabbit-Proof Fence* tells the true story of one aboriginal family's experiences when the government forcefully took three children from their homeland area, their subsequent escape from the Moore River Native Settlement, and their 1,500-mile trek back home on foot to Jigalong.

Health and Mental Health Issues

Today access to adequate health care and services for health-related problems are some of the greatest challenges facing contemporary tribal communities. Prior to colonization, Native peoples addressed and administered their own health needs. Different tribal members specifically addressed health challenges, specializing in some combination of plant medicines and healing ceremonies.[11] Health needs and *health disparities* continue to be two of the most critical issues facing Indigenous peoples and tribal communities today. Life expectancy rates have hit an all-time high in the United States, with overall life expectancy at 78.1 years of age in 2006 (80.7 years of age for women and 75.4 years of age for men). Native people today have the lowest life expectancy of any ethnic population within the United States, where Native men have a life expectancy of 69.4 years and Native women have a life expectancy of 77.6 years.[12] Cancer, heart disease, accidents, and diabetes are the four leading causes of death for Indigenous peoples in the United States.

Provision of health care by the federal government is considered a treaty right for federally recognized tribes.[13] Of increasing concern are the health disparities experienced by Indigenous peoples and the underfunding of treaty-promised health care for Natives in both urban and tribal community settings. In *A Quiet Crisis: Federal Funding and Unmet Funding Needs in Indian Country,* the U.S. Commission on Civil Rights chronicles the large deficit in spending for Native programs historically and describes the present state of health disparities for Native peoples. Most Native people living in tribal communities do not have access to the same programs, services, and resources experienced by other Americans, even though the federal government is obligated to provide such services. In many tribal communities, there are limited health facilities with inadequate medical equipment to provide health care services, and the average age of the facilities is thirty-two years. The majority of the Indigenous population lives in urban areas yet has less access to health care and health care facilities than others. Natives access health care less than any other ethnic group. For comparative purposes, the doctor visit rate for Anglo Americans is 239, Asian Americans 233, African Americans 211, and Natives only 54.

The Indian Health Service (IHS) is a federally funded government agency responsible for the delivery of health care in urban and tribal community settings. IHS serves approximately 60 percent of the eligible 2.5 million people. Funding isn't statutorily determined, which makes IHS funding vulnerable to annual discretionary appropriations, and it doesn't accrue annual increases to keep pace with inflation like Medicare and Medicaid funding. Over the past 30 years, a pattern of chronic underfunding has occurred, and this arguably contributes significantly to the disparate health status of Natives making them 20 to 25 years behind other Americans in health status. Consider the cost of health care in 2003: $5,775 was spent for the average American person, $5,915 for Medicare recipients, $5,214 for veterans, $3,803 per federal prisoner, and $1,914 per Native in the IHS system.[15]

Alcohol and drug use represents a serious challenge in the untreated mental health needs of Native peoples. Mental health services are severely limited and largely provided by the behavioral health program within Indian Health Service

(IHS). Suicide remains a critical concern for Native youth. Mental health problems persist in populations where poverty exists, and Natives are no exception. Many tribal communities have developed outpatient tribally run alcohol programs. Mental health services are even more seriously limited with regard to tribal children living in tribal communities.

HIV/AIDS has significantly affected many communities of color, including tribal communities. With limited health care and an overall lack of prevention programs, HIV/AIDS and other sexually transmitted diseases and infections have presented serious health concerns to Native communities. In recent years, funding has been available to provide some outreach, prevention, and educational materials developed to specifically address HIV/AIDS in urban and reservation tribal communities. Health programming that includes Native-specific images and HIV/AIDS walks and events can be found in a variety of settings. The National Native American AIDS Prevention Center (NNAAPC) works with a number of agency and tribal partners to address HIV/AIDS prevention for Native peoples.

Family

Family within an Indigenous worldview is inclusive of extended family members. Much importance is placed on family, tribe, and thus community. In a Native worldview, great emphasis is placed on the idea and importance of "other" versus the emphasis on "self" experienced in the non-Native worldview. Since family is held up as important, family is defined broadly and, in a general sense, many Native people define family via clan, blood, societies, marriage, and adoption (both formal and informal). Familial roles and the concept of family differ significantly from definitions of family and familial roles within the non-Native context. For example, the roles of aunts, uncles, and cousins, as well as the concept of adoption, can vary greatly within the various Indigenous communities. Extended family networks have been a source of resilience in tribal communities. Native families traditionally practiced kinship care and continue to do so today, evidencing strong family networks. Many grandparents are taking care of grandchildren to support single-parent family needs and rescue their grandchildren from serious challenges faced by their adult children.

Spirituality

Indigenous spirituality is diverse and, like other religions, provides an explanation of how the world came to be, the forces around them, death, and other great mysteries of life. Some scholars claim it may be more appropriate to refer to Native religion as the "sacred and the ceremony" since many tribes did not have an actual word for religion. Lack of true understanding of Native spiritual life has led to cultural misunderstandings and cultural appropriation of Native spirituality. Native spirituality is interwoven with Native cultural life and involves complex relationships with the natural world and the homeland environment.

Many urban and tribal human services programs include traditional practices and healing as a part of the services that are offered. Western-type mental health resources are often limited in tribal community settings and traditional healing offers Native people an indigenous approach to health, healing, and spiritual practices.

Indigenous spiritual belief systems are an area of fascination for many non-Natives. Previous federal policies outlawed many Native spiritual practices, some of which have been characterized as cultural genocide. As a result, many tribes do not allow non-Natives or non-members to participate in their ceremonies and cultural practices. In mainstream film and media, Native people are often stereotyped by their spiritual beliefs or practices. Given this fascination by non-Natives and past federal policies, it is important for social workers to approach Indigenous spiritual beliefs and traditional cultural practices with respect and refrain from prying into areas that people have not brought up or are reluctant to openly discuss.

Indigenous Women

Indigenous women have a history of egalitarian relationships and being viewed with respect within their tribal communities. Historically, in many tribal practices, Native women had decision-making ability over land, children, leadership, marital status, and resources.[16] Even in tribes that practiced strict sex roles, women were viewed in interdependent relationships with men and were accorded the respect that accompanied their roles within the tribal community. Many Indigenous women define their identities in terms of their relationship to the land and to family/tribe/community. Gender is mediated by tribal identity, in some instances motherhood, and family relationships within the urban or tribal community setting. *Heteropatriarchy,* the intersection of oppressions such that heterosexuality and patriarchy are presented as the natural order was a practice brought to the New World by colonists, and today tribal communities have struggled with sexism, homophobia, and gendered policies that have placed Native women, as well as members of the Native lesbian, gay, bisexual, and transgender (LGBT) community, in more marginalized situations. Various genders and gender identities were well established and accepted in many tribal communities before contact with settler populations.

Native women experience the highest rates of sexual assault, domestic violence, and stalking of any women within the United States. Native women are 2.5 times more likely to be sexually assaulted and 2 times more likely to be stalked than other women.[17] In a 2006 study, Native providers from around the country identified race/ethnicity as the major risk factor for sexual assault and other forms of violence. Native women discussed the idea that non-Natives are not knowledgeable and thus unconcerned about the violence and safety issues affecting tribal communities.[18] Native women stand out today as activists and program administrators developing sustainable initiatives to address violence against both women and children, as well as creating prevention programming for Native men.

Children and Adolescents

Native children have always been central to Indigenous life and community. Parenting practices may vary in tribal communities, but in general children are viewed as important within the family and thus tribal milieu. Many Native children today still have access to a cultural life and traditional teaching practices. Child maltreatment is a critical social issue since health care dollars and prevention programming resources are not as available as they are for other American children. Safety concerns are critical in many tribal communities, and unintentional injuries are the number one cause of death for tribal children.[19] Child maltreatment also poses serious health and safety risks, and Native children are overrepresented in child abuse cases, foster care placement, and fatality cases.[20] In response, a number of tribes have developed children's advocacy center programs and three national organizations—the Native American Children's Alliance, the Tribal Law and Policy Institute, and the National Indian Child Welfare Association (NICWA)— that provide training, resources, technical assistance, and public policy analysis regarding child abuse and neglect, particularly for NICWA as it applies to the Indian Child Welfare Act.

Violence and Criminal Justice

Indigenous peoples have historically had justice systems in place, and many modern alternative justice programs have features of Indigenous justice incorporated within them. In 1999 the American Indians and Crime Report made the front page of newspapers across the country announcing that Native Americans experience the highest violent crime rates of any people within the United States and that the crimes perpetrated upon them is committed primarily by non-Natives.[21] Crime and mistreatment of Native people is largely uncovered in mainstream media. Native people are statistically over-represented in the criminal justice system. Tribal sovereignty yields authority to create judicial programming in tribal communities, but chronic underfunding of judicial services and case law has crippled progress in rehabilitation and crime prevention. For some criminal acts on tribal lands, federal, state, and tribal law could apply, and convictions of most felony crimes committed on reservations will result in incarceration within the federal penal system. Criminal jurisdiction is a complex issue for tribal lands and people.

In tribal communities, there are infrequent incarcerations and historically little use of a penal system. And while there are some jails present in tribal communities, many communities do not have a system of secure confinement or jail facilities even for the most serious of crimes. Traditionally there were ways of punishing or providing a consequence to tribal members who violated social and moral codes of behavior. These traditional practices are part of *customary law* since they were traditional in a number of tribal communities. These customary practices include public shaming and ridicule, whippings, banishment from the community, termination of membership rights, restitution whether by financial payments or providing labor, and community service.[22] Mediation, family conferencing, and peacemaker courts, which reflect traditional Indigenous justices, are contemporary methods in a number of tribal communities. The Navajo Nation, for example, has a number of peacemaker courts in place, and mediation is used in many First Nations communities in Canada.

The Ecosystems Framework

Historical Challenges and Federal Indian Policy

Prior to contact (with the white population in the United States), the Indigenous peoples had a sophisticated culture, well-developed societies, and complex governmental systems in place. Successful in living off the land and maintaining healthy lifestyles, tribes were in a strong position when settlers came to the Americas. Recognizing the status of tribes, Spain, England, France, the Dutch, and later the American colonies entered into treaty negotiations with tribal nations. Settlers brought new diseases to America, and Native people died in large numbers from the introduction of those diseases. Once weakened by disease and reduced in numbers, tribes were vulnerable to colonist populations. Federal Indian policy began with treaty negotiations and changed over the course of the formation of the United States. These policies encouraged further oppression, removal, and diminishment of tribal nations. This process of colonization by settler groups is considered to be ongoing since the impact of many federal policies is still experienced today. The continued negative impact of federal policies is conceptualized as a form of structural racism. Given this treatment, there is a historic distrust and disconnection particularly with outside agencies, some state governments, and non-Natives.

In young adulthood, when young people become aware of the "American ideals" of justice and freedom that this country was founded upon, it presents a contradiction for many young Natives considering how very different that experience has been for Native people in the eighteenth, nineteenth, twentieth, and even twenty-first centuries. This revelation can be difficult for Indigenous youth, and many experience being torn between loyalty to country and loyalty to ancestors and tribal traditions. This disillusionment and anger at times is turned inward and can manifest as depression, or it may be turned outward and experienced as acting out.[23] One movement in the United States has been to reclaim all that is Indigenous, and cultural revitalization attempts are being introduced in both urban and reservation communities to embrace culture that was lost or taken away.

These experiences and other specific impacts of policy, particularly removal, assimilation efforts, and termination, were experienced in great intensity—especially for the direct descendants of war or for others who are the survivors of the forced boarding school era—and have culminated in what is referred to as *historical trauma*. There is a growing body of work and important interventions being developed to help address historical trauma for the Native population.[24]

Deloria and Lytle identify six primary "eras" of tribal–federal relations that many historians, legal theorists, and academicians turn to today to categorize the historical experience of Indigenous peoples in America. These six periods of time have vacillated between time periods with particularly harsh policies to fairly positive time periods for the treatment of Native peoples. We refer to these six distinct periods as 1) Discovery, Conquest, and Treaty-making; 2) Removal and Relocation; 3) Allotment and Assimilation; 4) Reorganization; 5) Termination; and 6) Self-determination.[25]

Discovery, Conquest, and Treaty-making (1532–1828) was a period that posed particularly difficult concessions and compromises by Native nations. Even though treaties are old and have been broken, they are still considered supreme law, are thus enforceable today, and represent the foundation of tribal sovereignty. The *Removal and Relocation* period (1828–1887) posed significant continued harm to Native nations as the new government rejected the notion that settlers and Native nations could live peacefully as neighbors. Nations were forced to migrate westward, and on many forced marches, such as the Cherokee Nation's "Trail of Tears," many lives were lost. *Allotment and Assimilation* (1887–1928) was the period of federal policy aimed at forcing Native nations to assimilate through private property ownership (by means of individually allotting reservation lands) and through forced boarding school attendance. During this period, the Native land base that had been provided through treaty was reduced from over more than 138 million acres to only 48 million acres. *Reorganization* (1928–1945) was a period of revitalization for Native nations. The Indian Reorganization Act called for an official end to the devastating allotment policy and provided opportunities for economic development and self-governance. During the *Termination* era (1945–1961), the federal government passed a policy to terminate the status of more than 100 tribes. Many of those tribes remain ineligible for BIA services and are still not federally recognized today. Termination policies were implemented by the government in an attempt to relinquish their responsibilities for Native nations to the states. Tribal sovereignty took severe blows during this phase as some nations lost their recognized status, while many others were brought under state civil and criminal jurisdiction.

Self-determination (1961–present) characterizes the current era of federal–tribal relations, recognizing the shift in emphasis in Congress that resulted from the socially oriented Great Society Programs of the 1960s. Finally, Indian nations are being given the opportunity to design, manage, and control their own federally funded programs. Tribal nations are more fully asserting their sovereignty now than in any period since the initial treaties were signed. While Native nations recognize the freedoms and opportunities of this positive phase, most are cautious in their optimism as they have an abundance of historical information that disallows a prolonged sense of security with the status of federal–tribal relations.

Environmental-Structural Factors

Many American citizens have changed their attitudes regarding both the historic wrongs and current treatment of Native people. However, injustices embedded in past and current policies are what were referred to earlier in this chapter as *institutional or structural racism*. State governments continually assault tribal sovereignty and pressure federal agencies and Congress to side with states' rights on many issues, thereby further diminishing tribal sovereignty. So while individual attitudes may have changed over time, there continues to be an ongoing impact that posits Natives in a seriously marginalized position resulting from the racialization of Natives carried out in ongoing policies and procedures. For example, there continues to be significant underfunding of health care, education, and justice systems in tribal communities, which contributes to lower educational attainment by Native youth, shorter life expectancy rates, serious safety risks for women and children, and the mounting untreated mental health challenges. Lack of federal funding has also affected the sustainability of tribal programs. The U.S. Commission on Civil Rights has characterized this level of underfunding as a human rights concern.[26]

Native communities continue to be isolated, with less access to resources and less access to the typical structures of society, including education, health, and welfare. Thus resources available to other Americans are not as plentiful or available to Native peoples. Even in the areas where Native communities are empowered and taking control of their economy or programs, progress remains slow, and tribal members are still subjected to acts of racism and marginalization within the states where their tribal communities are located.

The continued reference to Natives and tribes as imagery for fierce-looking team mascots and stereotypical advertising is a form of continued discrimination, and many Native people experience this as an unacceptable form of American racism. Americans take for granted, for example, the name "Washington Redskins," and are largely unaware of its potential for harm to Native people. The negative impact and potential for encouraging lower self-esteem for Native youth and their identity development is of concern when *Native imagery* is presented more as an "object" fixed in time or labeled with racialized terminology. In the twenty-first century, it is hard to imagine any other ethnic or racial group in America being labeled in such a way that is then embraced by the majority of Americans.

The trend is to be more inclusive of tribes and Native people's voices in social welfare policy initiatives, research, case management, and program planning. Universities and research centers are increasingly engaging in "community-based and participatory" research initiatives that allow for full engagement of the community. In this form of research, tribes are included as partners, and Natives are involved in each phase of a project. Many Native people believe this approach will lead to less *appropriated knowledge* (knowledge that has been acquired under the pretense of helping the Native community but that ultimately does not provide any benefits), and therefore the much needed benefits of the projects will return to the tribal community.

Cultural Considerations

There is tremendous diversity in Indigenous populations within the United States, and it is critical for social workers to consider and ask their clients about individual tribal customs and practices. Indigenous cultural considerations are complex and often shift depending on the context and nuance of the social or family situation, and some tribal practices are simply very different than the practices of other tribes. There are, however, some cultural values that are found in many different tribal communities. These include a sense of generosity, spirituality, emphasis on "other" versus the individual, and sense of time and place.

In a Native worldview, time is not viewed rigidly. Rather, emphasis is on personal relations, and considerable value is placed on taking the time for family and other necessary social interactions. Also, sense of place and connection to homeland areas resonates for many Natives, even those with relocated populations. Generosity, too, can be seen in formal and informal gifting, sharing knowledge, time, and helping to care for others. Finally, spirituality is considered central to health and happiness, and living in balance is a cultural value embraced in most tribal communities. In an Indigenous worldview, spirituality is connected with all other aspects of life, and this is how health and harmony is achieved. Many Indigenous people integrate Native belief systems with Christian practices. Thus, use of Western medicine may be fully embraced or mediated with the use of traditional healing methods and medicine people.

Family, Group, and Community Practice Considerations

Intervention techniques when working with Indigenous people should be client-centered, group focused, and concerned with the well-being of the whole. Thus the Ecosystems Model must be adapted to reflect the culture by addressing family, group, clan or tribe, and community simultaneously.

Family When there is a social issue to address, the family must define the problem and be active participants in identifying the solution. Great resistance will be encountered if a social worker (particularly one who is not of the tribal community) attempts to define the family's needs. It is important to note that many Native people are carefully trained in family relationships and traditions, and that person's social place is largely determined by family connections. For these reasons, family involvement in social work intervention is critically important as fulfillment of family obligations, and a comfort level with current family interactions is crucial for Native peoples' mental health. Important decisions generally require the approval of significant family members (spouses or elders). In particular, extended family approval and involvement is important when traditional spiritual help is being considered. One example of implementing culturally competent programming can be seen in a variety of treatment programs that incorporate tribal elders as consultants or advisors. There is great diversity in tribal responses and programming as it relates to the familiar roles and tribal customs and practices.

Native identity is also rooted in tribal membership. Native people often refer to themselves as members of the Native community, regardless of their geographic location. Many identify first with their nation or tribe, second with a clan or society to which they belong, and lastly as a Native or Native American. Social cooperation is often valued over independent decision making.

Group Group involvement in decision making is compatible with Native culture. For example, one of the authors previously worked with an American Indian graduate studies program at a major university in a metropolitan area. The Native students in the program were honored with full scholarships for their two years of study and were provided numerous professional development opportunities. The students often experienced these years in closely knit groups (primarily composed of Native students) who became their "community" away from home.

As with any group, the student needs were dynamic, and the programmatic responses were the same. A repeated theme was a student request for an organizing force that called together "elders" to assist and support "younger" students. Initially, without a second year and thus more experienced MSW student cohort in place, the program instituted a "host family" system wherein Native students were matched with affiliated mainstream families who lived in the area and could serve as a resource to the students (e.g., provide a warm meal, a homelike setting, information about the university community, and advice on how the students may meet their shopping and recreational needs). Over time, feedback indicated that this programming, dependent of course upon the families involved, could at times feel paternalistic, and it was suggested that the graduate program instead provide a "mentor program," wherein a second-year student would be randomly assigned to mentor a first-year student. Through this program, similar assistance would be provided to the new student, yet this programming would only involve the Native community. This mentoring program survived many years, yet it also encountered difficulties as it became clear that some students were in conflict with their assigned mentors or mentees, thus there existed inequities in the assistance the program was meant to provide. It is important to note there are historic and modern intertribal tensions and differences that may emerge.

Students were consulted and suggested a programmatic change to more informal mentoring, programmatic offerings of advice and referral, and a voluntary "secret pal" program was instituted. This final method of group interaction and support has proven successful. This example of dynamic group work illustrates a number of points that are important in working with the Native population:

1. The Native group members wanted opportunities for group participation and demonstrated responsibility toward others.
2. The community and its needs were dynamic and sought a dynamic environment in which to flourish.
3. Fluidity of style was important, though the group purpose remained the same.
4. It was important that the group felt empowered to voice modifications needed to address their concerns.
5. The movement over the years in the methodology was from an externally imposed framework to one of self-government (following the maturity of the program).
6. This group participation provided a culturally effective framework for addressing the cultural adjustment issues experienced by the students encountering the most drastic cultural and environmental changes.
7. Many of these groupings or pairings remained close long after departure from the program, indicating the sense of community this group work created. It allowed for a much stronger bond than typical student programming.

Community Working with Native communities is critically important in the development of programs, developing collaborative relationships, or gaining support for existing programs. Tribal communities are unique, and, while some issues and common challenges persist across tribal communities, it remains important to understand what accounts for the differences, as well as successful interventions, across tribal communities. Community readiness serves as one potential model for developing specific community interventions that take into account culturally distinct tribal communities and tribally specific approaches.[27]

It is significant that most Native programs base health- and healing-related interventions on their respective tribal culture, which, again, can be quite unique. The
Community Readiness Model (see Figure 23.1) integrates culture and tribally specific
solutions in the analysis. This nine-stage model recognizes as a key issue the community's readiness to define and develop an intervention or program. The model is based
on the theory of an individual's readiness for treatment applied on the community level.
Just as people progress through readiness stages for a particular treatment intervention,
communities also go through stages of readiness for program development. This
concept of readiness provides an effective framework with which to view a social,
economic, or policy-related issue. Developed initially to increase the potential for interventions to be effective in the area of alcohol and drug abuse, it is now implemented in
urban and rural tribal communities to address challenges ranging from health and

Figure 23.1

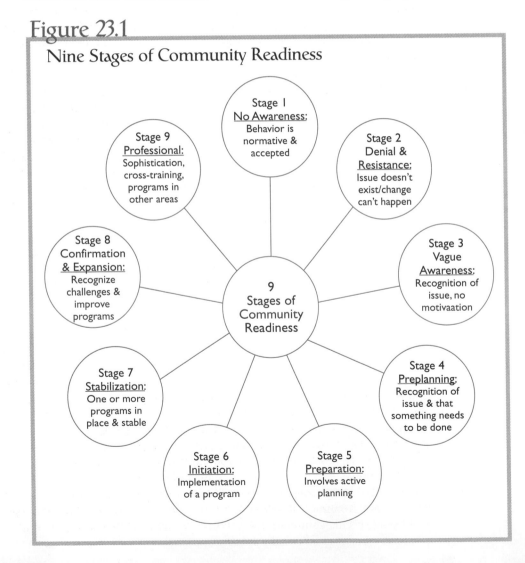

Nine Stages of Community Readiness

9 Stages of Community Readiness

**Stage 1
No Awareness:** Behavior is normative & accepted

**Stage 2
Denial & Resistance:** Issue doesn't exist/change can't happen

**Stage 3
Vague Awareness:** Recognition of issue, no motivaation

**Stage 4
Preplanning:** Recognition of issue & that something needs to be done

**Stage 5
Preparation:** Involves active planning

**Stage 6
Initiation:** Implementation of a program

**Stage 7
Stabilization:** One or more programs in place & stable

**Stage 8
Confirmation & Expansion:** Recognize challenges & improve programs

**Stage 9
Professional:** Sophistication, cross-training, programs in other areas

nutritional issues such as sexually transmitted diseases and infections to heart disease and diet, environmental issues such as water and air quality, HIV/AIDS intervention, child sexual abuse, sexual assault, and cultural competence. The model identifies specific characteristics related to different levels of problem awareness and readiness for change. To increase the potential for success, interventions introduced in a tribal community must be consistent with the history and awareness of the problem, along with the level of readiness for change present among tribal members.

The Community Readiness Model identifies nine stages of readiness. Stages of readiness are assessed by evaluating the community on six dimensions: A) Existing Efforts (programs, activities, policies, etc.), B) Community Knowledge of Efforts, C) Leadership (includes appointed leaders and influential community members), D) Community Climate, E) Community Knowledge about the Problem, and F) Resources (people, money, time, space, etc.). In recent years, a number of tribal communities have used the Community Readiness Model to assess existing programs or to determine if their community is ready to implement a particular program, including a Children's Advocacy Center and instituting a multidisciplinary approach to the investigation and intervention in child sexual and severe physical abuse cases. Once the tribal community has determined its level of readiness, it is time to develop strategies for moving the community from its current level to the next level of readiness to address a problem.

The selected interventions suggested here are by no means comprehensive but offer a very brief example of the types of interventions that are used with each readiness stage. For communities in the first stage, effective strategies are generally aimed at raising awareness that a problem exists. For example, interventions at the stages of "No Awareness" and "Denial" should focus on one-on-one and/or small group activities. Home visits can be utilized to discuss the issue and obtain individual buy-in for addressing the issue, and small activity groups, talking circles, and one-on-one phone calls are used in a variety of tribal communities effectively. At the "Vague Awareness" stage, communities can utilize small group events, pot lucks or potlatches, and newspaper editorials or articles. Although use of national or regional data may make little impression on tribal community members, local survey data may have impact, i.e., results of school surveys, phone surveys, focus groups, and so on. Communities at the "Initiation" stage might implement training for professionals and paraprofessionals, conduct consumer interviews to gain information about improving services, identify service gaps, and utilize computer searches to identify potential funding sources that match community needs.[28] In the context of child maltreatment, community readiness could be used to incorporate strategies that address intergenerational trauma and colonization that empowers and moves the community in a meaningful way to address child maltreatment in tribal communities.

This model suggests that effective community efforts must be based on a working knowledge of the historical factors in the community, a system-wide assessment, involvement of multiple systems, and utilization of resources and strengths within the community. Efforts must also be culturally relevant and accepted as long term in nature. The Community Readiness Model takes these factors into account and provides a tool that communities can use to focus and direct community efforts toward a desired result, maximizing their resources and minimizing discouraging failures.

Community readiness cannot be determined by the readiness of policymakers and providers it must relate to the readiness of the community to deal with the issue. There remain significant challenges to building effective program responses in both urban and reservation-based tribal communities. In the case of child maltreatment, for example, the importance of developing culturally competent approaches and providing education on the legacy of colonization, violence, alcohol and drug use, and historical trauma introduced via federal law and policy is fundamental in understanding contemporary challenges present in tribal communities today.

Individual Practice Considerations

The Ecosystems Model concludes with examination of factors affecting services provided to individuals. As identified in this chapter, the social issues experienced by Indigenous people often require the skills of professional social workers—whether the social worker is Native or not. This assistance includes tangible services such as assistance with obtaining financial aid, housing, clothing, legal advice, and so on. However, like other population groups, Native people require assistance from social workers in almost every field of practice, including mental and physical health, corrections, child welfare, alcohol and substance abuse, and youth services. The competencies learned in BSW and MSW social work education programs provide the fundamental skills for working with this population. However, application of these competencies is insufficient (and potentially harmful) without accompanying cultural competence and attention to social justice challenges. For example, the wishes and plans of individuals must be balanced along with the needs of family and community members. This emphasis on the group can lead to strong mutual support networks, particularly for those dwelling near or in tribal community settings. It is important to know that, when working with a Native individual, as in most communalistic cultures, almost all matters are of concern to the family, the extended family (in some instances clan), and on occasion, the entire community.

In short, when working with Indigenous people, the well-being of the whole (however that is defined by the individual in this situation) is paramount. Another key consideration is the long-term welfare of the group. Inherent in many tribal cultures is some form of recognition of the *seven generations* ideology. This is the understanding that we must consider what impact our every act is going to have upon our descendants seven generations from now.

Social Work With Native People: Case Examples

Applying the Indian Child Welfare Act

The Indian Child Welfare Act (ICWA) of 1978 represents one of the most sweeping statutes in the field of federal Indian law involving more litigation than any other federal legislation related to Native peoples. The ICWA was passed in an attempt to remedy a long history of child welfare abuses that occurred throughout the United

States, where Native children were taken from their communities and placed or adopted into non-Native families. The disparity of placement rates is shocking, and many families and tribal communities were severely affected by the permanent placement of their children, largely because social workers and other professionals were not trained in culturally competent ways to properly access the home environment. The ICWA remains an important piece of legislation protecting Native children, families, and upholding the sovereignty of tribes to make decisions for the welfare of their children.

Social workers and other professionals should receive ongoing training on the specifics of the ICWA and be prepared to comply with the act when cases involving Native children arise. When placement issues involve temporary placement, adoption, and pre-adoption settings for Native children who are eligible for tribal enrollment in a federally recognized tribe and have a Native parent who is also enrolled, these children are covered by the ICWA, and compliance with the Act is mandatory for social workers and others.[29] In these instances, preferences for placement are to first place children within their extended family, then with other members of the Native child's tribe, and finally with other Native families. Further, children should be placed in the least restrictive placement and within reasonable proximity of their own home.[30]

Working in an Urban Community

Urban Native populations are substantial in New York City, Los Angeles, Minneapolis, Oklahoma City, and Seattle, and the services afforded them are much more established. Yet, in other large metropolitan areas, Native populations are much less visible even though significant numbers of Indigenous people reside in these areas. The fact that the socioeconomic status of urban Natives is much lower than mainstream communities, combined with scarcity of resources for the urban population, creates a critical need for urban programming in a number of cities.

In this case example, we journey to one such metropolitan area. The greater metropolitan area of St. Louis is located in both Missouri and Illinois and includes nearly 3 million people. St. Louis was one of the original Native relocation cities in the relocation policy implemented in the 1950s and '60s. From the early 1970s through the 1990s, St. Louis housed an active Urban Indian Community Center, and then the center closed. In the years since, the Native community has struggled with the lack of services and the lack of a core community gathering place that the center had once provided. Thus, a community revitalization effort has been under way with the goal of once again creating a central place for community gatherings, a place to share cultural ideas and traditions, and a place to provide resources (or at least referrals) for the health, education, mental health, and welfare services for the Native community.

The community process for coming together did not involve the use of the Community Readiness Model, although in retrospect it seems the community moved through the readiness stages 1 through 3 (no awareness to vague awareness) and is working to move through stage 4 (preparation) and beyond. In 2005 and continuing into 2006, the Native Studies Program mentioned in the group work case (above) hosted many monthly community gatherings aimed at defining what revitalization could mean for this community. Initial efforts at engaging the various parts of the community found different stages of readiness, and certainly different definitions of need and five separate Native groups were identified within the community, each with different interests and needs. Some of the groups expressed a definite need for a community center, while others felt a community center would only bring harm and build a sense of distrust in the community, as there were too many varied interest groups with varied definitions of Native identity. A center might further divide the community around identity challenges.

After several months of successful community monthly gatherings with representatives of the groups (totaling about thirty to sixty people), the Native group hosting the meetings made significant attempts to move beyond the questioning and defining need stages and into more healing efforts. These efforts were met with significant failure (only eight were present for the Restorative Justice gathering and only six for the "Wiping of the Tears" ceremony). In considering the Community Readiness Model, it is clear that the St. Louis urban community was not ready for the healing type of initiatives that were implemented since the Native community itself was perhaps at a lower stage of readiness. It is interesting to note the community voiced with clarity its need to "just be together" and "learn once again to trust and enjoy each other's company" before moving into more formal planning and programming efforts. Later in the same year, the community was successful in promoting a holiday gathering involving more than one hundred people. Since that time, the community has taken a step back and decided to establish a coalition of the five different groups to determine the best steps moving forward, utilizing a Community Readiness Model so strategies that are implemented are culturally representative of the entire group given the tremendous differences that are often present in urban situations and position the community to move at a pace that reflects its level of readiness.

Concluding Comment

This chapter sought to provide a comprehensive introduction to the historical and contemporary complexities for working with Indigenous populations within urban, suburban, and reservation settings. Although the Native population is relatively small, it is important for social workers to become familiar with this group, as it is especially vulnerable to social problems and has preserved unique aspects of culture that must be addressed when providing human services. For example, the federal and many state governments have special relationships with Native tribes and nations that do not apply to other population groups, and social workers serving Indigenous peoples must practice within these differing legal requirements. As another example, when serving an individual, the social worker should recognize that a Native worldview will typically reflect a balance between emphasis on the individual and consideration of the interests of family, tribe, or community. These and other factors must be a part of the social worker's cultural competence if services are to be effective when working with Indigenous people.

KEY WORDS AND CONCEPTS

Sovereignty

Resiliency

Trust responsibility

Heteropatriachy

Community readiness

Indian Child Welfare Act

Institutional or structural racism

Self-determination

Colonization and historical trauma

Cultural competency

SUGGESTED INFORMATION SOURCES

Brave Heart-Jordan, M., and L. DeBruyn. "So She May Walk in Balance: Integrating the Impact of Historical Trauma in the Treatment of American Indian Women." In J. Adelman and G. Enguidanos, eds. *Racism in the Lives of Women: Testimony, Theory, and Guides to Antiracist Practice.* New York: Haworth Press, 1995, pp. 345–368.

Bubar, R., and I. Vernon. *Contemporary Native American Issues: Social Life and Issues.* Philadelphia: Chelsea House Publishers, 2004.

DeBruyn, L., M. Chino, P. Serna, and F. Fullerton-Gleason. "Child Maltreatment in American Indian and Alaska Native Communities: Integrating Culture, History, and Public Health for Intervention and Prevention." *Child Maltreatment* 6 (2001): 89–102.

Deloria, V. *God is Red: A Native View of Religion.* Golden, CO: Fulcrum Publishing, 2003.

Duran, E., B. Duran, and M. Y. H. Brave Heart. "Native Americans and the Trauma of History." In R. Thorton, ed. *Studying Native America: Problems and Prospects.* Wisconsin: University of Wisconsin Press, 1998, 60–76.

Evans-Campbell, T., T. Lindhorst, B. Huang, and K. Walters. "Interpersonal Violence in the Lives of Urban American Indian and Alaska Native Women: Implications for Health, Mental Health, and Help-Seeking." *American Journal of Public Health* 96(8) (2006): 1416–1422.

Harvard Project on American Indian Economic Development, Eric Henson, Jonathan B. Taylor, Catherine Curtis, Stephen Cornell, Kenneth W. Grant, Miriam Jorgensen, Joseph P. Kalt, and Andrew J. Lee. *The State of the Native Nations: Conditions Under U.S. Policies of Self-Determination.* New York: Oxford University Press, 2007.

Jaimes, A. *The State of Native America: Genocide, Colonization and Resistance.* Boston: South End Press, 1992.

LaDuke, W. *Reclaiming the Sacred: The Power of Naming and Claiming.* Cambridge, MA: South End Press, 2005.

Pilkington, D. *Rabbit-Proof Fence: The True Story of One of the Greatest Escapes of All Time.* New York: Hyperion Books, 1996.

Roscoe, W. *Changing Ones: Third and Fourth Genders in Native North America.* New York: St. Martin's Press, 2000.

Trask, H. K. *From a Native Daughter: Colonialism and Sovereignty in Hawaii.* Honolulu: University of Hawaii Press, 1999.

U.S. Commission on Civil Rights. *A Quiet Crisis: Federal Funding and Unmet Needs in Indian Country.* Washington, DC: U.S. Commission on Civil Rights, July 2003.

U.S. Department of Justice, Office of Justice Programs, Bureau of Justice Statistics, *American Indians and Crime,* Lawrence Greenfeld and Steven Smith, statisticians, (Washington, D.C.: U.S. Government Printing, February 1999), 4.

Vernon, I., and R. Bubar. "Child Sexual Abuse and HIV/AIDS in Indian Country." *Wicazo Sa Review* 16 (2001): 47–63.

Walters, K. L., J. M. Simone, and T. Evans-Campell. "Substance Use Among American Indians and Alaska Natives Incorporating Culture in an Indigenist Stress-Coping Paradigm." *Public Health Reports* 117(suppl. 1) (2002): S104–117.

Weaver, H. *Explorations in Cultural Competence: Journeys to the Four Directions.* Belmont, CA: Thomson Brooks Cole Publishers, 2005.

Wiebe, R., and Y. Johnson. *Stolen Life: Journey of a Cree Woman.* Toronto: Alfred A. Knoph Publishers, 1998.

Wilkins, D. E. *American Indian Politics and the American Political System*, 2nd ed. Lanham, MD: Rowman & Littlefield Publishers, 2006.

ENDNOTES

1. U.S. Census Bureau, "National Population Estimates—Characteristics," Table 3, 2007, http://www.census.gov/popest/national/asrh/NC-EST2007-srh.html, and http://www.census.gov/Press-Release/www.releases/archives/population/010048.htm.

2. U.S. Census Bureau, *The American Community—American Indians and Alaska Natives: 2004* (Washington, D.C.: U.S. Department of Commerce, 2007), p. 2; U.S. Census Bureau, *The American Indian and Alaska Native Population: 2000. Census 2000 Brief* (Washington, D.C.: U.S. Department of Commerce, 2002).

3. David H. Getches, Charles F. Wilkinson, and Robert A. Williams, Jr., *Cases and Materials on Federal Indian Law*, 5th ed. (St Paul, MN: Thomson/West, 2005).

4. U.S. Commission on Civil Rights, *A Quiet Crisis: Federal Funding and Unmet Needs in Indian Country.* (Washington, D.C.: U.S. Commission on Civil Rights, July 2003).

5. Eric Henson, Jonathan B. Taylor, Catherine Curtis, Stephen Cornell, Kenneth W. Grant, Miriam Jorgensen, Joseph P. Kalt, and Andrew J. Lee, *The State of the Native Nations: Conditions under U.S. Policies of Self-Determination* (New York: Oxford University Press, 2007).

6. Hilary N. Weaver, *Explorations in Cultural Competence: Journeys to the Four Directions* (Belmont, CA: Thomson Brooks Cole, 2005).

7. Stephen Cornell and Joseph P. Kalt, "Two Approaches to Economic Development on American Indian Reservations: One Works, the Other Doesn't," *Joint Occasional Papers on Native Affairs* (2005), retrieved from www.jopna.net.

8. Jeffrey Ian Ross, "Gambling, Native Americans and Lobbyist Jack Abramhoff," *The Examiner* (June 29, 2006).

9. J. Noriega, "American Indian Education in the United States: Indoctrination for Subordination to Colonialism," in M. Annette Jaimes, ed., *The State of Native American: Genocide, Colonization and Resistance* (Boston: South End Press, 1992), 380.

10. Getches, et al., op. cit.

11. Irene Vernon and Roe Bubar, "Child Sexual Abuse and HIV/AIDS in Indian Country," *Wicazo Sa Review* 16 (2001): 47–63.

12. U.S. Commission on Civil Rights, *A Quiet Crisis*, op. cit.

13. Office of Statistics and Programming, National Center for Injury Prevention and Control, CDC, "10 Leading Causes of Death: American Indian and Alaska Natives, Both Sexes, 1999–2000."

14. U.S. Commission on Civil Rights, *Broken Promises: Evaluating the Native American Health Care System* (Washington: U.S. Commission on Civil Rights, September 2004).

15. U.S. Commission on Civil Rights, *A Quiet Crisis*, op. cit.

16. T. Perdue, *Sifters: Native American Women's Lives* (New York: Oxford University Press, 2001), 4, 31.

17. P. Tjaden and N. Thoennes, "Full Report of the Prevalence, Incidence, and Consequences of Violence Against Women: Findings from the National Violence Against Women Survey," National Institute of Justice and Centers for Disease Control, 2000.

18. Roe Bubar and W. Bartlemay, "Native Women Left Behind: Sexual Assault in Tribal Communities," results from a National Pilot Study (Kyle, SD: Cangleska, 2006).

19. Office of Statistics and Programming, op. cit.

20. T. Morton, "The Increasing Colorization of America's Child Welfare System: The Overrepresentation of African American Children," *Policies and Practices of Public Human Services* 57 (1999); K. A. Earle and A. Cross, *Child Abuse and Neglect among American Indian and Alaska Native Children: An Analysis of Existing Data* (Seattle, WA: Casey Family Programs, 2001).

21. L. Greenfield and S. Smith, *American Indians and Crime* (Washington, D.C.: U.S. Department of Justice, Office of Justice Programs, Bureau of Justice Statistics, 2004).

22. A. Melton Pecos, "Indigenous Justice Systems and Tribal Society," *Judicature* 79, reprinted online by Tribal Court Clearinghouse, 1999.

23. M. Y. H. Brave Heart-Jordan, "Wakiksuyapi: Carrying the historical trauma of the Lakota," *Tulane Studies in Social Welfare* (2001): 21–22, 245–266.

24. Swinomish Tribal Mental Health Project, "A Gathering of Wisdoms, Tribal Mental Health: A Cultural Perspective" (LaConner, WA: Swinomish Tribal Community, 1991).

25. V. Deloria, Jr., and C. M. Lytle, "American Indians in Historical Perspective," in Vine Deloria, Jr., and Clifford M. Lytle, *American Indians, American Justice* (Austin: University of Texas Press, 1983), 1–24.

26. U.S. Commission on Civil Rights, *A Quiet Crisis,* op. cit.

27. Ruth W. Edwards, Pamela Jumper-Thurman, B. A. Plested, Eugene R. Oetting, and Lewis Swanson, "Community Readiness: Research to Practice," *Journal of Community Psychology* 28(3) (2000): 291–307.

28. Roe Bubar and Pamela Jumper-Thurman, "Violence Against Native Women" [Special issue], *Social Justice: A Journal of Crime, Conflict and World Order* (2004): 31, 70–86.

29. Indian Child Welfare Act (ICWA) of 1978, P.L. 95-608

30. Ibid.